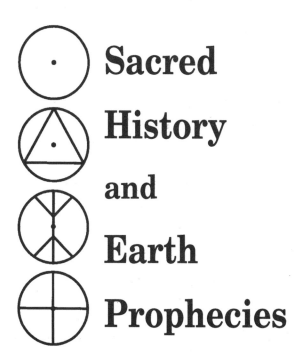

Sacred

History

and

Earth

Prophecies

Sept. '99

To Edith Thanapue

Phoenix, AZ

Sacred History

and

Earth Prophecies

by

Dinawa

IN PRINT PUBLISHING
Sedona, Arizona

Cover photo by Margaret Jackson ©1996

Cover design by In Print Publishing

Map graphics by Karuno

Typesetting by Karen Reider

Publisher's Cataloging in Publication
(Prepared by Quality Books Inc.)

Dinawa.
     Sacred History and Earth Prophecies / Dinawa : Khadar, illustrator; Sindja, editor.
     p. cm.
     Includes bibiographical references.
     Preassigned LCCN: 96-68507
     ISBN: 1-886966-07-9

1. Prophecies. I. Title

BF1791.D56 1997   133.3
                QBI96-40632

Manufactured in the United States of America by Vaughan Printing

Table of Contents

Introduction

Dedication

To the Friend, Dr. Bob.
To Beloved Gandarva.
To dearest Raven woman "the all seeing one"
thanks for your guidance.
To the unending generosity and encouragement
of New Fox.
To the editorial efforts and patience of
Sindja, Khadar and Karen.
To the fine folks involved with In-Print Publishing.
To everyone's mothers and fathers who provided
these physical vehicles.

*Whatever voice appeals unto thee is My truth for thee,
to nurse thee until I shall lead thee into all Truth.
(For) each brain believes a different doctrine and different
historical facts, and I feed them thereon, giving each the
best possible food for such a brain.*

*And thou art thyself a proof of My care;
For even in this I do not let thee believe what thou readest
unless that belief shall be the best food for thy brain.*

'X'

Introduction

Sacred History and Earth Prophecy is an invitation to discover the hidden treasures of ourselves, both as individuals and as a species. Blinded as we are by our fragmented and fragmenting culture, born of a dry theology, an empty, consumer-based life philosophy and economically driven science, we are led to a materialistic and soulless view of ourselves and our history. Through the medium of Sacred History we are given the opportunity to remove the blindfolds and see the "human condition" as a function of our evolution as a species and as individuals – and the even greater occasion to see the Divine at work in human affairs.

Although this story recounts historical events, it is not just a historical book of facts and dates. And although you'll find some possibly frightening predictions, this is not another "woe be unto us" doom and gloom forecast of humanity's demise. Rather, through the introduction of the concept of the Four Sacred Streams, you'll see past the illusion that human history is driven soley by economics and territorial instincts. Sacred History and Earth Prophecy *is* the story of the Divine's human adventure, from before recorded history to the present age and beyond; it is also your story.

The characters in this earth epic are the Four Sacred Streams through which the Divine tells Itself the tale of Its rise to awareness in humankind. Transcending the usual divisions of race, religion or nationality, these Four Great Streams of Consciousness weave a pattern which manifests through all aspects of human action and interaction. The empires which rise and fall, the cultures which come and go, and even our personal triumphs and failures are the eddies, whirlpools and rapids in the Four Sacred Streams. The holographic nature of reality allows these historical events to reveal the underlying pattern of human spiritual evolution, giving the revelations of Sacred History and Earth Prophecy both deeply personal and global relevance.

In times of uncertainty, Inuit hunters of antiquity relied upon a shamanic ritual in order to find a caribou herd. Placing a caribou bone in an open fire, they would watch as the cracks forming in the bone became a map of the landscape. Where those cracks crossed showed the exact location of the herd they sought. In much the same way, the insights and revelations we receive from Sacred History can cross the "cracks" in our personal journey, providing a ritual map of our spiritual landscape in these times of change.

As you acquaint yourself with Sacred History, some of you may get a sense of deja vu, a remembrance that this is knowledge already held in the heart. Others of you may react with outrage or disbelief. Whatever your response, be assured that after the storm of emotion has passed, the rainbow calm of your own knowingness will appear and you will receive from Sacred History exactly what you need.

Twelfth century Muslim mystic scholar, Ibn al Arabi, may have summed up Sacred History best, "History is the development of God to Self Consciousness which He (God) achieves at last in man (woman). The world was never created, it is the external aspect of that which in its inward view is God. The true lover will find and love the author of all beauty in any beautiful form."

Chapter One
Humankind's Aspiration

biding in the Silent Spiritscape, the landscape of Life, as the Eternal Source of the mind, the Seer witnessed a wind of thought stirring within the One Heart of the Supreme Being. The Seer shed a tear for the ordeal which humankind must embrace. A ray of joy lit the candle of speech, charging the soul and soil with fertile lifeforce. Yes, this revelation must be shared. It is time.

"No!" echoed into dark infinity, forever rippling through sheaths of matter yet to be born. "No, I don't want to do this. Why me?," proclaimed the Seer. Then, this "don't want," this preference, began to dissolve within the Great Presence. The "I" was liberated and all "whys" vanished like mist. Only a great calm remained, unruffled, as if no disturbance had occurred. The realization, "I am not the doer," dawned, revealing a Great Unknown as Source of all Doing.

There are Norse legends of the hero hanging upside down from a wind-blown tree, wounded by a spear, taking up the secret wisdom, screaming in pain, falling back up to life. An Indian Rishi seeress cognizes the hymns of truth as the activity of her own self-bliss. In both cases, seer looking to the Seer reveals all wisdom in this holy act. We will ask you too, to follow the example of these seers!

This vast tale has no owner or author. It is the recognition of the blissful pain of your own existence and evolution. Who I am doesn't matter. But I will send forth a silent and loyal guardian of humanity, to watch over each of you. Out of the endless sky I send you power to listen; out of the wind please receive the gift of touch, from fire the glory of sight, rain showers bring tastes and soil brings fragrant aromas. I enter you, hiding Myself from Myself. Receive My own power manifested in you as the activities of your body and senses. I imbed Myself in you as individual spirit, Life force, new mind, old mind, body. I await your recognition of the development of Myself as you throughout eons of time. Some of you will already know of this by the time this story is really heard. Others will not. It will not matter. It is not important. For now, relax and enjoy. Keep your mood up always, through all the circumstances of your own personal history.

This is our story, the story of the many diverse creations, cultures and events that are Sacred History and have given rise to prophecy. This is Her story, His story, Sacred History. In the silent void Mind stirs, asking the questions, "What is going on on this plane of confusion, earth?" And more basically, "Who Am I? What am I? Where am I? What's going on here? What, if anything, can I do about it?"

It will be useful to remind ourselves that this tale is as vast as the infinite space of the unbounded sky, universal, with no beginning and no end. Against the great backdrop of sky appears the bright blazing sun by day and the indirect, reflected light of the moon, and distant stars at night. The turbulent winds of change blow, bringing the purifying rains and raging storms of destruction upon the oceans of Life, the abundantly manifesting beauty of earth's myriad forms, beings, events, cultures.

Investigation into Sacred History and Prophecy comes with a loving warning. Do not continue; stop here; go no further unless you are willing to no longer participate in the mass programming manifested in an unconscious life and the false motivations and outdated identifications of a conditioned spiritual life. Even your most treasured beliefs will be tested and possibly uprooted. When the tapestry of your conditioned mind begins to unravel itself, don't panic. Be silent, as the Seer was silenced by the recognition that this is a process.

In order to understand prophecy we must see the forces and patterns at work in human culture. Birthing itself from various sources, growing out of infancy, struggling through adolescence and emerging as mature and wise humanity before a new seasonal change of death and rebirth; human culture is a process, not a goal.

Man/womankind is in a chrysalis state, a kind of puberty in which the pressures of growth are ripping apart the very fabric and order of life on this planet. Never before have so many complex factors gathered together on a global scale in an apocalyptic vision. Overpopulation, disease, environmental destruction, nuclear and biological warfare, electro-pollution, impending world economic collapse, weather changes and geologic upheaval all threaten to sound the death knell of the world as we know it. Combine all this with the confusion surrounding spirituality, metaphysics, religion and politics and we discover a story of epic proportions.

When butterfly-hood is upon you, don't panic. Man has not always been what he is today. Movements of civilization and the guidance of great personages have always facilitated human evolutionary transitions, pointing to the outworking of conditioned human patterns as the deeper, underlying cause of Sacred History.

A great experiment is at work, endeavoring to discover how the vehicles of human expression: mind, speech, body, family, community, education, religion, economics, ecology, etc., manifest in balanced and non-violent ways. The impending outcome of this experiment has humanity perched on the precipice of self discovery. Such has been prophesied by all great seers.

Sacred History is the story of humanity's collective unconscious becoming conscious. On the surface this story can seem senseless, tragic, heroic and beautiful. However, deep within the fabric of history are archetypal patterns that tend to escape recognition, lying just at the edge of awareness, as a vague dream does upon awakening. Seeing this will bring the clouded picture of prophesied events into sharp focus as pivotal points in human development.

All Sacred History is appearance, images reflected in a cosmic mirror, leaving no lasting impression. Because perception of reality depends upon the viewer, there is no objective historical reality. There is, however, a great mind-game of charades going on within each individual and each culture.

The cosmic play of Sacred History on the stage of time allows individuals and cultures to entertain and evolve themselves by enacting the unconscious ritual of striving for identity, expression and unity. It arises within the heart of the Supreme Being. He/She is His/Her history, creation and evolution, creatures and cultures. It is essential to understand before encountering prophecy that through this process of evolution a foundation has been laid for the development and merging of Four Great Sacred Streams of humankind. According to prophecy, this will occur in our lifetime.

The Four Sacred Streams are living, human embodiments of Life's process of manifestation. Their evolution is tied to emanation from Source, creation and the evolution of Earth herself. Everything in existence is related through the bio-spiritual web that is Life.

Before the Flood and the last Ice Age, the Four Sacred Streams were expressed wholistically through several ancient wisdom cultures (Mayan, Indian and Egyptian). Over time, due to evolving humanity's needs, climactic differences, geomantic effects and cross-cultural factors they evolved through natural selection into four distinct but mutually complementary Sacred Streams.

Each Sacred Stream represents certain principles of existence itself. Each offers itself as a gift for the development of human beings and is characterized by certain attributes and evolutionary strategies. The names of the Streams, (West, East, South and North) relate loosely to their geographical locations and were chosen partly for ease of identification. (See map #1.)

The first two Sacred Streams are like two octaves of the same note and represent the origins of life. Members of the Western Sacred Stream are the caretakers of the manifest spirit power of nature and represent Earth energy. Members of the Eastern Sacred Stream, signifying Heaven, are custodians of unmanifest spirit. Although they approach the One Divine from unique standpoints, the Western Sacred Stream (the Divine Manifest) and the Eastern Sacred Stream (the Divine Unmanifest) are quite complementary.

The third Sacred Stream, the South, comes out of the Divine Manifest Earth, holding the energy of the progressive development of divine forms – spirit expression through speech, the body and form.

The last Sacred Stream to mature is the Stream of the North, representing self. Coming out of the Divine Unmanifest, Heaven, this Stream is learning to caretake and develop intelligence and will as Divine forces of activity.

These Four Sacred Streams, which have existed under the illusion of separateness for most of Sacred History, hold the DNA strands of the new humanity, the Sons and Daughters of God. Through the events of Sacred History humanity undergoes its maturation process until the prophesied reunion of the Four Sacred Streams takes place in the the 21st century. By observing Sacred History with the knowledge that these Streams reflect maturing components within each of us, we can see ourselves more clearly and understand and assist our own individual growth. A healing of the past may then occur, giving us a greater ability to embrace and adapt to the future.

There are apparently (at this time in human development) four ways in which Truth makes itself known: first, realization, cognition, revelation or transmission, direct from the Source; second, through a lineage of Great Mentors or Awakened Adepts who pass on ancient teachings to devoted Initiates; third, through omens, signs and portents; lastly, through the suffering and struggling inherent in Life – evolution. Often, Truth makes itself known through a combination of all of these. There is no way of knowing how or when this will occur.

True wisdom is given according to the sacred needs of the time and cosmic requirements. Although all four of these forms of revelation occur simultaneously in all cultures, each human being and each culture can only receive according to their capacity and in ways framed by their particular temperament.

Souls, according to their various natures, incarnate into certain historical environments, cultures and religious eras in order to learn the lessons they require. This movement through Sacred History assists the soul's development as both a unique individual and universal being. Gathering experience, the soul builds and experiences through an ego identity until this is no longer necessary and re-identification with the Divine begins. It's all just a matter of time as to when each soul and each culture recognizes What Is. We are both the One and a portion of the Many. Our path will focus on either Being, Becoming, or both.

It is through this process that contributions to humanity are made. Inventions, political innovations, advances in science, technology, the arts, agriculture, etc., are often introduced by great souls who have no conscious awareness of their spiritual status. Such contributions made in the distant past remain anonymous because records were either nonexistent or destroyed. Countless others who have no destiny for public or historical recognition serve behind the scenes, keeping mostly to themselves or sharing their spiritual light with only a few. Whether they affect the outer world or the inner, they all further the development of their Sacred Streams.

Chapter Two
Our Mysterious Beginnings

here was a time in the distant past when all across the globe humanity lived in a world of visionary impressions and instinctive imaginations. They experienced themselves and their world through a type of clairvoyance that came before independent thinking and self consciousness had been completely formed and individuals were governed more by group identity than their own egos. The basis of human culture, which can be found in the mythologies of every society, was formed by these visionary impressions. Remnants of these shamanic societies or Lifeways which once covered the globe still survive today in the cultures of the indigenous/aboriginal peoples of North, South and Central America, Indonesia, the South Pacific Islands, Africa, Australia, Asia, and Siberia.

These hunter/gatherers (and the early pastoral and agriculturally-based peoples who emerged later) sprang from the Western Sacred Stream, the Stream we all share as human beings. They were (and still are) the Earthkeepers, guardians of the powers of the elements, communicators with animals and the healing spirits of plants; they are dreamers of the future.

In those ancient times, human beings were psychically and psychologically open to the energy and vitality of The Great Mother who birthed them. Their basic orientation to life was based on values we consider to be feminine. Harmony, cooperation and interrelationship, rather than conflict were understood to support the life force and were the guidelines for daily life. As evidence of this, most Paleolithic sites bear no sign or depiction of violence or warfare. It was only much later, with the emergence of the other

Sacred Streams and their patriarchal gods, that humanity's orientation toward life underwent a radical change.

We know The Great Mother by Her ancient names around the globe: Hopi Corn Maiden, Celtic Gaia, Gaelic Anu, Greecian Sophia, East African Oshun, and East Indian Aditi,/Ama, and Aima of the Hebrews. She is the Life Giver, the divine force of manifestation. As the embodiment of these natural, rhythmic mysteries, woman was respected and and in some cases, revered. Her intuitive connection to nature and familiarity with plant life led to her mastery of herbal knowledge and healing practices. Her magical awareness served to guide the people to places where nature supported them.

Through ceremony, Western Stream peoples experienced themselves as extensions of their environment, active participants in maintaining the balance of nature. In respect and reverence they lived harmoniously with the natural world. Psychologically, they lived not just in their bodies, but in the body of the earth with all her energies and spirits. They were, and are, the mergers of realities. Actually, these peoples had no concept of nature as something separate from themselves, for their perception of separation between the dimensions of mind, spirit and body was much less acute. Nature was them, in all its richness and interrelationship, and not something foreign and dangerously "other" to control and dominate.

Hunter/gatherer tribes migrated with the seasons, following the stars and animal herds. Their sensitivity to and communication with spiritual forces and personalities of the natural and supernatural worlds enabled them to recognize and establish sacred sites – places where earth energies and the energies of various other worlds interpenetrate and overlap one another and where great nonphysical beings reside or touch into the physical plane for a parallel energy exchange. For nomadic tribes of that era, sacred places (later immortalized in emergence myths) provided focal points for other-worldy communication, healing, precognitive visions and enhanced fertility.

Some of the energies or entities encountered at these sites may exist independently of humans, existing in vibrational frequencies beyond our sensory range or technical ability to perceive or measure them. Others appear to be manifestations of archetypal images held in humanity's collective psyche, or brought into our reality by our mental habits of belief - thoughtforms. Our thoughts and emotions serve as nourishment for these beings/energies and they are sustained by our worship and attention.

The ancients knew of forces, energetic embodiments of negative tendencies, that actually feed off mankind's collective neuroses. Even today wise people of the Orient and scholars of the Kabbala say that our destructive habits are magnetically held in place by psychic forces (entities) that thrive on our confused mental and emotional states. These are the biblical devils, the basis of black arts, that hold steady, through magnetic attraction, the terrible confusion within mankind. Our slow progression toward the heights of development can be credited in part to the influences of these beings. Some traditions also credit these forces with the initial splitting of unified humanity into the Four Streams.

The more scientific among us prefer to explain the almost universal belief in gods with the idea that they have a common archetypal lure for mankind as ways to explain the world or bring meaning to one's life in pre-scientific societies. On the other hand, the gods may be figments of man's imagination based upon cultural projections or they may be the next evolutionary step up from humans. It is even conceivable that they are extraterrestrials.

Legends and their own visionary experiences told our ancestors that their world was just one of nine interpenetrating, interrelated worlds. Hopi, Norse, Hebrew, Egyptian, Hindu, and Buddhist beliefs all refer to these realms. Ancient stories spoke of events that took place in the otherworlds, underworlds and overworlds. Ritual reenactment of those events suspended the hard, linear time of ordinary mind, providing entry into the concentric, sacred time of spirit.

Using shamanic techniques to bridge interdimensional spaces was a common theme among Paleolithic cultures. Through the use of sacred plants, ecstatic rituals and sexual magic, one could be transported from the ordinary world into the non-ordinary world of power. However, if one is not careful and wise, those same worlds of power can entrap one in the vicious snare of ego aggrandizement.

Recognizing themselves as part of the process of creation, our Western Stream ancestors understood that they could manipulate or influence the process by which the unmanifest One becomes the manifest Many. By making contact with deities and other interdimensional beings through the use of ritual, symbols, gestures, and words they received tangible, beneficial results in everyday life.

To dream and dance the hunt before it actually takes place is to use the magical power of emotion and mind to ensure success, just as sexual rituals magnified the fertile power of spring, ensuring a healthy harvest. These magical elements are the primordial source of all major world religions whose shamanic origins are hidden within their rituals and holidays.

Elaborate ceremonialism and magic permeated the lives of early hunter/gatherers and farmers. To them Life was a process of neverending change, keeping oneself in balance with unseen forces. Seasonal celebrations surrounding spring planting and autumn harvesting allowed one to embrace a larger view, healed and regenerated by actively participating in the rhythms of nature.

Because they saw that all of nature is sexual and connected to the cycles of moon and sun, ocean tides and earth energies, the natural fertility cycles of life (planting, harvesting, etc.) were considered sacred, as was human sexuality. These were celebrated as the merging of complementary, procreative forces. Creation on this plane takes place in the union of apparent opposites and all acts of creation are sexual acts. It is within the union of opposites, creation, that the state of joy appears. Sexual rapture is momentary self extinction, an experience of the soul's oneness with the life force of the Great Mystery.

Humankind seeks the experience of union with the great power of Life through many avenues, including religious experimentation. All activity offers a window to sublime reality and all activity is inherently unified when one forgets oneself. The momentary bliss of sexual ecstasy, the focus of creative concentration, intense fear, selfless service to another, or simple love and devotion to an ideal or a person, such as raising a child – all can afford an opening.

Holy medicine shamans received a calling and were designated by the people as guides and healers and interpreters of dreams. In practicing the principle of Oneness with nature, they were keepers of calendars, acknowledging their unity with the most obvious example of the living, energizing power of the Great Mystery, Sun Being. The natural world was perceived as an active manifestation of spiritual force. Birth, growth, maturity, death and rebirth were honored with the appropriate rites. People of the First Sacred Stream understood that we don't break the natural laws, we break ourselves against them.

Theirs was an oral tradition of legends, ritual and sacred sites, unlike the imposed authority of written scripture that came along later. The tradition, received from supernatural sources through visions, was kept alive through carefully prescribed songs and stories. Without written language, living memories permeated their present. The language of stone (expressed through megalithic structures such as Stonehenge) dance, symbols and dreams played a crucial role in preserving the culture. Profound reverence for the Unknown Source and Its powers and agencies (later known as angels) characterized these peoples.

Forms of divination developed as a means to predict the outcome of important events well before they matured into overwhelming consequences for the future. In order to coordinate oneself with spiritual forces and powers, one would seek oracular guidance and wise approaches to a situation while it was still malleable to human will. The Chinese I Ching, the Mo of Tibet, astrology from all parts of the world, Egyptian Tarot, East African Ifa, and Celtic Runes are all examples of this art.

In divination there are no good or bad prophecies, or moral/ethical do's and dont's. Everything has its perfection, its utility. Everything is used to gather experience, to bring one into alignment with the great mystery of existence. If one understands that the universe is an immense bio/spiritual feedback system and knows what to look for, anything can be used for divination. An attitude of prayerful attentiveness and assuming responsibility for one's actions will help one make the most of whatever information received from the built-in synchronicity of circumstances.

Somehow, as if out of nowhere and perhaps simultaneously with Earth-Based peoples, the River/Water cultures arrived on the global scene with well-established religious societies, mystery schools and technologies for harmonious living. The agricultural civilizations of the Egyptian Nile, Indian Indus, Chinese Yellow, Middle Eastern Euphrates rivers and the tropical rainforests of the Central American Yucatan appeared as if they had sprung fully grown from a watery womb.

Whether these nomads, early farmers or more fully developed civilizations represent an evolutionary chain of human communities from prehuman ancestors, or were remnants of mythical Lemurian or Atlantean colonies is open to question. According to the stories told in the great epics of the past such as the Ramayana, Popul Vuh, the Old Testament of the Bible and ancient folklore, songs and myths, the existence of ancient Mother/Fatherlands was an acknowledged fact in ancient times. Undeniable, striking similarities in stories, myths, symbols, architecture and languages whose peoples share no obvious connection lead one to the conclusion that there was a common source for humanity; either here on earth, or as some legends state, perhaps somewhere in the starry heavens. Many shamanic cultures trace their pre-Flood origins to the Pleiades star system, or Sirius, the Dogstar, the brightest star in the galaxy.

Ancient stories from around the world tell of colonies established all over the globe tens of thousands of years ago by highly advanced civilizations. Refugees fleeing the last major geophysical upheaval, which destroyed those great cultures, went to live in the colonies, mainly those located in South and Central America, North Africa and India. Other sites included New Zealand and the Hawaiian islands. From those ancient colonies, humanity populated the earth.

Myths and legends aside, there is linguistic evidence that, contrary to current anthropological theory, the first Americans did not come across the Bering Strait during the last Ice Age. With the exception of Navajo, Apache and Eskimo, the languages spoken by the "indigenous" peoples of North, Central and South America do not relate to Asian language groups. This could indicate that these peoples really are remnants of Lemurian and Atlantean peoples. In fact, Aztec stories about 'Aztlan' Atlantis), refer to it as one of the "previous worlds" of their creation stories. (See map #2.)

Over time, smaller outposts which lost contact with the major colonies sank into primitive lifestyles, retaining remnants of their past in legends and stories of previous "worlds." Other settlements, much larger and better equipped, such as those in Mayaland, India, and Egypt kept their civilizations and wisdom intact over much longer periods of time.

The seafaring people of ancient southern India, Lemurian immigrants whose modern descendants bear a strong physical resemblance to Australian Aborigines and the Veddas of Ceylon, settled along the Indus River, building the Vedic cultures of Mohenjo Daro and Hareppa (the ancient Indian equivalent of Egyptian Nile culture). They traveled to Mesopotamia, trading with the Semitic peoples of Sumeria and after establishing colonies in what is now Oman, on the Saudi Arabian coast, they landed in Ethiopia, helping to populate the southern Nile in Egypt in an area known today as Sudan.

The northern Nile was colonized by Atlantean adepts under the leadership of Thoth (Hermes Trismegistus), who established

Hermetic initiation centers based upon the Kybalion Laws[1] (Hermetic principles).

Others, a collection of disparate peoples of Atlantean and Lemurian origin, called Habirus[2] (later known as Hebrews), are said to have settled in north central Asia, possibly leading to the legends of the once-fertile land of Shambala, north of Tibet. The wisdom brought to this mythical kingdom from Atlantis and Lemuria may have been the source of the Indian Vedas, Egyptian kybalion, Hebrew Kabbala, and Chinese Way of the Tao. All have strong emphasis on the great Oneness of all things. It is interesting to note that during this time period people in different parts of the world used very similar- names for the Absolute (Hopi Taiowa, Chinese Tao, Mayan Teol and Hindu Tat).

perhaps even deliberately destroyed along with other ancient wisdom in the "book" burnings which took place in Alexandria many centuries later. By some accounts, the Kabbala was brought to

The Kabbala's traceable origins are lost in the sands of Time, Shambala by Atlantean refugees, then carried by Habirus (Hebrews) into the Middle East and Africa. Other accounts credit the Egyptians with originating the work (called the kybalion) and sharing it with the Hebrews.

Although the Kabbala and the Vedas are best known through their Jewish and Hindu proponents, they are not the exclusive property of those cultures. The wisdom contained within their traditions existed prior to the two groups that carried them forward.

---

1 • *Very similar to each other, the Kabbala and kybalion (the Greek name for a very similar work) express the same concepts and axioms using different imagery. Hermetic axioms are visually displayed in the Kabbala as the sephiroth on the Tree of Life. The Substantial All is One of the kybalion and the Limitless One (Ain Sof) of the Kabbala are one and the same. Both works point to this as the substance underlying all outward manifestation. Both kybalion and Kabbala have the axiom, "As above, so below" as a basic principle.*

2 • *The word "abir" in Hebrew means "great," "hebir" means astrologer. Given that they may have spent a good deal of time in Chaldea, well known for its astrologers, this implies a profound connection between these people and the ancient mystical arts. Astrology affords the precision that is required for the ritual (13 month) lunar calender of the Hebrews to be coordinated with the cosmic motions of the celestial bodies. The ceremonies on earth loose their effectiveness ˙when a man-made work week dictates the convenient times for celebration of holidays rather than the heaven's cosmic timing.*

inspired script and sacred languages. It is also interesting to note There are striking correspondences between the teachings of the Indian Vedas and Hebrew Kabbala and both are written in divinely that the Sanskrit word for knowledge, "veda," bears a strong similarity to its Hebrew equivalent, "yeda."

YHVH, the Hebrew sacred name of God, is identical in meaning to India's Agni, the Vedic mystic fire, is the first sound/word of the Rig Veda. Both represent and vibrationally express the understanding that creation emanates/extends/manifests out of the Boundless Unmanifest – Ain Sof to the Hebrews, Brahman to the Indians – through a "point" of contraction – Binah, in the Kabbalah, Bindu, in the Vedas.

The ancient Kabbala has its western equivalent in the Hopi Kachinas ("ka' tsina" refers to their gods) – carved, cottonwood depictions of supernatural beings. The Hopi Sun Feathered Head (Taiowa ka'tsina) is an anthropomorphized Tree of Life, representing the Limitless Light (Sun) of the Ain Sof, Source of the Tree of Life, radiating in all directions from the risen (activated) Life energy at the crown, just as do the Mayan feather-headed serpent, the Indian Naga cobra and Chinese dragon. The symbolized knowledge of the Kabbala's sephiroth is further repeated in the nine worlds of both the Hopi and the Teutonic wisdom systems. In the Kabbala, however, a tenth world contains the first nine.

Great Truths brought from Atlantis, Lemuria and hidden Shambala, became the foundation for later civilizations with which we are more familiar. Spiritually-based societies and learning centers were established in India, Egypt and Mayaland. Under the Solar Dynasties of those great civilizations, secret mystery schools taught the eternal truths as the bases for studies in science, medicine, religion, philosophy, music, timekeeping, architecture and sacred geometry. Incorporating a balanced relationship between the individual and society, the wisdom cultures of old exemplified a wholistic view of life, incorporating all four Sacred Streams.

All three of these great cultures acknowledged the existence of great beings who guide the development of humankind. Known by many different names around the world (Adityas in the Vedas, Spirits on the Throne of God to Christians) these solar beings are depicted as either historical or mythical beings who have already gone through earthly human schooling and were understood to reside in the sun, from time to time incarnating into a prepared human form.

The belief that the sun is the eye of God was quite widespread. Out of the eye of God come the saviors of mankind, the solar deity or deities, as omniscient creator gods; one of which is known in Vedic India as Varuna. According to the Indian Vedas, these beings rule the universe, upholding cosmic law, evolving the human race as part of the experiment of humanity. They possess and control the magical powers of Maya, manifesting the evolving universe out of unmanifest reality.

The deeper knowledge of these beings slowly deteriorated after the global cataclysm until simple sun worship took its place. Amazingly, many ancient cultures (India, China, Japan, Egypt) claimed their rulers were descended from solar deities. The influence of this understanding can be traced through every major civilization on this planet, particularly those of India, Mayaland and Egypt.

The secret behind the sun worship found in so many ancient cultures is that there is in each of us a soul or spirit which, when the barriers to the Infinite Source are removed, shines as if a thousand suns are blazing. Either by association or actuality it is apparent that our spiritual individuality and the physical Sun are of the same Light Source.

Originally, the people of ancient (Vedic) India understood that in Truth, human beings, their art, sciences and religions are the dream creations of Brahman, God's Yoga, whereby He unifies Himself with His creation thru maya-shakti (energy extension). At that time it was understood that humans are literally the thoughts (imaginings) of God and we are one in essence with That Source. It was only much later that this understanding was twisted into the idea that Life itself was an appearance or illusion.

As in Vedic India, Truth was directly revealed and realized in ancient Egypt but was imparted through the use of prescribed initiatory tests, congruent with a neophyte's development on the inner planes of awareness. Through careful preparation and instruction by priests and the use of consciousness-enhancing geometry and mind-expanding substances, the inner journey was activated and accelerated. Buildings were carefully constructed using sacred proportions known to evoke certain emotions and states of consciousness. Also, the senses were engaged by the use of the corresponding vibration in music, color and scent. All this, so that temple initiations were the same as those received on the inner planes in alignment with the metaphysical axiom, "As above, so below." This important Truth was later deeply misunderstood, leading some to attempt to gain some worldly benefit by simple mimicry and imitation of higher initiations – sorcery and magic.

In Mayaland the Divine chose a different cultural channel for Its expression. Hunab Ku, the One Sacred Source of All Movement and Measurement, was the Mayan equivalent of Vedic India's Brahman. For them the One Source was Dynamic Activity, a field of immense power and motion. Hunab Ku, the Source as Energy and Matter, was to be calibrated, measured, used by human civilization. Deep investigation on their part resulted in uncovering the link between space/time and consciousness.

Astronomical observations, calculations and recordkeeping were the most outstanding feature of the Multi-Stream culture of the Mayans. These astounding mathematicians lived in a world where time was a deity to be honored and lived through and each hour of the day was revered as a god. Mayan temporal calculations extended thousands of years into the future and millions of years into the past. Their calendar, which was held sacred, was intimately tied to the orbital paths of Mercury, Venus, Jupiter and Saturn.

The "plumed serpent" of Mayan lore is a symbol of the activity of Hunab Ku's primal power in the human species. This serpentine symbology, signifying the rise of the life energy up the spine and the opening of the energy center at the crown of the head (referred to in India as the thousand-petalled lotus), is yet another example of the connection between the ancient wisdom cultures. The kundalini energy of Indian Shiva/Shakti, becomes Naga, the cobra. In Egypt, the cobra is found on the Pharaoh's headdress, indicating a state of higher consciousness. This same energy is represented by the dragon in China and certain deities are often depicted riding a dragon.

From Jesus' admonition, "Be as wise as serpents," to the cobra emerging from the Pharaonic headress, to the plumed serpent god of Central America, to Shiva/Shakti nagas of India, or Damballa, West Africa's python-creator-god, the snake has been a worldwide symbol of wisdom and power. Oddly, in Judeo-Christian culture this same serpent came to represent evil forces and was seen as God's enemy and the promoter of sin. In the Biblical creation story, Adam blamed Eve and she blamed the serpent for their disobedience to God's admonition to not eat the fruit of the Tree of the Knowledge of Good and Evil. This was the beginning of "passing the buck," the abdication of responsibility, and indiscriminate use of the human power of choice. Humanity chose duality over life and (in Judeo-Christian mythology) blamed power and wisdom (the snake) for influencing them in the wrong direction. The ensuing confusion, delusion and conflict has dominated human history ever since.

The languages of ancient wisdom cultures also shared special properties and purposes. Language was often used to safeguard Truth from the uninitiated and to communicate on surface levels, in depth and in secret simultaneously. The Mayan language served as both communication and numerical/mathematical system. Just as in Hebrew, each syllable has a numerical value. Messages of deeper Truth were often hidden within the outer message. In their own language, Maya means the few, the initiates, the chosen. Interestingly enough, Vedic scriptures refer to a distant people whom they called the Naga Maya.

Certain syllables appear to have carried a sacred theme through sound and meaning for diverse cultures. In order to examine these linguistic connections between ancient sage civilizations and others, let's look at the syllables that make up the Mayan word, Hunab Ku and compare their meanings among several cultures.

"Hun" in the Mayan language means "one," "the center of everything." The Hawaiian term "huna" has much the same meaning. Hawaiian Kahunas (shamans) were "keepers of the secrets." In Arabic, we find the expression "hu" referring to God's answer (the cosmic sound current) to our prayers (Allah Hu). In India, "hu" is the ending of mantric prayers, signifying the completion of an offering in honor of the deity.

"Ab" relates to the Aramaic word for Father or Source, "abba." The Hebrew term, Kabbala, which means "to receive hidden wisdom," incorporates both "ku" and "abba." "Kabbala" contains the Arabic word for the name of God, "Allah." The Sanskrit word, "kevala," surprisingly similar to Kabbala, means "indeterminate Absolute." A variation of that word, "kaivalya," denotes "psychological source."

The New Mexican Acoma term, "Ha Ku," meaning "a pre-existing special place" (spiritual or physical), relates to the Chinese and Tibetan, Ku, which means "universal substance," or "That Which Is."

Other sounds also appear to have spiritual significance to cultures with no obvious connections between them. In Hawaiian,

"Aloha" expresses the idea of universal love as synonymous with a supreme being and the breath. This is remarkably similar to the word "elohim" of the Old Testament which refers to the creative aspects of God. From the Aramaic root "Allaha" (astonishingly similar to aloha) comes the Arabic word for God, "Allah." In India, the word "Halla" is a Shaiva sect name for the Supreme Being. In Hebrew we find Aheya or Eheyeh ("I AM") is the divine name for the 1st emanation of God, Kether. This word comes from the root word "haya," meaning "to be" or "being."

Sanskrit, viewed by many as a sacred language, is also considered to be a perfect language because of the condition of "devata" – a Sanskrit term meaning that the name of a thing is the same as that thing's vibrational essence (sound). Science has proven the validity of this cognition of the Rishis by using technology to give visual representations of the sounds of Sanskrit words. They found that the sounds, when correctly pronounced, produced the same shapes as the Sanskrit letters used to write them. The same phenomena was shown to hold true for Hebrew but, to date, does not apply to any other language. The Hebrew and Sanskrit languages are said to have been divinely inspired, coming to their recipients as fiery flames or divine vibrations.

The concept of the Logos (the Word made manifest in the flesh – physical reality), has its origins in devata. In Vedic India, the power of speech is an aspect of Agni, the mystical fire of transmutation, therefore speech and fire can bring life, manifestation and change to the world; they were viewed as creators. Languages such as Sanskrit and Hebrew, which are true to the original vibration of a thing or concept, help preserve the people's connection with Source by cementing it in consciousness through constant use. This is the basis for the ancient development and use of mantras and chants, as well as magical incantations. This is also the foundation for the more modern use of affirmations.

The sounds of these languages, when properly pronounced, impart "blueprint vibrations" to the human energy centers, affecting consciousness. It is during this natural process that communication becomes prayer and the spiritual faculties located in these energy centers can be activated. This concept has far-reaching implications for the conscious use of human speech as a spiritual tool; the potential is immense.

In Hebrew, the actual forms of the letters are considered supernaturally imbued, every letter expressing a numerical value and containing many meanings, as well as representing the essence and inner workings of the Divine. For example, the secret coded meanings and numerical values of the Hebrew words for "One" and "Love" are the same as are those for "God" and "Nature." The identical numerical values point to an equality of spiritual concepts and their unity. Meanings were often purposely disguised to reach the soul comprehension in the same way a Master's phrase or instruction is interpreted uniquely by the conscious requirements of each individual present. At those times each person may have the feeling that the Master is speaking only to him, regardless of the number of people present.

Letters of a sacred language, like notes on the musical scale, express certain proportions and symmetry when properly arranged. This sense of balance and harmony is easily grasped in fine art, music and architecture and can also be found in pyramids and other buildings erected with the principles of sacred geometry in mind. Proper use of these principles organize chi, the life force managed by Chinese Feng Shui and can be made to apply to one's mind and life.

A step removed from the "devata" of Sanskrit and Hebrew, the Egyptian and Mayan languages used idea/pictures or ideograms to form their written language. Today's Chinese and Japanese (derived from Chinese) characters are an evolved Asian version of the hieroglyphs used by those ancient cultures. All three reflect a consciousness that relates more directly to the world, rather than the distancing, objectification and separation from real meaning that occurs when a culture uses phonetic script.

Using a pictorial representation of a thing or a concept to communicate it promotes continuity of cultural ideas, beliefs, understandings and meaning. For example, the Chinese characters for "China" literally mean "middle country" and show a plot of land, centrally located. Like many ancient peoples, the Chinese saw their land as the center of the earth. "Middle country" meant that they were central to life on this planet. All of these concepts come across in the ideogram. In the same fashion, the characters used for "sun" and "moon" are combined to form the word "bright." Suddenly there is much more cultural information available than just a reference to wattage.

Cultures that use languages such as Sanskrit and Hebrew, with sacred sounds and script, or with culturally sacred script, as found in Chinese and Japanese, keep a stronger connection to reality itself, because their language is an extension of it, like heat is to fire. In cultures where the language is based upon phonetic representation, there is little or no connection between the sound/word or script and the thing they communicate. These languages and the cultures that use them are farther removed from the vibrational reality of the thing or concept they attempt to convey.

Phonetically represented languages, such as English and most other languages in use today, are the farthest removed from the condition of "devata" and don't incorporate the vibration of the thing or concept they describe. While encouraging greater linguistic fluidity versatility and convenience, phonetic writing can also lead to cultural discontinuity and a sense of rootlessness. Modern Western Euro-American culture, relying entirely on written language which is a step removed from the reality it attempts to describe, has no real sense of its origins. For example, most people today have no idea why on Halloween[3] children dress up and go door to door for candy, why we have an "Easter Bunny" that lays eggs, or a jolly old fat man dressed in red, bringing gifts once a year. The origins of these customs and their symbolism are lost to us. Just as we have no idea why some of our customs exist, we also have no idea why we think about the world as we do. We are encouraged by our written language and cultural imperatives to continue the form of a thing with no understanding of its substance. This has led us to develop a "non-culture" based on meaningless rituals, such as those described above, now used to perpetuate endless consumerism.

The ancient Greeks believed there was a hidden danger in relying upon reading and writing. It doesn't allow one to experience oneself free of the mind-data of others. It imposes a template on the perceptive faculties, making it nearly impossible to ascertain reality cleanly and clearly, covering up what is. Reading and writing tends to overmentalize a society, while at the same time sculpting the mind, discouraging unhampered thought and supporting the

---

3 • *Halloween ("Holy Evening") was originally a pagan holiday (samhain) which celebrated a time when the veils between the physical and non-physical worlds were lifted and one could commune with the dead or even the gods. The confusing symbology of Easter (Mr. Bunny bringing Easter eggs) stems from the adoption of springtime fertility symbols from several different cultures. The story of Santa Claus was an amalgam of a Turkish folktale about a generous saintly man, European legends about "the little people" and pagan winter solstice festivals. Ironically, St. Nicholas replaced "Old Nick," a term variously used to refer to the Divine Mother's randy consort, a water goblin, or much later, the "Evil One."*

prevailing paradigm. It causes one to peer at reality through a veil of ideas and concepts, leaving little room for real originality or uniqueness to emerge.

How reading and writing (and today's computers, television and movies) are used is of vital importance. Unconsciously parking our minds (and our children) in 'neutral' in front of the television set or at the movies has had serious consequences on twentieth century society. The worldwide moral decline we are experiencing has been directly proportional to our obsessive reliance upon the media to sculpt and interpret reality for us. The philosophers of Greece felt that the decline of their culture came along with their reliance on written tradition. The same can be said for us.

Because our evolution requires the gradual unfoldment of the ability to more fully express Truth, there are stages or seasons in any religion, philosophy or lifeway. Each is suited to the receiver/participant's development. The preparatory level, consisting of outer, exoteric laws, observances, rules, commandments, precepts, etc., is designed to establish order and control behavior. Next, the inner, esoteric level opens the spiritual faculties and functions through stages of initiation, using symbols, magical/alchemical rituals and purification techniques. The third level occurs after all the vows, laws, techniques and other personal efforts have been exhausted and grace dawns. At the fourth level, Truth becomes something so natural and obvious that there is no need to do anything to attain it. One is so ingrained in embodying Truth that one feels as though it has always been this way.

After a golden age of purity, the cycle of the seasons turns again, during which a new blueprint or concept is given and a period of expansion and propagation follows. This phase is usually associated with the rise of cults and distortions of the original principles. The living Truth becomes fragmented into systems, hierarchies, sects and institutions grasping for power, wealth, territory and control.

Then fanaticism and narrow-minded fundamentalism signal the beginning of a decline, which can cause the mother religion to give birth to an evolutionary seed model. This either purifies and regenerates the old, evolving it or gives rise to a new religion/system, which is renounced by the old. This pattern is seen in all great traditions; for example, Buddhism sprang out of Hinduism, bringing the Eastern Sacred Stream back to wholeness. These cycles, phases and tendencies are repeatedly demonstrated throughout Sacred history as the cosmic play unfolds through the rise and fall of all empires, both religious and secular.

Unlike the Phoenix that rises reborn from the ashes of the old, some cultures whose time has passed never give rise to an identifiable new form, but they do leave monumental reminders of their immortal quest, such as the pyramids of Central America or the mysterious Sphinx which guards the great pyramids of Egypt.

With the passing of the Vedic Golden Age, India's wholistic, multi-stream orientation was lost and the Eastern Sacred Stream was born. The natural inclination of the Eastern Stream towards directly experiencing the Divine in non-physical ways later evolved in India as a tendency to withdraw into the non-physical dimensions. The pristine understanding which had included all Life, Sanatan Dharma, as preserved in the Vedas, had become something else, subject to the effects of the cosmic seasons of time, or Yugas. Hinduism, a much later development, is the result of the devolution of the original Vedic world view of Bharata (India).

There are in Vedic tradition four Yugas, time cycles lasting hundreds of thousands of years, which through their differing qualities of purity affect human development as our solar system appears to move backwards through the signs of the zodiac. Our journey through each sign or in this case, age, of the Zodiac takes approximately 2100 years. The present Yuga, Kali, named for the goddess of destruction of ignorance, is dominated by the tamasic qualities of spiritual darkness, degeneration, conflict and violence.

Like wheels within wheels, each main Yuga is affected periodically by short visitations from one of the others. For instance, as we leave the Zodiacal Age of Pisces for Aquarius (individuality and cooperation), our Kali Yuga (432,00 years long) will be interrupted by a 400-year sub-cycle of the Sat Yuga, bringing a temporary reprieve from the Kali Yuga's intense ignorance and negativity with the sattvic qualities of spiritual light, purity and truth. The golden age of Aquarius predicted and expected by so many for so long is, according to Vedic reckoning, a comparatively brief interlude of increased spiritual light. Next in line on this cosmic clock is the Treta Yuga, in which spiritual light diminishes to 75% of what it had been during the much longer major Sat Yuga cycle. The Dwarpa Yuga which follows brings another 25% reduction in Truth potency, providing a 50-50 spiritual atmosphere for humanity.

Our Modern era, said to have begun around 3,000 B. C., is governed by the Kali Yuga's rajasic (high emotion, reactivity, desires)and tamasic (degeneration and lethargy) tendencies. The extreme contrast presented by the overwhelming negativity and small percentage of sattvic qualities is said to be particularly favorable for accelerated development of human beings. These incredibly long spans of time covered by each Yuga could explain the Mayan obsession with astronomy and chronography. They, like their Vedic brethren, may also have been keeping track of the Ages in order to make better use of their time.

Unlike the peoples of the Western Sacred Stream, who celebrated the physical world of nature and experienced Divinity through living fully in harmony with the Divine Manifest in the natural world; the people of India developed a culture which partially invalidated physical reality and negated earthly life and the body. Earth-based peoples did not experience themselves or their world as illusory or separate from the Creator. The Heaven-oriented people of India, however, began to see the physical world as a deception of perception, an illusion, Maya.

With emphasis on leaving manifest reality behind, a bhakti (devotional) culture arose, which clung to devotion to Spirit, exclusive of material reality or progress. Indian sages devised and maintained an inner technology of consciousness in order to promote and accelerate union (yoga) with the Divine through the mastery and purification of man's tools of perception and experience, the body/mind. The different natures of humankind and attributes of the Godhead were reflected in the diverse forms of Yoga that arose.

Jnana yoga is a path in which discrimination, deidentification with the body, images and the so-called objective world and self enquiry take the place of the more devotional ritual worship of Bhakti yoga.

Unfortunately, Jnana often degenerates into purely philosophical schools with no living embodiments of the Self (masters). In true Jnana, the tools of words and worship are eventually discarded as the aspirant finds a spontaneous surrender and automatic enquiry, the magnetic pull of the Divine drawing the mind into Itself.

More active natures gravitate towards Karma yoga (union through performance of worldly duties), which purifies the heart by promoting forgetfulness of oneself through selfless service (seva), ceremony, making pilgrimages to sacred shrines, or holy places, etc. Hatha yoga focuses on rigorous discipline (postures, breath control, austerities) as the path to realization. Raja Yoga, designed for royalty, seeks union through becoming ruler of one's own mind by defeating its enemies – passion or lust, anger, greed, delusion, pride and jealousy. The eight-limbed path designed by Patanjali for this purpose includes techniques of breath control, mantra (repetition of sacred sounds), and postures in order to raise the kundalini energy.

Tantra, which predated the other forms of yoga, was a natural extension of ancient fertility practices. Early on Tantra wasn't a system, it was a way of life. The Tantric view was that Life itself was intrinsically "mergeable." A person's awareness could easily become synchronized with the underlying oneness through merging with something – beauty, a lover, the land – all was seen as holy, God. To them, all activities carried an inherent potential to act as gateways to God-union. Even some unexpected shock or "tragic" event could trigger an instantaneous awakening. Later, a system for attaining realization sprang up from the tantric lifeway which respected and used all aspects of life, including sexuality, for purification and spiritual development. Practitioners (known as Tantriks) engaged in visualization, breathing exercises and specific sexual practices to gain control of the kundalini (life/sexual energy) and other energy pathways, opening them to handle greater spiritual power, leading to realization.

All these paths may require an apprenticeship with a qualified Master or Guru in either reclusive or worldy settings. Eventually, all the yogas merge into one when their goal is realized: awakening to the pre-existing union (yoga) with Divine Source, God.

At a certain stage of advancement with any type of yoga, the Master or Guru (and even the world) is actually cognized as only the Self, masquerading as a teacher who simply pushes you back onto your own divinity. This cuts the tie with mind-projecting habits and the need for an external guide or image, reasons or ritual. The individual returns to God through the illusion of separation, the dream of the mind's waking veils and various religious and mystical avenues, removing mis-identification with either the outer world of the body, sense objects and karmic circumstances or the interior world of emotions, mind, intellect, or even bliss. This is the delicate shift of the dual path (duality) dissolving into the non-dual path (wholeness) and requires an unconfused mind and surrendered heart. Thus evolves the "play" of the Divine's rediscovery of Itself.

Despite the inevitable degenerative cycles of time, India has maintained her role as the emissary for the Eastern Sacred Stream, the Divine Unmanifest Source - Heaven. Today, India is the only remaining culture with a living, unbroken, spiritual tradition, stretching from the distant past into our present. Mother India has had countless revivals of her ancient wisdom, providing a continuous stewardship of the spiritual heritage transmitted through the sacred Vedas and Upanishads and the great epics of the Ramayana and Mahabharata. India's ancient spiritual glory is exemplified in such classic statements as, "I am the Self which abides in all beings." (Bhagavad Gita, 10:20); "All this is the Brahman, this self is the Brahman." (Mandukya Upanishad, 2:7) and "Whence shall he have grief, he who sees everywhere oneness?" (Isha Upanishad, verse 7). Today, nearly every historically recorded Indian spiritual path lives on in the cultural monument that is modern India.

Chapter Three
The Word and Worship

I t would be too simplistic to assert that Vedic civilization led to the migrations that spawned the great civilizations of Greece, Egypt and the fertile crescent stretching from Palestine to Babylonia. However, the migration of the Aryan people of Vedic Northern India was a major contributing influence, exhibited by the fact that Sanskrit is the source of Indo-European languages, extending across Persia into Greece and Europe. As a modern day example of this influence, the language of Lithuania is still 80% recognizable Sanskrit.

Contrary to popular European theories, the Aryans, whose name means "wise" or "noble," didn't invade India from the north but simply inhabited the northwest area of Vedic India and what is now known as Afghanistan, just as the Dravadians inhabited the southern portion of India during that same era. More than likely, European theories of Aryan invasion into India are based upon a vague collective memory of their journey from Shambala into India.

Rulers of northwest India, the Aryans were considered to be of the warrior caste, referred to in Vedic times as kshatriyas. Kshatriya defiance of the Brahmins, India's priestly caste, tarnished their image as the "noble lords" of the Vedic Age. They became known as the undivine, demons, enemies, those who opposed the 'divine' priests. This is possibly one of the historical events that support the Hindu mythological references to "asuric forces" clashing with " devas"(divine powers) in the subtle realms beyond our world, and whose battles echo back into our own psyche and manifest within society.

From India, the Aryan warriors embarked upon a great migration, from Varanasi, on the Ganges river, to Kashmir, enroute to the Caspian Sea (where they became the Kassites) and branching into the Middle East, where they influenced the Hittites and Assyrians. Spreading further west, they became the Mycenean Greeks of the Mediterranean and the Celtic peoples of Europe. Continuing north, they moved up to the Ukraine, reaching Lithuania and the Baltic Norselands. (See map #3.) The Aryan migration occurred simultaneously with the demise of the navigational culture of Crete and may have forced Abraham out of Chaldea, sending the Hebrews into Black Egypt ahead of the Hyksos invasion. This migration might also explain the war-like nature of the peoples of Europe and the Middle East and provide an explanation for the spread of the Sanskrit-based, Indo-European languages from India into the Steppes of southern Russia and across Europe.

The names of the gods worshiped in the cultures along the migration route make the Aryan journey easy to trace. Vedic Asura[4] becomes Persian Ahura, Assyrian Ashura and Germanic Aesir. The Sanskrit word asura, is also the root for the Germanic rune Ansuz, which relates to magical incantations, songs and poetry.

The religious influence of the Aryan migration can best be seen in Zoroastrianism, a religion with obvious ties to Vedic India. An offshoot of a Vedic cult which worshiped the sun god Surya Ishtara,[5] this religion branched into the Indo-Iranian plateau (there the founder was known as Zarathustra), giving rise to many successive Zoroasters meaning sun-priests in Persia.

Greek records say Zoroaster existed in 5500 B.C., preceding even legendary Krishna's time (3200 B.C.). Zoroaster, born of a virgin, like Krishna, was considered the son of the Lord of Light (God). He was later referred to as the "Ahura Mazda" - "the wise lord." The name "Ahura" comes from the Sanskrit word, "asura," meaning "almighty" or "lord." "Mazda" in ancient Persian means "wise One." In a flash of lightning, Zoroaster was finally consumed

---

4 • *The meaning of the word "asura" underwent drastic change in India over time. Originally meaning "almighty" or "lord," later it came to be a derogatory term, meaning "demon" or "enemy." The reason for this radical shift remains a mystery.*

5 • *Vedic India originated the tradition of the , "ishta devata" or worship of one's chosen deity. As a purificatory aid or intermediary bridge to realization of the Radiant Self/ Sat Chit Ananda a broad spectrum of deities or divine powers would be chosen to suite the individual or even cultural temperments : Mother Divine, Brahma , Agni, Mitra or Surya (Zarya). Surya (sun) ishta, or (Zara thustra) was chosen in the farthest reaches of ancient India's western borders (Persia) and over time became the goddess Ishtar in Babylonian, Astarte in Phoenicia.*

and ascended to the heavens. Synonymous with the later Persian version, Mithras, he was often symbolized by a "winged disc" in the Hittite, Egyptian, Assyrian and Sumerian cultures. In name and qualities Mithras is very similar to the Vedic Varuna Mitra, both considered "almighty lords, or solar deities, Adityas. Both were credited with having sovereignty over all beings, referred to in Sanskrit by the term Dyaus Pitar, meaning Heavenly Father. In name and qualities Mithras is very similar to the Vedic Mitra, one of the 12 solar deities.

The obvious similarities between the story of Jesus and that of much older Zoroaster are hard to overlook. However, this doesn't necessarily discount the fact of Jesus' existence or divinity. It may just point to a pattern through which the solar deities operate.

Despite the fact that there are more Egyptian archeological remains than all other ancient civilizations combined, Egypt's mystery has remained an elusive enigma to modern culture. This is partially due to the fact that European scholars refused to accept the Black African roots of European and Greek culture, something that, due to racism and ethnocentricity, Euro-American anthropologists, archaeologists and historians have either avoided, altered or misinterpreted. Because of this, Egypt was conveniently "left out" of Africa by "orientalist" scholars. This same idea persists today, with most people thinking of Egypt as something separate from and other than "African," in other words, "Oriental" or "Middle Eastern."

In ancient times, Egyptians called themselves "Kemet," from the Egyptian root Km, meaning black, like the dark, fertile soils of the Nile and were known by Indian traders as Kem. Pre-Semitic southern Egypt was populated by a mixture of the Black peoples of the Sudan/Ethiopia and the seafaring traders, often referred to as Dravadians, from Southern India and the Indus River valley. This group, Lemurian in origin, made up the Upper (southern) Kingdom of Egypt. (See map #4.) In all likelihood Egyptians worshiped the solar deity of the land of Km, K'Mit Ra. This name, reminiscent of the Vedic god Mitra, was later shortened to Ra.

Those currently thought of as "Egyptian" – lighter-skinned North Africans whose ancestors came from the Middle East – arrived well after Black Egypt's ascendancy. Ancient Egypt's dominant racial foundation was Black African, which was later mixed with Asian and Caucasian peoples during migrations, trade and warfare. They could be compared to those people of mixed race found in great abundance today throughout the United States, the Caribbean and certain parts of South America.

It is a modern curiosity that any trace of Black African blood qualifies a person as a member of the Black race, whereas to Egyptologists studying the Black African people of ancient Egypt, any trace of non-Black blood qualified one as a non-Black (oriental) Egyptian. If this same outlook was applied to the African-American population, they would have to be classified as non-Black. This obvious misapplication of the "rule of thumb" they themselves established to categorize the people they studied was actually used to bolster a racist, ethnocentric point of view. It clearly shows the powerful influence of cultural conditioning, misuse of the intellect and lack of rationality on the part of those decifering the messages of the past.

The Lower Kingdom of Egypt in the north was originally under the leadership of Atlantean Thoth, later known as the god of writing, who is still revered today as Kwoth, the principle deity of Sudanese Nuers. The mysterious Egypt of antiquity was formed when the lower and upper kingdoms were united under the rule of the Black Pharaoh Menes around 3500 B.C.

Egypt's spell over the European mind is founded in the desire to understand the mystery of Life/Spirit which Egypt represents. The misinformation about the origins of ancient Egypt and her mysticism has led to a spiritual romanticism, glamorizing all things "Egyptian" without knowledge of what they really were or where they came from. In order to truly understand the mystery of ancient Egypt one must enter into the Black African cosmic principle of harmony, Ma'at.

The African equivalent of the Chinese Tao, the cosmic harmony of the goddess Ma'at was understood as the underlying unity between the individual and the universal, the senses and sense objects, between humans and all of nature. To the worshippers of Ma'at, the universe is the result of the union of complementary elements – cosmic unity in diversity; the procreative embrace of the sky and earth, past and future, the immortality of the womb and the tomb, even the upper and lower kingdoms of Egypt. Even today, Zulus echo this ancient understanding in the declaration, "I am river, mountain, tree, love, emotion, beauty, lake. I am cloud, sun, sky, mind, One with One."

Problems in one's life were seen as simply the manifestation of the need for education in the ways of Ma'at. Disorder and disharmony were seen as the only evils. One could come to understand the causes of disorder and disharmony by studying oneself. The saying made famous by the Greeks, "Know thyself," was actually birthed in Egypt and is inscribed on a Karnac temple in Luxor.

The principles of Ma'at which were central to Kemet beliefs so long ago are still woven in and through traditional communities of today's Black Africa. Love of children, valuing fertility, extended families, societal good before individual desire, caretaking the environment, festivals for agriculture, rites of passage, and honoring ancestors and elders, are all based on an understanding of the principle of Ma'at: innate harmony.

The name Ma'at bears striking resemblance to the Sanskrit word Mahat, meaning "the first individualizing principle of Cosmic Intelligence, emerging from Purusha (universal Soul) and Prakriti (universal substance). We also find a similarity in the Mesopotamian goddess, Tiamat ("She who gave birth to them all"), and Mayan "Na'at," meaning intelligence. Divine intelligence is necessary in order to give birth, to emanate the apparent differentiation of all unique expressions of the Divine, which is within Its own creations as their very forms and processes; just as heat and light are contained within the sparks of a fire. This relationship is Ma'at. The Hebrew term Da'ath, meaning "divine knowledge" plays a parallel role in the Hebrew mystical tradition of the Kabbala.

Ma'at's influence in African culture was expressed in ancient times through the recognition and use of the power of oratory, careful organization and just ruling of society. It was also replicated in temple architecture.

African Egypt was well-versed in the use of sacred geometry in architecture. Because of their understanding of Ma'at, the Egyptians recognized that the operative laws of the spiritual world manifested in the physical world ("As above, so below"). They saw this in nature and the human body, and used this knowledge in their architecture to record and communicate data and affect their environment and state of consciousness. It was understood that the shape of a thing affects the vibratory rate of its contents. Pyramidal shapes, for instance, are great energy conductors and prevent deterioration of anything put inside them.

Egyptian temples and other important buildings were designed as interdimensional bridges and arenas of spiritual training and initiation into the spiritual realities standing behind the forms. The Great Pyramid[6] is one such device. Devoid of hieroglyphs, its geometrical measurements and proportions activate cosmic energies and represent, among other things, prophecies of future events.

Beyond the sacred geometry of architecture, the power behind the spoken word was held in equally high esteem. To the followers of Ma'at, the power of speech was a sacred, creative process, proceeding from Harmony and bringing the Truth of things into Form. The Biblical passage, "In the beginning was the word and the word was with God," speaks to this very basic Truth that creation emanated from vibration. Harmonious manifestation of Truth in speech was considered to go far beyond not lying. Speech was never to be used for struggle or confrontation but explicitly for bringing about or expressing Harmony. In this way, sacred oratory was the African understanding and use of "devata." Spells, incantations, affirmations, chanting, and mantrams are examples of the use of this understanding.

In order for one to become a proper orator, and therefore a just ruler, one must know Ma'at. The orator well-versed in the principles of Ma'at connected the past to the present and unified himself with his audience. Outstanding modern examples of this Southern Sacred Stream power are found in the oratory of Martin Luther King, Jesse Jackson, Louis Farrakhan, and even Rap music.

When the creative power of speech is used disharmoniously, sickness manifests and society slowly disintegrates. Laws and rules, enacted to prevent social deterioration are ineffective in "curing" societal ills; these measures work only on a limited scale. Because an intuitive, working knowledge of the soul and cosmic laws is essential for any effective remedies to be recognized and/or enacted, healing the vibrational disturbances of one's own or another's thoughts and speech has always been the domain of shaman/priests.

---

6 • *The Great Pyramid is sometimes referred to as the Pyramid of Enoch. It is interesting to note that according to the Aztecs, one of the first men on earth was Tenoch, who searches for the feathered serpent. Is it just coincidence that as the sun sets in Tenochtitlan, Mexico, it rises at the Sphinx, at the base of the great Pyramid?*

The knowledge of sacred geometry, the power of speech and other metaphysical matters gave rise to the secret guilds that calibrated and built Solomon's Temple, as well as the celebrated temples of Greece, and all Middle Eastern mosques and European cathedrals. Later known as Freemasons, these groups trace their roots to ancient Egypt. They developed European mystery schools that produced the architects of the United States constitution. Today, evidence of Freemason influence on the birth of the United States can be found in the secret hermetic symbols used on American currency. Ironically, apparently unaware or in denial of their Black African roots, American Freemasons routinely excluded African Americans and other people of color from membership in their organizations.

Worship of the Cosmic Synthesis of Oneness, Ma'at, through the Nine Deities of the Nine Worlds (called the Ennead by the Greeks) was common. The cosmic forces and principles that sustain nature were called "neters" by the Egyptians (which in Sanskrit means guides). The sun god, Ra[7], (considered self-created) masturbated, creating Air (Shu) and Moisture (Tefnut). Air gave birth to Sky (Nut), and moisture subsequently gave birth to Earth (Geb), all of which continuously created the world through their interaction. Osiris, Isis, Seth and Nephthys – the other four, better known deities – aided the Pharaohs in regulating justice in human affairs.

Through association with more experienced initiates and participation in ritual initiation, Egyptian neophytes came to know and eventually embody, the neters. They actively pursued the mission of the Southern Sacred Stream: expression of the divine in form through the body, speech, architecture, just society, immortality of the soul and bodily resurrection. At first, anyone who had the aptitude or showed signs of being ready was welcome to participate in the mysteries; much later, all that changed.

The Egyptian story of Osiris (known to the Egyptians as Ausar, similar to Vedic Asura) provided a template for the future development of Christian belief in a resurrected savior and the regeneration of humanity. Osiris was dismembered by his brother, Set,[8] who then scattered his pieces all over the world. Isis, both wife and sister to Osiris, saves the day by finding his scattered pieces and restoring him long enough to become pregnant by him with Horus, the sun god, who then kills Set and becomes the new Creator-god.

---

7 • *Ra's symbols were the same as Indian Lord Shiva's, the bull, sun and cobra.*

Osiris, worshiped as the embodiment of goodness, represents, among other things, resurrection and regeneration of the body, eternal life and spring fertility. His story reflects the ancient belief in the need for a sacrifice in order for regeneration of life to take place in springtime. This theme was common in ancient Western Stream cultures, manifesting in some regions as spring sacrifice of males.

Ritual sacrifice of some kind played a vital role in most ancient cultures, growing out of the nomadic hunters' ceremonial magic and continued with the development of agriculture and the domestication of animals to insure a healthy harvest and livestock. Possibly triggered by the observation of the renewal resulting from women's menses, ancient peoples recognized the benefit of the release of regenerative supernatural life force through the spilling of blood and ritual calendars were closely tied to the phases of the moon.

Throughout the world (including Europe and the Middle East) gifts of foodstuffs, wine, animals, and sometimes humans, were made to the deities in exchange for blessings, to atone for some trespass, or to avert a calamity. In Vedic India worship rituals were based on sacrificial offerings of milk, animals and intoxicating plants, accompanied by hymns. Biblical passages refer to such sacrifices made to Yehova, and Abraham, father of the Jews, is said to have been prevented by an angel from sacrificing his son. The ritual of circumcision may have evolved out of this practice in order to appease the need for male sacrifice without actually taking a life. Much later, ritual sacrifice continued in more symbolic form in Christianity in the story of Jesus' crucifixion and resurrection, the martyrdom of early Christians themselves, and the celebration of the Catholic Mass.

The spiritual glory that was Egypt had begun to deteriorate, giving rise to a distortion of the Southern Stream tendency to put forward successive innovations in spirituality. This was exemplified by a succession of regional and dynastic Egyptian gods, which led to diverse and often conflicting legends/mythology. When a new ruler came to power, he/she would often rename the local gods. For example, Ptah was at one time substituted for the creator god Atum, who like earlier Ma'at was considered to be immanent in all life.

---

8 • *Originally Set was known as a benevolent god, but with the shifting of political/priestly power, the god of the conquered region, in this case, Set, became associated with evil. This same process occurred in India, changing "asura," "almighty lord," into "evil demon."*

However, regardless of the name given to divine successors, the powers and principles of Ma'aṭ always shone through. In this case, with Ptah, divine order came into being through what the heart thought and the tongue spoke. The manifesting power of oratory ("the Word made flesh"), a Southern Sacred Stream trait, was still very much a part of the picture.

Egypt was conquered by Semitic invaders, the Hyksos and after a brief return to power when the Hyksos were finally routed, the Pharaohs slowly lost their demigod status. Temple initiation was first restricted to the royal family, and later (around 1400 B.C.) abolished altogether by Pharaoh Akhenaton (Amenophis IV, of the 18th Dynasty), replacing direct experience of knowledge with the use of oracles.

Akhenaton's major contribution was the introduction of monotheism to the common people of the Southern Sacred Stream through the exclusive worship of Aton. Formerly Atum, the sun god of the Ennead, Aton was represented by a winged solar disk. Prior to that time, the people's understanding was limited to the idea of theological bureaucracy – many gods, each handling his/her own little corner of reality. Aton was actually the Southern Stream's attempt to return to the idea of oneness, which over time had been lost among the uninitiated.

The downward spiral of deterioration which brought about the renaming of gods, then prompted the loss of temple initiation and the deeper understandings that came with it, spelling the end of Egypt's golden age. The knowledge and understanding of Ma'at was removed from the world, and put outside of everyday life and individual experience, resulting in Egypt's eventual downfall. Ma'at's principles of Oneness, truth, harmony and oratory power would, however, be preserved for later generations by another Southern Sacred Stream people. As the "Word of God" made manifest through commandments and prescribed action dedicated to the Divine, the mission of the Southern Stream would be carried forward by its next flower, the Children of Israel.

The ancient Habiru tribes, later known as Hebrews, who arrived in Egypt along with the conquering Hyksos, were made up of disparate Atlantean peoples. After first immigrating to central Asia, they made their way to Sumeria through the Iranian plateau, brushing up against remnants of the Vedic culture (which at that time extended into what is now known as Afghanistan), then on to

Egypt on the heels of the Semitic invading armies of Hyksos, some say carrying with them the oral tradition of the mystical Kabbala.

The pre-Mosaic patriarchs of the early Hebrew tribes never used holy books for guidance. Divine revelation manifested itself in their hearts through waking epiphanies, dreams, and visions, such as the biblical report of three archangels entering into Abraham's tent. Like Western Stream shamans, Hebrew prophets interpreted occurrences in their lives as mystical encounters with spiritual and natural forces.

The role of the Hebrews is singular among humanity for uniting all Sacred Streams through their migrations, exiles and persecutions. Flowing first through the Western Stream central Asia, touching Eastern Stream Vedic India, Southern Stream Egypt and now Northern Stream Euro-America, the Hebrews influenced and were influenced by the cultures they passed through. Now carrying the knowledge and purpose of the combined Streams to Euro-America, they may help bring about the completion of the Tetragrammaton, the full manifestation of the Divine in physical reality. It is also interesting to note that Black Africans have accomplished the same feat, albeit in a different way, due to their sojourn in slavery.

Abraham, the progenitor of those later known as Israelites and Arabs was of Hebrew descent. His name, Abram (later Abraham, "father of many nations"), incorporated elements from Sanskrit, Egyptian and Semitic languages. Abba, meaning the One Source, or Father, has its roots in Semitic languages. Ram, an Indian Solar King, was said to be an incarnation of Vishnu, a god of the Indian pantheon. (Amen) Ra was also an Egyptian sun god. In Sanskrit, the word "abrahm" could mean "not a priest." We shall see the significance of this shortly.

Abraham's teacher, Melchizadek, was part of a mystery priesthood which survived the destruction of Atlantis. In Hebrew the word "tzadek" means "righteous holy person." Abraham was initiated into these mysteries as a "tzadek."

Abraham and his descendants represented a departure from a system run by priests – they became a *priestly people,* instead of being subject to the rule of a chosen few with spiritual authority. The Israelites considered themselves a God-chosen people who would serve as an example to the other Semitic tribes, resisting the segregated authority of a priestly caste, such as that found in those times in India or Egypt. This theme was lost, however, when the Israelites themselves established their own priestly castes of Levites and Cohens.

Abraham rejected the idol-worshipping ways of the Chaldean colony of Dravadians among whom he lived. He kept to himself, and with his wife Sara and servant girl, Hagar had two sons. One (Sarah's child) became the founder the Israelites, the other founded the Arabs. These two lineages carried the Southern Sacred Stream forward where Egypt left off.

Abraham's rejection of idol worship reflects, among other things, the understanding that the image of a thing is not the thing itself. Just like the fact that a word is not the thing to which it refers. It is humanity's imagination, the ability to image, conceive, reason and self-reflect, which differentiates us from animals. It is also this very faculty that causes us to believe we are separate from God. We "imagine" our paradigms, both religious and secular.

Because so few of us have the ability to use mental images and physical idols to truly merge with abstract spirit, we require worship, development and education to attain that level of consciousness. Worship in the form of song, music and prayer, especially in a sacred language or rhythms and octaves that affect the consciousness centers (Hebrew or Sanskrit, for instance) bridges the gap between the Real and what the mind imagines by tapping the longings of the heart. Through this process the experience of the Divine is so all-embracing that the idol/image can be seen as an extension of the divinity the worshipper reveres because in Truth, It IS all things. Idols, art and the products of the imagination (mental pictures, concepts, reasoning), or living examples such as teachers, gurus or saviors are stepping stones that lead to or develop the ability to leave image or imagination behind and enter into the Real, the thing itself.

In India, merging with the guru was revered as the gateway to God. Becoming one with the manifest form (the guru) leads one to forget oneself, emptying out self importance. Then, through the grace of the guru, the formless Presence reveals Itself as your very own nature. We come to know that God became us, individualizing Itself, in order to experience its Creation and thereby know Itself. It was for this realization that all the rules of conduct, initiations and rituals of religious/spiritual practice were created.

After the Egyptians ousted the Hyksos regime and regained control of their empire, they kept the Israelites as slaves. Although there is almost no mention in Egyptian history of their 400-year stay in Egypt, the culture, language and religion of the Israelites were heavily influenced by their Egyptian masters and the neighboring Semitic peoples. The psalms of King David and the Book of Proverbs bear strong resemblance to the writings of an Egyptian Pharaoh named Amenemope. Even the Hebrew name, Adam, which means "the perfected one," "the living light of all emanations of God," is suspiciously similar to the name of the Egyptian sun god of the Ennead, Atum.[9] The Hebrew Adam Kadman[10] – the archetypal, perfected human – is said to hold all the attributes of God.

This Egyptian/Hebrew name (Atum/Adam) is also the same (astonishingly so) as our name for the power of the sun – the atom. Our attempt to harness the power of the atom – nuclear energy – may represent our vain attempt to, in a sense, control God, or the solar beings.

Israel's god had archangel assistants with Egyptian names, evidence of the cross-pollination of Hebrew and Egyptian cultures. MaHaEl (Michael), the Great God, KhaBriEl (Gabriel), the Desire God, RaFaEl (Raphael), the Sun God, URaEl(Uriel), the Space Sun God and ShamAEl (Shamuel), God of light/matter are actually names of the vibrations of different aspects or agencies of the Supreme Being, borrowed from the Egyptians.

The very name IsRaEl is full of Egyptian meaning: ISis (goddess of the moon and femininity), RA, (Egyptian sun god), EL (common word for god in Semitic languages). According to the Bible, when Abraham's son, Jacob, wrestled with the angel he was renamed Israel, meaning 'holy struggle with god' in Hebrew.

Moses, who led the Israelites out of slavery, is yet another example of how deeply they were influenced by their Egyptian captivity. The son of Israelite slaves, yet raised and educated as an Egyptian prince, he was well-versed in the Kabbala (Egyptian kybalion/Hermetic mysticism). Like Joseph (Jacob's twelfth son who was sold into Egyptian slavery by his brothers), he may have been married to an Egyptian priestess. The name Moses, which was in common usage in those times as an ending for Egyptian names, meant "begotten from" (e.g. Tutmoses, begotten from Tut, Rameses begotten from Ra, etc.).

---

9 • *It's a short leap from Atum, a name for the Egyptian sun god/solar being, to Adam, the perfected human, pointing to the mission of the Southern Stream and the task of the solar beings.*

10 • *Later, the term "son of man," meaning son of the Adam Kadman, was used to refer to men who exhibited divine qualities, such as Ezekiel or Jesus who were called "sons of man" in the Bible.*

Strangely, Moses chose to keep his Egyptian name when he took up the cause of his people, but dropped the first half, which would have indicated who his Egyptian (adoptive) father or patron god was. His name, "begotten from," acknowledged that he was a child of Egypt, while denying any particular patrimony. He was, in a sense, claiming all of Egypt as his father and disassociating himself from any past images of god. His name also indicated that he was no one special – "begotten from" pointing to the mere fact of being born just like everyone else – from no particular father, lending greater mystery to his already unusual background, while at the same time declaring his ordinariness.

To the Children of Israel living as captives in a failing Egypt, the fading glory of Amen Ra or Aton, who replaced Ma'at in Egypt's later years, seemed much too limited compared to YHVH, the "One without a second," the Unknowable whose name could not even be uttered.

YHVH, known as the Tetragrammaton, comes from the verb, HY or haya "to be" and contains the secrets of the Kabbala's Tree of Life and prophecy within its letters. It is a graphic representation of the axiom, "As above, so below." To those who understood, YHVH was the name of the All Reality of God, from unmanifest to manifest and the key to creation. For them, YHVH was not simply a tribal god, but a secret code for the manifestation of the All Reality on earth. One's atunement to YHVH allows one to receive the fruits of the Tree of Life.

The Shema prayer, "Hear O Israel, YHVH, (the Lord) our God, YHVH the (Lord) is One: (Det. 6:4) is a sacred confession of divine unity. The declaration, "Thou shalt love YHVH, thy God, with all thy heart, with all thy soul, and with all thy might," is actually a prescription for realization of that unity. The whole man, the Tree of Life is consecrated to the Divine.

The Kaballa's Ain Sof (Limitless/Boundless) is the Hebrew version of Vedic Brahman, Egyptian Ma'at, Mayan Hunab Ku and the Chinese Tao. YHVH, one of the 10 names of the sephiroth (the emanations, names and aspects of Ain Sof, arranged as the Tree of Life - See diagram A.) also contains the spiritual keys to understanding them. The 22 letters of the Hebrew alphabet and the 10 numerals are derived from this Tree and comprise the 32 "paths of wisdom" on the Tree of Life, describing the process of manifestation – bringing form out of the unmanifest.

The intrinsic unity of the 10 sephiroth[11] in the name YHVH could be seen only by abiding in the essence of one's own being, unified with the Supreme Self. Otherwise, from the level of mind interpretation, the sephiroth are distinct qualities or attributes. These attributes are all present in man, therefore, the divine man, the Adam Kadman, (the son of man) is superimposed over the Tree of Life, demonstrating that man is made in the image and likeness of God. (See diagram B.) However, man has yet to use all his gifts; as Jesus stated,."... and he will do works greater than these...," John, 14:12.

YHVH (Yehova or Jehovah), also one of the 10 divine names of the Ain Sof, is the word/name relating to the 3rd emanation from the Ain Sof, Binah (the divine feminine wisdom/intelligence). The ancients recognized that nothing can be manifested or created without Her dynamic, active power and She was worshiped by the Habirus, along with the Father principle. Her spoken Hebrew name was Aima which is also a word or seed mantra used in India to invoke the Divine Mother.

The idea of the "wise lord," found in the Kabbala's Yehova presiding over the Wisdom emanation of the Tree of Life, can also be found in Vedic Varuna (Asura), Persian Ahura Mazda and Norse Aesir. The similarities, sometimes in name and always in concept, point to not only cultural diffusion but clearly relate to a true Divine Principle or Attribute appearing simultaneously or consecutively in various places around the globe. (See map #3.)

According to the Kabbala, Metatron (Mitatra), the highest solar archangel and "servant of the Lord God of Israel," is also the immanent counterpart of the Adam Kadman. In Persia this same relationship was expressed through Ahura Mazda and his servant, Mithras; in Vedic India Asura and Mitra fulfilled those roles respectively.

Under threat of the pain of death from Moses and the sons of Levi (3,000 idol-worshipping Israelites were slaughtered), the "Chosen People" left behind sun and idol worship during their forty years of isolated wandering in the Sinai Desert. The majority of the people, however, didn't understand what YHVH meant. In order to span the chasm between the Reality and their understanding, the Israelites constructed a tribal demi-god out of transcendent concepts.

---

11 • *The 10 emanations of the Ain Sof (the sephiroth) are actually a more detailed description of the same power referred to in Vedic terms as the maya-shakti power of Brahman.*

The fear inspired by Jehovah's priesthood – and many, if not all other authorities – was (and still is) a power play. Obedience inspired by fear is not true humility; it is self preservation, eventually leading to resentment and some form of backlash/reaction focused against the controlling agent. Awe in the presence of true spiritual greatness is a natural response based on deep appreciation and acknowledgment of the Divine, tending to humble the human ego. Leaders, religious or otherwise, lacking in true spiritual greatness will use fear to "inspire" their congregations, followers, or subjects to obey the rules, toe the mark, and usually, empty their wallets.

The Children of Israel became worshippers of an inverted version of the ever-accessible Ma'at. Invisible, mysteriously exclusive, patriarchal, jealous, and warlike, Jehovah, although surrounded by angels with Egyptian names, was outside the Egyptian pantheon. Ma'at, now known to the Israelites as 'the glory of God', the Kavod, was to be received only in Temple, at the Ark of the Covenant. Repeating the pattern of their Egyptian Southern Stream forebears, the people shifted the emphasis away from acknowledging and worshipping both the masculine creative and feminine wisdom-power of God, towards the more limited, strictly male Jehova.

Unlike the Egyptians, the Children of Israel placed less emphasis on the Oneness of all things. Their emphasis was on worship of the One God. Rather than focus on purification of the body/mind and eternal life, they focused on making themselves and their lives pleasing to their god. This god and worship of him became tied to a specific geographical location, the land of Israel, rather than being present in all earthly existence as it had been for the early Egyptians. Later, the land of Israel, its people and its god were understood as One, similar in principle to the all-encompassing view of Egypt under Ma'at, but on a much smaller scale. In this way the Israelites brought the concept of Ma'at's oneness down to a much more personal level. The move toward a more personal deity was required in order for people to find and develop their own individual identity.

The Hebrews' geocentric approach to spirituality is common in most Western Stream cultures which, as we have already mentioned, hold certain high energy places to be sacred. For the ancient Greeks, Mt. Olympus was the home of the gods. For the North American

Hopi, Kachina Peaks in northern Arizona is a place where the Heavens touch the Earth and the divine penetrates the human realm of matter. Religious pilgrims in India approach the body of Lord Shiva by circumambulating sacred Mt. Kailash in Tibet and Arunachula in southern India.

The tribulations of the Israelites in Egypt, just prior to the Exodus, represent the trials of the soul that must come to pass before it can return home. Each person must make his own exodus out of slavery according to his or her own nature and timing. We all are in bondage, sold into slavery by our family genetics and social agreements. We will be in exile from our true home until we stop being victims to the mental suggestions of others and cease our own mental interference (criticism and judgment). This process is reflected in the Jewish diaspora, as humanity apparently exiled itself from God, and only through humanity's actions can we return.

Wandering through countless incarnations, the soul makes its journey to the Promised Land, at last finding that God manifests on earth as each of His creations. And just as God revealed his Glory to Moses (the hallowed man) in the wilderness of the unknown, and as Krishna unveiled His Divine Radiance to Arjuna on the battlefield of Life, so it shall be revealed to each of us.

Almost five hundred years after their flight from Egypt, 10 of the 12 tribes of Israel were forced out of the area we now call Palestine by the Assyrian army and scattered throughout Mesopotamia and from the Black Sea to Afghanistan (c. 721 BC), becoming the Lost Tribes of Israel. As usually happens in these circumstances, some Assyrians in Palestine intermarried with some members of the remaining 2 Israelite tribes; this group became known as Samaritans. This probably brought the Children of Israel into contact with the principles of Zoroastrianism. Almost two hundred years later, the 2 remaining tribes (later referred to as Jews) were conquered by Babylonians and taken to Babylonia as slaves in 586 BC.

During their captivity in Persian Babylonia (586-531 BC) the Jewish priesthood rewrote the Torah (1st five books of the Bible), apparently first set down during their long association with the Assyrians, and as had happened in Egypt, the people's culture and religion were deeply influenced by their captors. The updated Torah now incorporated some new elements, obviously affected by the Zoroastrian beliefs of their previous conquerors. The idea of an eternal battle between a God of Good (light) and an evil Lord of

Darkness, moral and physical purity, the dedication of one's life and works to righteousness – all of which are central to Zoroastrianism, were combined with a Babylonian creation story. Persian Ahriman merged with the Egyptian Set to become Satan. What previously had been understood as the distinctions between the real and unreal of the Kabbala's Tree of Life had now become the differences between the good and evil of the Tree of Knowledge. Dualism had entered the flow of the Southern Stream and centuries later these ideas were passed along to Christianity. [12]

The drastic polarization of good and evil adopted by the Jews during their Assyrian and Babylonian captivity had its seeds sown in a war raging within the collective soul. This strongly manifested in a radical shift in religious belief, born in the Persian culture of fire-worshipping Magis. Goodness and Light, called Ahura Mazda by the Persians, was pitted against Evil and Darkness, represented by the temptations of the sensory world. In sharp contrast to Indian devotional spirituality and Afro-Egyptian dedication to the perfection of form, adherence to the principles of righteousness and law and striving to avoid evil and gain good came into being. As described in Genesis, humankind became immersed in eating the fruit of the Tree of the Knowledge of Good and Evil, rather than understanding the Kabbala's Tree of Life. Striving to become a companion to the Spirit of Light and vanquish the Prince of Darkness became the most important spiritual goal.

When people are unable (for whatever reasons) to manifest Truth in their lives, they must fall back on doctrinal religion, following laws which distinguish for them between what is good and what is evil, acceptable and unacceptable, moral and immoral, rather than relying upon their own inner knowing and goodness. The Tree of Knowledge's good and evil satisfies the mind's penchant for duality. Distinguishing between the real and unreal (the Tree of Life) is Spirit's province. Lao Tzu, earliest recorded proponent of Taoism, recognized that the passage of large numbers of laws eventually leads to increased lawlessness. True laws or true religious ethics don't exist to regulate the lives of the people but to ensure an environment in which the inherent power and talents of the individual can unfold and aid in the maturation of society.

---

12 • *The Christian belief in Judgment Day echoes Zoroastrian Frashokereti, a time when the dead shall be raised for final judgment and evil will be purged from the world.*

The Jews had a myriad of mitzvahs – rules of behavior to ensure one's acceptability in the eyes of God, (originally designed as psycho-spiritual stimuli or technologies that positively affected the soul's awakening). Within Mosaic law we find once again an attempt to imitate the Divine in order to be more like It. It is said that God rested on the Sabbath, so the Hebrews rest, reinforced by observances of holy law (ritual) and scriptural recitations. Through worship and study the sanctity (and some of the rules) of the Sabbath Day were extended into the ordinary rhythms of life, thereby bringing holiness into the everyday routine.[13] By comparison, in India a person is considered inherently holy and in no need of "salvation." This point of view is exemplified by the time-honored greeting, "Namaste," which means, "I honor the light of the divine that shines through you to me."

The original Torah (first five books of the Bible), gathered together by scribes about the same time as the Vedas were written down, (c.1000-700 BC). The major theme of the Torah is recognizing the sacredness of man's life and being, lifting up all of one's life to God. This is letting God in, the profane is closing off to Him. The gulf between the two is part of human experience and, according to the Torah, is crossed when one performs actions dedicated to the Divine, entering into the hidden mysteries (Kabbala) behind the outer codes of behavior. Actions dedicated to the Divine are what change society. This idea is aptly expressed in Proverbs which says, "Know Him in all thy ways. Find Him. Serve Him."

After Africa's Egyptian custodianship, the Southern Stream was further matured by passing to the Hebrews. By introducing Hebrew, a sacred language which contained the hidden knowledge of the Kabbala, the oratory power of Ma'at was held in both sacred script and everyday language. In addition, the laws designed to purify behavior made Ma'at's principles the spontaneous effect of adherence to the Torah.

Through the Jews the Southern Stream developed the necessary genetic and cultural configuration required to manifest the Divine into a "gifted" human, Jesus. However, this event is not limited to

---

13 • The observation of the Sabbath has origins probably surprising to Jews and Christians alike. The word is derived from sabbatu, meaning "heart's rest." Originally, each quarter phase of the moon was marked as a sabbatu on which Ishtar (goddess of love, wisdom and war) menstruated. On these days the people refrained from certain activities, just as if they were menstruating women. The prescribed rest of the Sabbath day, therefore, reflects the ancient Middle Eastern custom which restricts the activities of women during this phase of their menstrual cycle.

just one person or people but is available to all humanity. The story of Jesus is a template for the full manifestation of divinity in all humankind. Over the centuries this Truth was misinterpreted and limited to one man and the people from whom he sprang.

Manifesting the Southern Stream strategy of isolation in order to regroup, regenerate or transmute, the Jews isolated themselves in unconscious preparation for the Christ Event (bringing a solar being into a human body), emphasizing their perception of themselves as being chosen or special. In their isolation, they tested the technology of the Torah to produce a priestly people and a god-man, bringing about the Essene[14] communities and a mystical text of the Kabbala called the Zohar (The Book of Splendor).

Passing from people to people, culture to culture, the Southern Stream has flowed in and through Ma'at's Black Egypt, Jehovah's Middle Eastern Children of Israel and later, Jesus' Judeo/Christianity, which went to Europe, and Muhammed's Islam, which spread throughout the Far East. This sequential strategy of the Southern Stream lends itself well to the task of full manifestation of divinity in humanity by flowing this energy through the cultures it adopts to every corner of the globe.

The story of the endurance, ingenuity and adaptability of the Jewish people, born of their persecution is reminiscent of the Greek tragedies or Shakespeare's dramas. Even today we wrestle with the same harsh realities as those mentioned in the Old Testament Bible: inequity, rape, incest, jealousy, murder, assassination, betrayal, adultery; things haven't changed all that much over the last 4,000 years.

Along with the demise of polytheism for the Jews, personal, individual worship died with the establishment of more institutionalized religious structure and forms of worship. Local shrines were dismantled in favor of a centralized worship of Yehovah at the temple in Jerusalem. The 500 gods of Baal on Mt. Zaphon, the Egyptian ennead and the ever-present Ma'at were

---

14 • *Some say the Essenes were aware of their Southern Stream task and consciously prepared themselves for centuries in order to accomplish it, and that Mary, the mother of Jesus, was one of their own.*

replaced with a collection of laws and a covenant with their god as expressed in the Torah.[15]

The Jews have been credited with establishing a basis for monotheism for the Christian and Islamic faiths. The Southern Stream oratory power was carried forward in the sacred script of Hebrew and the poetry of Torah law. Fairness and equality became standardized, applied whether or not a person was related by blood or clan. Later, Biblical law was used as the basis for secular law in Europe. The basic principles of Ma'at – that we are accountable for our actions and that we have a responsibility to make a contribution to our community (personal righteousness) – was upheld by law and balanced by the idea that each of us will be judged by God.

Our "struggle with God" is an eternal challenge with ourselves. Each of us is a Jew, a chosen one, unique, never before created, each on a perpetual personal diaspora. Our self-created exile from the Garden, our wandering through the wilderness will not cease until the mire of our personal history, so brilliantly condensed in the metaphorical narratives of Biblical history, is offered as holy sacrifice to the Lord God.

Putting the spiritual component of man in the forefront, making each action a sacrament by acknowledging and dealing with that same spiritual component in our fellow human beings, irrespective of status, race or religion, this is the true gift of the Jews to the Southern Stream. If this methodology does not bear fruit, then it is incumbent upon the Divine to inspire new revelations and bring about a new innovation, whether that be a reform that clarifies the Law or an intermediary or a savior that shows the way, or a religion that rekindles the spirit of Truth.

---

15 • *The covenant between the Children of Israel and Yehova may have been born out of the treaties they must have had with their captors - an attempt to promote harmony and bring unity between conqueror and conquered.*

Chapter Four
The Divine Responds

reek culture exhibited a very different strategy for creative spiritual expression. Rather than using form to replicate the qualities of other dimensions, as the Egyptians did, or enacting the strict laws governing behavior as prescribed by the Jewish Torah, the Greeks understood the ideas of the Good and the Beautiful within the physical to be perfect archetypes and ideas of the Divine. Their understanding that beauty is not only harmony and proportion but also the unseen divinity behind and within things later inspired the Arab world and then through them, the Renaissance artisans of Europe.

The people of Greece are a mixture of many peoples who through their interaction produced the golden age of classical Greek culture, the foundation of Northern Stream western civilization. Beginning around 2000 BC a series of migrations occurred, bringing people from Mediterranean Crete and the area around the Black Sea to Greece. Subsequently, they gave rise to the Achaeans, Myceneans, Dorians, Ionians and Macedonians, all making their contributions, paving the way for the classical period.

Under the tutelage of Pythagorus, who spent 20 years in Egypt and was educated by Zoroastrian Magi, the ancient Greeks quantified the principles of Ma'at into harmonious numerical ratios applied to art, color, music and medicine. Health was considered to result from a harmonious balance of the humors (elements). Art became the medium to express Spirit in form, the basis of pantheism. This was in contrast to Truth as understood in India as a cognition beyond form, or in Egypt as manifested in form.

The true wisdom of the Greeks was in their ability to pour agape (unconditional love), spiritual beauty itself, into art, music, athletic competitions, theater, poetry, philosophy and democracy. All true art inspires one to move towards the Divine. Once one lives in the Divine, art becomes an expression of that realization, just as the artistic intelligence, so obvious in nature's handiwork, impels us to recognize divine genius. The same pure joy of sharing and celebrating life brought by the mastery of art will in the future be brought about by the mastery of one's life, which will lead eventually to the mastery of civilization. For the Greeks the irony is that although agape was obvious in their works of art, it was absent in their interactions with their neighbors. They lived amidst the almost constant turmoil of their own internal wars and continual sparring with Persia and Troy.

In the manner of other Western Stream cultures, Greek temples were dwelling places of the gods, serving to anchor certain energies from other worlds. Those seeking assistance went to the temples to hear the oracle (often a woman) speak to their problem. The temple priest would then interpret the frequently obscure message. One such site was Delphi which was considered by them to be the "omphalos" (navel) of the world.

The Greeks had both an esoteric and exoteric side to their spirituality, reflecting the varying needs of the people. For the more metaphysically inclined, the Trinity of the One that was True, Good and Beautiful reigned, while others worshiped their favorite member of the pantheon, which was much like the Egyptian Ennead. By anthropomorphizing the attributes of the One, the Greeks humanized the Divine, creating more humanly accessible gods and heroes with flaws, passions and amusements. The stern, mysterious Jehovah of Israel and demigod Pharaohs of Egypt found no place among the more down to earth Greeks, who perhaps understood that we humans are indeed gods' in tragi-comic hiding.

Of the three best-known Greek philosophers (Socrates, Plato and Aristotle), Aristotle's (384-322 BC) impact upon western philosophy and civilization has been immense. A student of Plato and tutor of Alexander the Great, his concept of leading "the good life" emphasized moderation, virtue and contemplation. For him, the apex of the Greek trinity (the One) was the Unmoved Mover. His teacher, Plato (428-347 BC), placed Form at the center of his philosophy. To Plato, Form, an immaterial, independent object, unperceivable by the senses, is that which makes a thing what it is. The dialectic of Socrates' (469-399 BC), Plato's teacher, dealt with the mysteries of the One, but allowed entry only to men who had been prepared though physical training and the study of mathematics and music. Unfortunately, the pillars of Greek society took a dim view of Socrates' well-rounded approach to learning and life and forced him to commit suicide. Through the teachings of these three Greek giants, the Good, True and Beautiful made Its mark on the Northern Stream.

The influence of Greek civilization was greatly widened by the efforts of Alexander the Great whose Indo-Hellenic empire (c. 333 BC) stretched from Greece to NW India, promoting cultural exchange. The interaction of the two cultures brought a sympathy towards Buddhist thought to Greece and produced the Indian Ghandharan style of art which imitated Greek sculptures of Apollo.

Around 531 BC, following the Jewish exodus from Persian Babylonia, a great global influx of Wisdom swept the planet, finding expression in Greece as the Golden Age of Classical Greek culture and in Judea in the rewriting and restructuring of the Torah. It also moved through teachers such as Pythagorus, the Buddha, Lao Tze, Mahavira and Zarapas who planted the seeds for recognition of the sacredness of the individual. These extraordinary people developed and taught ways for every human being to find his own salvation, liberation and completeness outside the confines of religious, tribal, racial, or national identity.

One of these was a Nepalese prince named Siddhartha, later known as Gautama Buddha, the Awakened One. He taught release from the effect of suffering by removing the cause – desire – through the Four Noble Truths and the Eight-fold Path, an innovation on the eight limbs of raja yoga. For the Buddha, freed desire becomes divine inspiration. Unencumbered by ego it becomes the delight of manifestation and creativity, spontaneously harmless.

The Buddha's pragmatic psychological system was a response to India's overemphasis on abstract metaphysics and Vedic ritualism. His Middle Way balanced the extremes between India's ecstatic and acetic traditions and between ritualism and metaphysics.

Along with Jain, the great ethical teacher, Madhavira, Buddha rejected the Vedas, condemned the caste system and at one time both were followers of a wandering Tantric Shaivist (worshipper of Shiva), Gosala, who carried on the tradition of Ajivikas, known for ecstatic music and dance.

Buddhism may have remained just another small religious sect in India without the intervention of King Ashoka. In 257 BC, following his triumph in a particularly horrible battle, he converted to Buddhism. With missionary zeal he promoted Buddhism among his subjects, sparking massive conversions away from Hinduism. Buddhism's popularity soared, eventually leading to its spread throughout the Far East. King Ashoka was to Buddhism what Emperor Constantine was to Christianity.

Ashvaghosha (1st century AD), a Hindu convert to Buddhism, is credited with the introduction of the bodhisattva ideal (the basis for Mahayana Buddhism). He lived during a time when the Roman Empire's Greek governors of the Northwest regions of India brought the idea of the "soter" (ruler/savior) to their Indian subjects. This may have precipitated the development of the bodhisattva ideal – postponing one's own enlightenment until all sentient beings have reached that state of consciousness – a radical shift away from the pure tenets of Hinayana Buddhism, which spoke only to one's own attainment. More traditional factions considered developments such as Mahayana a serious defection from Truth. This led to a split between Buddhists who adhered to the Greater (Mahayana) and the more traditional proponents of Theravada or the Lesser (Hinayana) Buddhism.

Calling one branch Greater and one Lesser actually did a disservice to all of Buddhism by making a value judgment of one form over another – something very un-Buddhist! Mahayana was not, however, the only innovation. By 300 B.C. there were 18 varieties of Buddhism in India. Once again we see how humans adapt Truth to suit their natures. Nearly every religion has done the same thing as the deterioration phase of the cycle runs its course.

Mahayana was taken on the "Silk Road" through central Asia to China while Theravada (Hinayana) flourished in SE Asia. The austerity of Theravada never really took hold in China, a country historically dedicated to the "stately art" rulercraft and paternal responsibility of the monarch for the people. For them, the bodhisattva ideal was much more appealing and appropriate. *Ch'an,* the Chinese forerunner of Japanese Zen, was just one of many Mahayana Buddhist sects firmly established by the 6th century AD, about the same time as Christianity gained a strong foothold in the West.

The spread of Mahayana Buddhism into the Western Stream cultures of northern Asia led to the addition of more Western Stream ideas and forms of worship to the sparseness of Buddhism. The concept of Maitreya (the merciful next incarnation of Buddha or coming savior) appeared at this time, becoming Amitabha or Amida Buddha for Asian peoples. Cults worshipping various buddhas, dakinis and bodhisattvas sprang up in much the same way that the cult of Mary and the Saints appeared in Catholicism half a world away.

Four or five hundred years after the advent of Gautama Buddha's teachings, in India the "emptiness" of Buddhism and the abstract, impersonal truths of the Upanishads created a growing need for a more personal experience of the Divine, spawning a revival of ritual worship. The gods of Puranic Hinduism, which fulfilled the needs of the devotional nature of the people, were very similar in principle to those of the Egyptian, Greek and Roman pantheons. Worship of Vishnu (Vaishnavism) and Shiva (Shaivism) came to dominate worship of even the old Vedic deities (Brahma, Agni, Indra, Rudra). With the resurgence of Hinduism, the thousand-year reign of Buddhism in India slowly came to a close, becoming nearly non-existent by the 13th century.

On the wings of Buddhism the Eastern Sacred Stream (Heaven), with its emphasis on unmanifest Source, spread from Mother India to China and Japan, later influencing all of Southeast Asia.

In China, the Eastern Stream emerged from Western Stream shamanic origins with the appearance of Taoism. The Tao or Great Way refers to the hidden principles of the universe. Harmonious interaction with the universe is seen as more important than some externally imposed moral code because such "right action" guarantees correct behavior. The cosmos is believed to be kept in balance by the harmonious interaction of two main forces-yin (female, watery, cold, moon winter) and yang (male, solid, heat, sun, summer). The I Ching, or Book of Changes, thought to be the oldest book on the planet, deals with the more mystical side of Taoism and has been used for centuries as a tool for divination and an instructional guide for statecraft. Lao Tzu (604-531 BC), who is credited with having founded Taoism, and Confucius (551-479 BC), who denounced it, both used the I Ching as a primary source of inspirational wisdom. They believed that by surveying a situation from a cosmic standpoint one can move in harmony with the cycle of events. For them, man is part of a trinity formed by humanity, heaven and earth.

The spiritual climate in 5th century BC China emphasized that longevity was required to reach complete attunement with the Tao because human understanding often took such a long time to develop. Higher consciousness and immortality of the soul were believed to be possible only if one had developed a fully conscious lightbody or rainbow body while in physical form. Therefore, health, medicine and methods to prolong life became vastly important to those who sought to become one with the Tao. The legendary Eight Immortals of Chinese folklore were purported to have achieved that goal. These beliefs led Chinese spiritual seekers to value the body, giving them more in common with the Egyptian followers of Ma'at and Indian Tantrikas than with most other Eastern Stream masters and yogis.

The Chinese creation (manifestation) story begins with the Anterior Heaven of the Changeless Tao, from which come the 8 states of change (the trigrams upon which the 64 hexagrams of the I Ching are based). From these eight states terrestrial existence emerges, made up of the 5 elements: water, wood, fire, wind, and metal. Being transmutational, the elements are in a constant state of flux and require harmonization with their Source, the grand flux of the Tao. In a sense, this is the Chinese version of YHVH, the recipe for manifestation. For the Chinese this thread of wisdom extends directly from Source into every aspect of creation and being – from the cosmos to nature and man, entering the realms of statecraft and agricultural and architectural methods.

Understanding the nearly alchemical movements/interactions of the elements led to the development of the Five Element Theory, the foundation of Chinese medicine. When Hippocrates, the father of European medicine, was formulating his theories, the Chinese were practicing an already ancient, extremely sophisticated method of healing that included acupuncture and herbology, dating back to a time before the Yellow Emperor (c. 2500 BC).

Confucius, who rejected Taoism, emphasized personal virtue, devotion to family and social justice as superior spiritual values. Morality based upon the nature of man, the needs of society and sublimation of the individual for the benefit of society were his major themes. The importance of individual awakening, so much a part of Taoism, was supplanted by devotion to a moral, ethical and just nation. The rise and spread of Confucism and the groupist allegiance it cultivated to the extreme actually laid the groundwork for Communism, which transferred that allegiance and obedience to the State.

Mo Tzu (470-391 BC), an anti-Confucian philosopher, attacked what he saw as the empty formulas of the Confucians, promoting frugality, universal love and the rejection and condemnation of warfare, the core elements of his teachings. In his view, government should undertake only those things that are of clear benefit to the people.

One hundred years later, philosopher Chuang Tzu (370-300 BC), an avid proponent of Taoism, asserted that while Confucism's emphasis on compassionate, moral duty and ritual veneration for family, society, heaven and earth, might lead to "wisdom chih," it was a far cry from the spontaneous way of the Tao, where only *wu wei*, or non-doing, was in alignment with the Tao. Wu wei prepared the way for the introduction of Ch'an (Zen) by promoting a "non-doing" stance in life that shares common ground with Ch'an (Zen) philosophy.

The 3rd and 4th centuries BC were periods of unrelenting turmoil in China. Empires, philosophies and religious ideals rose and fell in the political quest for power and the spiritual quest for understanding. Out of this chaos came two new elements, Legalism and Buddhism, to take their place in the alchemical crucible that is China.

The political unrest, wars and squabbling which had plagued China was eventually laid to rest when China was united under the rule of Ying Chen, ruler of the militant state of Chin. He and his administrators subscribed to a political doctrine which had no use for the harmonious flow of Taoism, nor the moral rectitude, humanitarianism or reverence for ancestors of Confucism. The Legalists adhered to a strictly enforced code of law, believing that government could only be effective if it left behind the useless abstractions of piety and tradition. First century philosopher Wang Ch'ung summed up the Legalist approach to government in this way, "Make standards clear, give precedent to achievement. If the 'good' are not profitable to a nation, don't supply rewards, If the 'unworthy' aren't harmful to good order don't apply penalties."

With the advent of the Legalists, totalitarianism was born in the Eastern Stream. Their adherence to the exact, unrelenting letter of the law laid the groundwork for the fanatical fascism which later tainted Chinese communism. Although a dominant theme in China, this pedantic approach to law/authority is also found to some degree in nearly every religious and political system. Those who aren't spiritually mature enough to take responsibility for their own actions call forth authoritarianism, totalitarianism, fanaticism, and fascism to do it for them. Control is enforced from the outside when it is not sufficiently understood or developed on the inside.

Buddhism arrived in China on the heels of Legalism, at a time when China had lost its Eastern Stream foundation in Source to military rule and social expediency. The passive nature of Buddhism found receptivity in a China ripened in the past by the yielding, receptive, openness of Taoism. The similarity between the two was so unmistakable that it spawned legends which stated that it was Lao Tzu, who after vanishing from China, reappeared in India to instruct the Buddha! Buddhism, however, never completely transformed the Chinese spirit, only softened its extremities with prayer, contemplation and ritual, intermixing with Taoism's far older elements, eventually resulting in Ch'an (Zen).

Today, most non-American Chinese people participate in a spiritual amalgam of shamanism, Taoism, Buddhism and Confucism, using whichever system appears to be most appropriate to the situation at hand.

In contrast to the apparent static nature of the Eastern Stream in India, China, like the Tao, manifests a state of constant change. It is as if these two great manifestations of the Eastern Stream have assumed the qualities of the two great principles of Heaven/Source: movement and non-movement, eternal change and changelessness. For the last two thousand years, the Eastern Stream in China has been expressing through Taoism, Confucism, Legalism and Buddhism, with the recently added influence of techno-culture, interacting in much the same manner as the five elements, each state leading to its successor in an inexorable dance of transmutation.

Even though China's "Silk Road" provided the rising Roman Empire with many cultural influences and precious products from the East, Buddhism's highest teachings were out of reach of most members of the Northern Stream because of their heavy reliance on the ego/mind. It was not until the 20th century, after much exposure to Eastern Stream Truth, that any but the most advanced members of the Northern Stream were able to see beyond their own minds into the no-mind of Buddhism. Some say this was due to the high number of reincarnated Buddhists who found themselves born into Northern Stream countries after the turn of the century.

Chapter Five
Love Reveals All

he Northern Stream represents the newest developing faculty of humanity, ego-driven mind, focused on externals. It is the nature of ego-mind to believe in its own supremacy and exert aggressive influence to establish dominion, secure survival and pleasure and avoid defeat at all costs. Intellect powered by the beliefs, "I am more important and valuable than anyone or anything else," and "I and my needs come first," is the energy raging in today's nightmarish ecological devastation, wars and ethnic cleansings, national pride, and racial prejudice. It is this infantile "spin" on intellect, not intellect alone, which has created the paradigm in which most of the world now lives.

The seeds of the Northern Stream were planted long ago with the birth of the human ego. These same seeds were nourished and brought to fruition around the globe, but found particularly "successful" expression in the peoples of Europe, the Middle East and the lands surrounding the Mediterranean. These highly aggressive peoples possess a competitive spirit driven by the ego/mind's desire for wealth, honor, power and territory. This purpose ran through the power of classical Greek thought and artistic excellence in all things, but perhaps found its greatest ancient expression in the unstoppable Roman war machine which produced the most extensive and powerful empire of its time, controlling all these bases for the Northern Stream.

Before the Roman Empire existed, the Celtic and Teutonic peoples mirrored the Western Stream character of their ancient Greek cousins. Organized in loosely knit tribes with a liking for raiding, trading, warring, feasting and magic, they too had migrated from south central Russia, but they scattered north to the Baltic Sea and as far west as Iberia (Spain). Like the early Mycenaean Greeks, Ionians and Dorians, who found their common thread in Ares, the god of war, the Norse-Germanic peoples were united by their family of gods of war, law and magic, Aesir.

The ascendancy of the well-organized Roman war machine made it fairly easy for them to quickly conquer and absorb the more loosely knit peoples of Europe into their empire. First through Roman rule and later Roman Christendom, the Northern Stream supplanted the Western Stream tendencies of Europe. Centuries later, these conquests were later supported by the Church as a prelude to the coming empire of God. Despite the basic teachings of Jesus that the Kingdom of God is within, Church clergy professed that a physical empire must exist before a spiritual kingdom could be established.

The aggressive, focused energy directed towards subjugating Nature and other individuals to suit one's own needs is a human evolutionary step reinforcing a strong sense of self as separate from a group and from other individuals. At this level of awareness, leaders are made when those with powerful, magnetic egos develop a charisma identified by those less powerful (average members of a tribe, nation, religion, political party, etc.) as their own. Throughout history to the present time this misdirected expression of the need for the Divine has fueled the struggle between group mind and individual ego assertion – the source of conflict.

Against the backdrop of a tumultuous period in the Roman Empire, the ancient stronghold of the Northern Stream, ego/mind met its master, Love, through the ministry of Jesus and would rebel against this harmonizing force for another 2,000 years in order to fulfill prophecy and evolve humanity.

The Christ Event reestablished by living example the foundation principle of the Southern Sacred Stream: the Divine in Form as the Word made flesh. Also, the teachings of Jesus reintroduced the concept of universal brotherhood: all people being children of one Heavenly Parent, in this case, a father.

It is speculated that like Pythagorus and Plato, Jesus was educated and received initiations in Egypt, traveling to India for further instruction. During Jesus' time, India was experiencing a well-established Buddhist renaissance which rapidly expanded into Southeast Asia and Ceylon. He may have dialogued with great Buddhist scholars in Kashmir and learned of Nagarjuna's Middle Way, the Madhyamaka.

Many of Jesus' teachings resemble doctrines found in earlier Eastern Stream spiritual systems, especially Buddhism. Converting adversity to wisdom, turning the other cheek, effacing the ego through humility, forgiveness and compassion towards fellow human beings are very basic Buddhist principles. Jesus' Sermon on the Mount has much in common with many of Buddha's discourses. The concept of loving your neighbors as yourself, a very Buddhist idea, is also a tenet of Judaism, and can also be found in Zoroastrianism and ancient Vedic texts.

Even though Jesus was apparently influenced by Buddhism, he was, first and foremost a Jew, teaching perfected Judaism, and for this reason many Christian principles grew from Jewish roots. Meritorious action and charity are Jewish mitzvahs. The Christian Golden Rule, "Do unto others as you would have them do unto you," was known earlier as Rabbi Hillel's rule. The Jews believed that when 2 or more people gathered together in the name of God, whether in the synagogue or the marketplace, the assembly would be in the presence of the Shekinah, the active, feminine aspect of God. This same belief is found in Christianity, albeit phrased a little differently.

The first followers of Jesus were not Christians. The word 'Christ', upon which the word Christianity is based, is a Greek title meaning "anointed One," or "Indweller," indicating a high level of spiritual development. But the use of this title for Jesus did not come about until much, much later. Christianity was not something that Jesus put together. It coalesced over the course of several hundred years around religious ideas, beliefs and rituals borrowed from very diverse groups of people and was finalized by a religio/political structure which promoted their own select ideas about what took place in the life of Jesus and what it all meant – with a view to establishing order and maintaining control.

For close to a hundred years after the Resurrection there was no such thing as a religion called Christianity. Before that time there were simply followers of Jesus – mostly Aramaic-speaking Jews[16]

16 • *Some Jewish followers of Jesus survived for 500 years in the remote mountains of Syria under the name Ebionim, meaning, the poor, combining Jewish law with piety and poverty. Descended from actual disciples of Jesus who took refuge in Jordan after the Roman destruction of Solomon's temple in 70 AD, this group was deemed heretical in 200 AD by Church officials who themselves were considered illegal by Roman law. Living in relative isolation, the Ebonites, though banned by official Christendom, were left unmolested and remained true to the unalloyed teachings of Jesus for five centuries.*

from Gallilee who split off into various sects, including a Southern Stream lineage under Mary the Magdalene and apostles James and Thomas, some of which later became known as Gnostics. These early groups, often under female leadership, were a silent rebuke of the male-dominated society of that time. They put God into action as a loving brotherhood, not a complex system of doctrine, dogma, and liturgical law, laying the foundation for a spiritually-based communalism.

Embracing an eclectic spiritual view based upon personal experience founded in the hidden teachings of the mystical Kabbala, Gnostics were loosely knit groups of metaphysicians who made these teachings available to all who sought Truth. Over time, these spiritual fraternities spread from Alexandria to Athens and from Jerusalem to Bagdad. Much later, led by people such as Simon Magus and Valentius, their numbers included Platonists, both Jewish and non-Jewish Christians, and Essenes. Eventually, Gnosticism, like Judaism, drew persecution and charges of heresy from the Christian church which over time had apparently forgotten from whence it had come.

Gnosticism developed during the spiritual ferment which marked the change from the Age of Aries to Pisces. Translations of the Old Testament (of which the Kabbala was a part) into Greek brought about the spread of Gnosticism to the then-known world. Independent spiritual investigation and mixing of different religious systems thrived, with the Roman Empire serving as a great melting pot for this religious soup. Elements from many different religious systems were sampled then, very much akin to what is happening today during our change from the Age of Pisces to Aquarius. Distrust in the deteriorating orthodox religious and political establishments, complicated by creeping apathy, pervade the world of today's metaphysically inclined. Very much like the Gnostics of old, today's spiritual seekers draw upon a synthesis of direct experience from all the mystical/religious traditions of the world. Modern communication technology and ease of travel to sacred areas and pilgrimage sites affords even better opportunities for philosophical/spiritual exchange and mixing than did the Roman Empire during its heyday.

Some time after 70 AD, the early Christian assembly took up the mantle of Christian theology. The formation of the Church and its subsequent councils, judgments of heresy and philosophical schisms is a graphic example of how the mind functions under the influence of ego's survival needs. Jesus' Truths became subject to the interpretations of his Jewish and Greek followers and the later editorializing and mistranslations by Church councils and troubled Church fathers, such as St. Augustine. Christianity was fast on its way to becoming what Jesus preached against: hierarchy, denial of the Divine Feminine in favor of a "logoic" intermediary, exclusive, intolerant behavior and savior and idol worship!

Contrary to Southern Stream Gnosticism's foundation in the direct knowledge of God, the beliefs of the religious lineage founded by Paul relied heavily upon the authority of priests and believed in the necessity of martyrdom. It was this Gentile Christian lineage that would serve the evolving mentality of the Northern Stream.

Paul, a Jewish Pharisee, Roman citizen and persecutor of Christians, became a follower of Jesus after a profound conversion experience on the road to Damascus. Unlike the apostles who preached only to Jewish communities in Turkey, Greece, Cyprus, and Syria, Paul focused his missionary efforts on converting mostly Northern Stream Greeks and Romans. Although he never met Jesus, Paul's religious fervor and zeal to make conversions was such that he indulged in mistranslating and image sculpting in order to increase the number of adherents. Under his influence the Jewish/Buddhist Jesus of Gallilee became the Christ of Theology.

Tarsus, Paul's hometown, was in an area in which the savior idea of Mithraism and the Dionysian legend of the miracle of "filling empty vessels with wine" were well known. This atmosphere, combined with his epiphany, compounded by his non-Jewish audience and rejection by apostolic Jews because of that audience resulted in zealous proselytizing of some interesting additions to Christian doctrine. For Paul, Jesus was the redeemer, one who could erase human alienation from God's love, if one surrendered to him. Later, Jesus' crucifixion became a substitute for animal sacrifice – now bringing purification, atonement and regeneration for all of humanity, quite a tall order, yet equal to the difficulty of the times and the degenerate condition of the Northern Stream.

In order to attract large conversions among Greeks and Romans, Jesus' story was fashioned after the main figures in the dominant religions of the Roman Empire and most of Europe: Persia's Mithra and Greco-Egyptian Serapis (a composite of Apis, the Sacred Bull and Osiris) – both resurrected saviors. Their mythologies were prototypes for what later became Christian dogma surrounding the enigma of Christ. That image was then reformatted into something very close to the Hindu concept of the avatar – the incarnation of God. It is therefore not surprising that hundreds of years later fanatical Christian sects declare that Jesus is God! The important thing to remember, however, is that none of these "images" of Jesus – savior, logos, avatar – existed during his own time. The legend of Jesus was developed long after his crucifixion.

The Persian prophet Mani (c. 216-276), founder of the Manichaeans, may have had something to do with the image-sculpting of Jesus. Raised in a Jewish/Christian community known as the Elkesaites, through his ministry Mani attempted to merge the beliefs of his upbringing with Zoroastrianism and Buddhism. Deeply entrenched in dualism, and considering himself a prophet of Christ, he preached that the material world is inherently evil, produced by an invasion of the powers of darkness into the spiritual realm of light. For Mani, rescuing the imprisoned particles of divine light was to be done by messengers such as Jesus and himself. The idea of a savior was a core principle to Manichaeans, helping to create the picture of Jesus we have today. After his execution by the Zoroastrian priesthood, Manichaeism continued to spread and flourish until the 10th century, some claim influencing the heretical Christian Bogomils (Bulgaria) and becoming the state religion of the Turkish people in central Asia around 700 AD.

In the social climate of his own era Jesus wasn't important at all. In fact, the most respected Jewish historians of that time remained mysteriously silent on the historical Jesus. Official records written by Josephus, a famous Jewish historian, contemporary of the apostles and governor of Galilee, bear minor references to the deeds of Jesus. Only obvious forgeries of his work written by church officials 400 years later recount stories of miracles. Apparently Josephus' works were not the only ones doctored up to inflate the references to Jesus, bending history to theology.

Philo, a devout Jew and Platonist around 30 A.D., contemporary to the time of Jesus, wrote extensive accounts of the Jews but never mentions Jesus at all let alone any miracles or ministry. In fact it is Philo that is credited with the development of the popular concept of the Logos, God's Mind. Philo's logos was a Platonic adaptation of the Kabbala's Adam Kadman. This idea was easily distorted nearly a century later, by the Gospel of John into Jesus as the Logos,

God's Son, mankind's Intermediary – a convenient way for the Church to gain greater notoriety and conversions among the Greeks.

One hundred years after the crucifixion there was still no New Testament, as such, only apostolic and evangelical letters disseminated throughout the Roman Empire – Matthew in Rome, Luke in Greece, John in Edessa, and Mark in the Holy Land.

And thirty years later (150 A.D.) Justin Martyr, a historian who gathered 300 early Christian writings, never once mentions the four Gospels, only apocryphal texts (Old Testament works whose origins as genuine, divinely inspired works are suspect). The Gospels of the New Testament, upon which modern Christianity is based, are synoptic texts, meaning they were taken from older, unknown documents whose authors remain lost in obscurity. They were the work of many hands (most unknown) over hundreds of years of translation and revision.

Some untampered texts still survive as a testament to the Truth taught by early Christianity. The Pershittas of the Syrian Aramaic Church and The Dead Sea Scrolls have never been mistranslated, edited or reformatted and therefore maintain their purity. Some scholars believe that another untampered find, the Coptic Nag Hammadi Texts, which contain the writings of St. Thomas, a disciple of Jesus, were written earlier than the others. So far, they appear to be the only record of what the living Jesus spoke, yet they are excluded from official Christian canon. Strangely, there is no mention of the crucifixion or resurrection in St. Thomas' works, supporting the idea that the stories surrounding these events may have been gleaned from earlier stories of Osiris, Ahura Mazda and Mithra. They are also decisively less zealous and missionary in approach than Paul's Gospel, which came much later. All of these texts, although much older and uncontaminated by mistranslation, editing and misunderstanding, have never been accepted by the Christian establishment.

In Thomas, 1:13 of the Nag Hammadi Texts, we find a classic pronouncement of pure Eastern Stream wisdom, "The Kingdom of Heaven will not come by waiting or watching. It is spread out upon the earth and the people do not see it. You enter the Kingdom of Heaven when you make the two one, the inside like the outside and the outside like the inside, above like the below and male and female one and the same. You will find the end in the beginning and will not experience death." This statement clearly points to the nondualism found in earlier Buddhist discourses and echoes the power of satori emanating from Japanese Zen koans, which came along much later.

The atmosphere in which Christianity was created was filled with economic, social and political uncertainty. Civil unrest was prevalent and Rome found itself fending off invaders from without and sabotage from within. Among the uprisings put down by the Romans were two particularly bloody Jewish revolts, of 66-73 A.D., which ended with the fall of Masada, and the Bar Kochba uprising (132-135 A.D.), which left 1/2 million Jews dead, and one thousand villages destroyed.

Too busy dealing with Jewish insurgencies, at first the Romans were indifferent to the isolated and obscure non-Jewish Christian minorities. On the other hand, both Jewish and non-Jewish followers of Jesus were considered dangerous. Having no altars, priests, or temples they followed Jesus' true teaching of personal sovereignty and refused to offer worship to the Roman gods while awaiting the "end of the world." In so doing they violated the devotion to the state and the maintenance of order in society, psychologically threatening the Roman status quo. It was for this very reason that Jesus was crucified and later, Christians were persecuted and martyred.

When the world did not end at the expected time, the balance of power among early Christians swung to the more organized Paulist Gentile bishops of the church, away from the less structured presbyters, whose itinerant ministerial tradition was of Jewish extraction. The new church fathers, with an arrogance typical of Northern Stream ego-mind, professed to act in place of the apostles, in the name of Christ, sowing the seeds for the later doctrine of papal infallibility. With this shift in leadership, Christianity's first steps away from its Southern Stream roots and toward Northern Stream tampering were taken. In a strange turnabout which seemed to demonstrate their contempt for their roots, bishop/historian Irenaeus of Lyons, Gaul (c. 185), labeled all remaining Jewish Christians (such as the Ebonites) heretics.

Imitating the structure of Roman geo-political provinces, Cyprian, a North African bishop, created church patriarchates in Alexandria, Antioch, Rome, Constantinople and Jerusalem, uniting all the bishops in 250 A.D. Still following the Roman empire's lead, rivalry between patriarchates became customary in the same way as competition between regions of the empire was common. The institution of the papacy owes its beginnings to the fact that the eastern Empire had four patriarchates and the west had one – Rome. Because of this, the eastern wing of the Church could never centralize the way Rome did. They were also more Southern Stream with less inclination to organize like their Northern Stream Roman brethren.

By this time (c. 300), with increasing conversions, persecution of Christians was replaced with the healthier policies of repression and tolerance under Emperor Galerius. However, once the persecution stopped and the policy of tolerance was adopted, Christian bishops began persecuting Gnostics, another Christian group with Southern Stream leanings. At this point, all so called "heretics" went underground, just as the early Christians had done almost 300 years before.

Amidst all the tumult, variety in Christian belief flourished and in those politically unstable times, it was this very proliferation, and the fear that without management Christians might become uncontrollable, that engendered a response from the Roman Empire.

Constantine, in his battle to wrest control of the whole empire from a Roman opponent, attributed his success to a vision of the sun superimposed by a cross. Interpreting this as a "sign," he converted to Christianity and further put the Roman Empire's stamp on his new faith by consolidating the many Christian sects into one Christian cult, modeling himself as the absolute one ruler after the one God. With Constantine's conversion in 312A.D., Christianity received imperial protection and promotion on par with other state religions.

After his conversion to Christianity, Emperor Constantine moved Christian headquarters from Rome to Constantinople. He also closed the official Church canon, placing political pressure on any Christian sect that deviated from his doctrine, such as the Gnostics and Arians. Even though Constantine still worshiped Apollo after his conversion, all Christian sects deemed to be heretical were banned. Seven panels, beginning with the Nicene Council,[17] first organized by Constantine in 325 A.D., (ending in 431 A.D.) standardized Christian doctrine, dogma and liturgy in order to encourage the spread of the new religion throughout the empire. Edited versions of the Gospels from which the Southern Stream influence of Gnostic Christianity were deleted, were officially adopted by the Council as Church doctrine. Later, copies of early texts that were not sanctioned by the official Church were destroyed, a strategy successfully employed by Caesar centuries earlier with the ancient library at Alexandria.

It wasn't until the rule of Emperor Theodosius I (c. 380) that Christianity became the official state religion by imperial edict. With the installation of a Roman state religion, Christianity's ascendancy on the grand scale of other Roman achievements (conquest, administration, public works projects, dissemination of the dominant culture, etc.) was virtually guaranteed.

Heresy laws and the judgments of further ecumenical councils, convened to clarify confusing dogmas, were used primarily to preserve the ever weakening empire's unity. The councils became legal courts, arguing the merits of various points of dogma. Losing debators, such as Arius and Nestorius,viewed as insubordinate to the stability of the crumbling empire, were banished or jailed by general consensus.

A number of doctrines were added to the teachings of Jesus by Constantine's Nicene council and those that followed. One of these was the official doctrine of the Trinity, borrowed from the Kabbala. The Kabbala's trinity is composed of the nondual, transcendent Source, Ain Sof (Father), which gives rise to the force of Beauty and Love, Tiperath (Son), received by Divine Immanence, the Shekinah (Mother) in the multiplicity of creation. Not unique to Judeo-Christian tradition, the principle of the triune nature of God can be found all over the globe, possibly due to humanity's own threefold nature (spirit, mind/emotion and body). For example, the Greeks acknowledged the trinity of the One that was True, Good and

---

17 • *The Nicene Council was also responsible for introducing the confusing creed professing that Jesus was "Lord, Jesus Christ, the only begotten Son of God," The Jews called Jesus "Rabbi, son of man" and not "son of God," which is a later church council's version. The cultural idiom "son" signifies "likeness of God." This is a secret reference to "a son of the divine man," Adam Kadman, which holds all of God's attributes as depicted on the Tree of Life. Such individuals who have realized their God essence radiate a holy presence or purity which is often depicted in religious art as "golden halos."In actuality," son of man/God" is a Biblical metaphor akin to the Hermetic metaphysical axiom, "As above, so below" but incorporates a sense of familial intimacy with the "as above" our "Heavenly Father" – "as below" our "earthly child."*

Beautiful. For the Norse peoples, the trinity which gifts mankind with spirit/breath (Anda) and inspiration (Odhr), consists of Odin, Hoenir and Lodhurr.

All trinities can only represent three letters of the Tetragrammaton, YHV, but the Kabbala presents a trinity giving rise to an eventual quaternary expression of the Divine. Humanity's fulfillment lies in the completion of the sacred name of God, YHVH, a four-fold manifestation consisting of Father, Mother, Son, and Daughter, which will make itself known during the Age of Aquarius, along with a new human faculty, heart intelligence.

Given humanity's level of evolution, the triune, partial manifestation of godhead was an inescapable (and perfect) error. The Christian trinity, however, presented a special case. Under the influence of the Age of Pisces (ruled by Neptune, the planet of delusion and deception), the Divine Mother, disguised by Northern Stream Christians as the Holy Ghost, lost human recognition of Her role as manifester of the power of life. Because of this, the power of God later received by countless saints and martyrs was perceived to come from Jesus; whereas this power was previously recognized as a function of the Divine Feminine – the Gnostic trinity's Divine Mother, Hindu Shakti, or Jewish Shekinah. Jesus Christ and the Holy Ghost had become spiritual intermediaries to which only the Church clergy had access. The essential Totality of the Father/Source became even more unreachable to the average person.

Those who did not ascribe to this or the other new creeds were considered heretical and officially denounced. Arius, leader of a very popular Coptic (Egyptian) Christian sect, found himself in direct conflict with newly established Nicene doctrine. He preached that only the Father is Divine and Jesus Christ, as imaged by the Church, was merely a substitution for the resurrected Egyptian god Serapis, a composite of Osiris and Apis. For his beliefs, Arius was condemned and excommunicated and his followers were banished.

The Nicene claim that Jesus was God's "only begotten Son" attempted to negate the validity of those earlier saviors whose stories furnished the foundation for the image carved by the Church. It also proclaimed the authoritative "exclusivity" of the Christian God, divorced from all His Mithraic, Jewish, Gnostic, and African/Egyptian roots, thus obscuring Christianity's Southern Stream foundation and denying Eastern and Western Stream influences. Later persecution of Jews, mystery schools and "heretics" served to further erase the origins of Christian dogma and claim original authority for the Church.[18] These political moves in no way refute the possibility that Christed Jesus may have actually been a special emanation, an avatar or vehicle for one of the 12 Solar Deities, it merely points to the spiritual immaturity that allows misuse of Truth to further one's own ends.

Christian doctrine strayed even further from the teachings of Jesus with the Church's preoccupation with the sinfulness of sexuality. This had little to do with the Master's way, but much to do with the fervor of two very devout Christians with a great deal of sexual guilt. In 400 A.D. St. Jerome translated Greek texts into Latin, forming the version of holy scripture authorized by Rome, the Latin Vulgate (Holy Bible). His abhorrence of the body and sexuality deeply affected his revision of the texts and led to Christianity's puritanical orientation. St. Augustine, a convert from Manichaeism, also had a great influence on the formation of Church doctrine. His own struggle with sexual self control, in combination with Mani's belief in the inherent evilness of physicality, caused him to over-emphasize the idea of original sin and espouse the wickedness of sexuality.

Christian spirituality became associated with a celibate, reclusive lifestyle. Taken out of its proper context as a temporary stage or preparation for the mystical union with Christ, celibacy was mistaken for the only means of salvation and the "temptations of the flesh" were considered an evil hindrance to religious life.

In contrast to Christian belief, the ancients recognized that at different times in the journey, certain bio-spiritual temperaments require either abstinence from or indulgence in the procreation, pleasure, healing, joy, and cleansing power of the sexual act. A long and healthy life was attributed to the divine, transformative power of sexuality and it was fully integrated with spiritual/religious views.

Multi-Stream societies viewed sexuality as healthy, therapeutic, and a spiritual expression of the Divine. The Mayans held that

---

18 • *It is interesting to note that the term Nazarene, was not specific to only Jesus. Mandeans or followers of John the Baptist, Manicheans or followers of Persian Mani, the acetic, communal Essenes , and some Gnostics all called themselves Nazarenes. Derived from the Hebrew "nazir" meaning dedicated to God, this term was generally given to all types of Eastern Christians (not those of Greek or Roman extraction)*

several marriage partners over a lifetime or polygamous relationships were natural and in many instances necessary for the alchemical opening and healing of various spiritual centers. This view was also held among Western and Eastern Stream peoples and some Eastern Stream regions abound in erotic scriptures, temples, sculptures, and paintings of divine sexual embrace. Indeed, it is the sexually explicit statuary at Khajaraho, India and art depicting Tibetan Buddhist spiritual masters in ecstatic sexual embrace that are used to symbolize the spiritual union of emptiness and skillful means. Spiritual practices which focus on tapping, harnessing and enhancing sexual energy are found among many Eastern and Western Stream peoples. India's Tantric yoga, China's Taosim and Tibet's Vajrayana all instruct aspirants in the art and science of spiritual sexuality.

The magnetic sex attraction is a natural power of creation and presents (on a bio-magnetic, and for humans, a subconscious level) the opportunity for wholeness. The mistake lies not realizing that sexual attraction is only a symbol, maybe the most powerful, of the true wholeness or completion brought about by spiritual marriage or union within. Nearly all spiritual traditions say that with the purification and transmutation of the ego, grace brings this about. Tantra and Taoism, two wisdom traditions that deal directly with sexuality as an aid to spiritual realization are both very difficult to practice because most people just don't have the dedication to development of consciousness needed to use their sexuality in this way, getting caught up in the sensuality and/or unresolved sexual issues.

The Christian condemnation of sex as sinful may have been collective humanity's reaction to the previous Pagan view of sex as holy. In this swing from one extreme to the other we see an example of the interaction of avoidance and indulgence in human consciousness, forced by the absence of true wisdom. This reproach of sexuality was also a prelude to the extensive use of guilt and religious fear, a control mechanism which characterized Northern Stream Roman Catholicism in Europe.

History itself gives sad testimony to the idea that sexually repressed societies produce both degenerate or pornographic sexual practices and the most violent and aggressive behavior. The puritanical repression of Northern Stream Europe produced horrific expression as the Church's religious power expanded into military and economic power as well. The alienation of the mind from the body and nature promoted by Church doctrine manifested itself as Northern Stream projection of the parts of themselves which they had disowned and condemned upon Western and Southern Stream peoples, who for them, represented Body and Nature. The Crusades, witch burnings, the Inquisition, slave trade, genocidal colonialism, the Holocaust and Apartheid are just some of the devastating effects of the rift in the European psyche between spirit and ego-driven mind, the Northern Stream's spiritual dis-ease.

Blindly mixing new and old customs from varied sources, the Church ignored the fact that every religion, including their own, is birthed from the secret doctrines and cultural imperatives of its predecessor and is invigorated with an evolutionary principle suited to the mentality of the people and the cosmic needs of the times. In this case, apparently partly due to political expediency, it was from Mithraism, the cult of Serapis and Judaism that solidifying Christianity drew much of its lore, rituals and holidays. An offshoot of Zoroastrianism, Mithraism, which excluded women from worship, was practiced throughout Europe and the Mediterranean, stretching from the Iberian peninsula (Spain) to Persia and beyond. As time passed, Mithraism never collapsed, per se, it was simply absorbed by the newer, government-backed Christianity.

Along with Persian Mithras, Greco-Egyptian Serapis, god of divine Sun and earthly Nature was also a prototype for Christian dogma concerning the history and nature of Jesus. Created by the Greco-Egyptian Pharaoh, Ptolemy I, (c. 330 BC), Serapis was a composite of Apis, the Sacred Bull, representing the soul of Nature and Osiris, the Wise Solar Deity of eternal life and goodness.

Christian baptism was drawn from Jewish ritual bathing (mikvah) the annual atonement, Yom Kippor, became confession. The belief in a struggle between the forces of Darkness (Satan) and Light (God/Jesus) was taken directly from the Avest Gathas (the revelations of Zoroaster). December 25th, adopted by the Church as Jesus' birthday, was previously Natalis Solis Invicti, a new year festival which included an exchange of gifts, celebrating the birth of the sun deity, Mithra. On a deeper level this was more than just a substitution of Jesus for Mithra. Now Mithra, the traditional Lord of

Light was merged with Jesus, Lord of Love, by sharing the same birthday.[19]

The Christian idea that Jesus died for our sins was adopted from beliefs already deeply established in Middle Eastern (and other) cultures for thousands of years. Sacrifice of a male was part of long-standing Western Stream practices connected to the yearly regeneration of vegetation. Germanic Odin, reborn as Balder, North Africa's Ammon, Phoenician Adonai of spring fertility rites, all reflect this belief and practice. It is no accident that the celebration of the crucifixion and resurrection takes place in springtime, reminiscent of ancient sacrifices of perfect males to ensure a good harvest. The Christian name for the celebration of the resurrection, Easter, comes from the name of the Germanic Goddess of Light, Ostara, whose festival was celebrated (not surprisingly) in April.

The gentle lamb became the symbol of Christ, replacing Persian Mithra's Bull and the Jewish Ram. No longer would lamb or ram be the common sin offering for Gentile or Jew. Jesus' sacrifice was all that was or would be needed. Now that the world has its permanent sacrificial lamb, Jesus, we have lost our understanding of the need to "give back" to what gives to us – the very basic foundation for ritual sacrifice. We have become disconnected from the land and its fertility and the Oneness that substantiates it, having no concept of what truly sustains us. And because of this we have become shamefully ungrateful and disrespectful of the chain of life that supports us. It is interesting to note that in our modern spiritual ignorance, lack of prayer and rejection of myth and sacrifice, we sacrifice not only animals but ourselves in the desecration of the biosphere.[20]

It wasn't until the 7th century that the symbol of the crucified Jesus was substituted for the docile lamb.[21] At this point a symbol of

---

19 • *Armenian, Greek Orthodox, Coptic and Aramaic Christian churches, considered dissident by the Vatican, celebrate January 6 or December 22nd as the birth of the Jesus.*

20 • *Possibly the most difficult sacrifice is that of the conditioned mind, done before the death of the body. This is the great work of the alchemist, this is the "born again" of the Christians, the "moksha" of the Hindu and "nirvana" of Buddhists, the Promised Land of the Jews, and the Paradise of Islam. When offered to the sacrificial fire of the Self's blazing furnace, the mind is likened to the moon which disappears in the radiance of the noonday sun.*

suffering and death supplanted one of growth and possibilities. The effect of this pivotal point in Christian history has pretty much gone unnoticed. From 650 to 1500 Christian Europe underwent a most difficult, bloody time. Suffering and death were the hallmark of many people's lives and the Christian focus in that direction seems almost prescient – or maybe causative.

Ironically, belief in Christianity's Jesus and his "story" became the justification for some of the most cruel and murderous activities in all of recorded history. Humanity missed the opportunity for self determination offered by the spiritual teachings of Jesus and instead, fell into the trap of resting the burden of spiritual responsibility at the doorstep of the Crucifixion and later, the Church. The Church merely reinforced an age-old human pattern that monarchies, warlords, emperors and priesthoods everywhere already had firmly in hand. As a species we had (and still have) the desire to have someone else take care of us, tell us what we need, what to do, what to believe, what to fight and die for. In the Northern Stream this tendency was kept afloat through efforts made by the Church and throughout later political innovations because it wasn't (and still hasn't been) resolved by humankind's collective consciousness.

Theological controversies raged over the nature of Jesus (Was he human or Divine or both?) and the trinity, springing from the desire to stamp out "heretical movements" and increase conversions, thereby consolidating Church power. This of course did nothing to serve the needs of the faithful or increase their level of understanding. These philosophical arguments and the decrees they spawned were simply another example of misuse of Truth to increase power and authority. However, the final Church definition of the nature of Jesus was actually a beautiful description of the state of illumination common to all enlightened beings, not just Jesus. Truth was there, just misused.

"Christ is a Divine Incarnation. He is perfect, both in his divinity and in his humanity, truly God and truly man. In divinity, begotten of the Father, in his humanity begotten of Mary, Mother of God, for

---

21 • *Due to the fact that the crosses used for crucifixion in Jesus' time bore little resemblance to the cross popularized in Christianity's crucifix, more than likely, the popular Christian cross was an adaptation of the Celtic cross of the ancient Druids, associated with the resurrection of the sun after winter solstice, regeneration of life and the promise of spring renewal.*

us and for our salvation. He must be acknowledged in his two natures, without change, or division or separation, that the distinction between the natures is in no way removed by their union but rather that the specific character of each nature is preserved and they are united in one person and one hypostasis." – Tome of Pope Leo

The unfathomable mystery of nondual Infinite Divinity manifest in myriad finite forms is impossible to grasp outside the company of one who lives in that state of realization. The grace that proceeds from association with enlightened beings is the most direct, time-tested method for being "saved" by the "Lord" through realizing your own Son Self. Theologizing about it is a futile effort, bearing no spiritual fruit. The papal decrees, judgments of heresy and official crystallization of Christian thought, further entrenched the Northern Stream mind in its own narrowminded ideas, interpretations, pride and arrogance and removed it even further from Truth.

The confusion associated with Christianity throughout the ages (church corruption, hypocrisy, masquerading as something that it's not, etc.,) could be attributed to any number of causes, given the conditions under which it was formed. However, the most likely cause arises from a rather obscure event in the formation of Christian doctrine. In 4th and 5th century North Africa, one of the many Christian sects existing at that time gained considerable popularity. The Donatists, named for bishop Donatus of Carthage, were for a time the major Christian movement in North Africa. Stressing the separation of church and state, and social revolution and responsibility, their beliefs were particularly troubling to both the trembling political structure and the newly formed Christian church. Donatists were also adamant in their belief that those responsible for giving the sacraments of the Church (clergy) must be of high moral fiber and spiritual development, otherwise the sacrament received was without spiritual value. Their influence was ended (ironically) by (St.) Augustine of Hippo when they were formally condemned in 412 A.D. With this one condemnation, probably based upon the possible dangers posed by a politically and socially active congregation, the Church also renounced the necessity for righteousness among the clergy charged with tending to the spiritual needs of the flock, blocking the Southern Stream influence on Christianity.

The ramifications of such a cynical decision are chronicled in the next few hundred years of Christian history. No longer required to "walk their talk" or adhere to the spiritual qualifications or attainments required of aspirants to other religious/mystical traditions, Christianity was left to the rule of canonical law and the ego-based vagaries of those in positions of power in the Church.

Denying the connection between what one is and what one does paved the way for biblical forgeries, selling fake "relics," absolutions and dispensations and a myriad other questionable activities, not to mention the truly heinous Crusades, persecutions and inquisitions. This renunciation of integrity cemented into the Northern Stream mentality a fundamental belief in the "machine" – that personal righteousness is of little consequence because the power of the structure would carry one through. Personal responsibility and spiritual power were overthrown in favor of the System.

Changes in official church doctrine continued and in 431 AD, against the vigorous protests of Nestorius, the leader of a Persian Christian sect, the council of Ephesus raised the status of Mary, Jesus's mother, to Mother of God. It was theologized that since Jesus was from the same beingness (homo ousia) of God, the Father, they surmised that Mary must be Mother of God. The Mary cult which arose around this logic served two functions. On one hand it allowed a return to the Goddess, the Great Mother who had been the object of widespread worship for thousands of years, but had been all but eliminated from Church doctrine by replacing Her in the trinity with the neuter image of the Holy Ghost. Humanity's collective consciousness required that the Divine Mother or Shekinah be present, and although it may not have been consciously recognized by the Church, this need was met by the Ephesian Council's decision to call Mary "Mother of God."

On the other hand, through the Church's denouncement of sexuality and Mary's virgin status, as well as Her dethronement from the Trinity, the Divine Mother was put "in Her place" by making Mary, Her representative, subject to the will of Father God as indicated by the story of the Immaculate Conception and the Assumption.

As with many other Church holy days, the Feast of the Assumption of the Virgin was used to supplant the ancient festivals of the holy virgins Isis and Artemis (Diana), Aug 13th. Around the same time the Communion of Catholic Saints was substituted for worship of the Greek and Norse demigods, because the people were long accustomed to praying and making sacrifices in order to obtain favors from their God or Goddess, even though such worship was certainly not validated by scripture.

When the mentality of a culture either degenerates or requires focus on an object to develop the mind, or worship through ritual is required to satisfy a strong emotional component, detours from Truth arise, such as devotion to the Virgin Mary or the saints, or focus on the Crucifixion arose in Catholicism. Although practices such as these were forbidden by Jesus, the apostles and the Jewish patriarchs, they were, perhaps, necessary in order to redirect inappropriate behaviors that strict laws only suppressed. In the cosmic scheme of things, everything has its place and is valid in its proper timing.

As Christianity entered this darker phase, with its denial of the need for personal spiritual attainment on the part of clergy, tainted holy scripture and focus on suffering and Mary iconography, Europe was torn with revolutions, quarrels over (irrelevant) diverse church doctrines, biblical interpretations and struggles between corrupt kings and popes.

Jesus did not intend to start a new religion. And his purpose may not even have been to reform Judaism by returning to more basic Mosaic Law. However, it was inevitable that something new would arise from his ministry because his own realization of the Kingdom of Heaven was too expansive to fit into the Jewish hope for a political messiah or the longstanding savior-style beliefs which riddled Mediterranean culture during his time.

The deep, abiding compassion gleaned from his understanding of the pure tenets of Judaism and his exposure to Buddhism manifested in that to those who had the capacity to receive it, the living Truth was introduced and transmitted directly by Jesus. After such a transmission, absolute faith is bestowed and one never again lives in doubt. One's daily affairs are thereafter permeated with profound wisdom and praise of God.

Jesus' bestowal of grace to all who could hear, understand and embody Truth was a radical departure from the established standards of rigorous tests and purification rites practiced in the ancient mystery schools of Egypt, Greece and Babylon. External observances and study of Hebrew law were not prerequisite to receiving the teachings or transmissions of Jesus. Even the demonstration of the qualities of integrity and virtue were waived. All that was necessary was an opening. Be present and leave the rest to the Divine Grace of the Father. For, ."..of himself he could do nothing." It is the Father/Source through him, within him that acts.

For those who were unable to receive grace directly, Jesus, like the Buddha, spoke to the mentality of his time through the symbolism of parables, stories and adages. It was only later, after the formation of a clergy, that doctrine, dogma, liturgy, rules and vows were established through the organized efforts of that clergy.

The transfiguration, crucifixion and resurrection of Jesus was a greater act than Arjuna's sacrifice of his relatives on the battlefield, chronicled in India's Mahabharata. He could not perform this physical sacrifice, an act of supreme obedience to God, until self love and selfless service had been firmly established. However, we now know that no longer encumbered by the body and its physical laws, Christed Jesus could imprint love into human consciousness and await its fruition during the next 2,000 years as the Northern Stream exhausted itself in its attempt to subjugate the world. Without the Northern Stream's opposition and chaos, Divine Love might have remained only a concept in the unmanifest spiritual realms and the ego/mind might never develop beyond its infantile state. By first embodying the Divine Plan then facing his destiny in crucifixion, Jesus allowed the blueprint of a spiritually evolved humanity to be released into physical manifestation.

The love brought to this realm by the physical presence of Jesus polarized the aggressive, warlike conditioning of the Northern Stream's main attribute: mind/will force. This, of course, led to his crucifixion. Earthquakes and rainbows that were said to have occurred during this ordeal were a sign that a Body of Light and Love had been produced by a great adept.

Although considered by Westerners to be a one-time-only event, possible only for Jesus, the production of a rainbow body is an advanced technique found in the secret Dzogchen ('complete perfection') teachings of Tibet and considered quite common among the holy people there and in India. With a resurrected body made of the rainbow light frequencies of the elements, one is able to travel freely, appearing at will to all beings who need and are ready to receive spiritual assistance. Some say this explains the appearance of the bearded white gods, Quetzalcoatl and Kulkucan, in the Americas.

Jesus' ascension, as reported in the Bible, may have been an initiation both for him and for his disciples. No longer defendant upon a teacher, they would be forced to integrate and embody the teachings themselves. What was reported as the Ascension, may have actually been Jesus' dematerialization in Israel and rematerialization in India. Undoubtedly, the return of Jesus the "soter or savior" profoundly influenced the development and spread of the bodhisattva ideal in a predominantly Buddhist NW India. Tibetan Buddhist records, regarded by Muslim scholars as authentic, report that Jesus, known by the Kashmiris as St. Issa, lived the rest of his days in India and that Kashmir, India, once inhabited by a lost tribe of Israel and the source of the Dzogchen teachings, is the final resting place for both Jesus and Moses. St. Thomas, who is said to have returned to India with Jesus, is now entombed in Madras.[22]

The power and purity of the Christ Being planted the seed of the concept of a common humanity bonded by Love. This Love is still waiting for humanity to recognize it as THE guiding principle. It is hovering in the atmosphere, at an unmanifest level, totally available to those who can rise above their strong attachment to the ego/mind's paradigm. Especially concentrated over Israel, this energy brought into the world by Jesus awaits, but humankind's strong attachment to identification with tribal loyalties (nations, religions, etc.), collective memories and beliefs, formed (and still form) hard resistance to the reception of Truth.

Love so pure can polarize the evolving mentality, causing spiritual toxins to rise to the surface, exposing elements in need of purification, facilitating an alchemical transformation. The worst (as well as the best) in human nature has made its appearance on a grand scale through the interactions of Christian religion and culture and the rest of the world, making this process obvious and fairly easy to see. In order to facilitate the completion of this alchemical transformation, Christianity must go to confession, applying its own message of admission, forgiveness and redemption to itself. This will liberate it from the ideas to which it has become attached

---

22 • *Some Northern Stream legends report that after his resurrection, Jesus led a quiet life with Mary Magdalene, founding the Merovingian kingdom in Gaul (France). According to Dzogchen precepts, an adept can simultaneously emanate as many bodies in as many locations as he or she desires, making these legends entirely possible.*

and will help accomplish the goal of the Christ Event, not by the will of the Church, but by God's Will. Otherwise, the Second Coming may never happen.

How can this Divine Love unify all peoples given the vehicle of Christianity? Surely, Christianity must admit that it is a conglomeration of many, many non-Christian influences and internal conflicts. Originating in Southern Stream Afro-Egyptian antiquity, absorbing principles and rituals from Judaism, Western Stream Paganism, Eastern Stream Hindu and Buddhist systems and Persian Mithraism; and then being propelled into the world and promoted by Northern Stream power and authority, Christianity has certainly touched all peoples. This is one way the mission of Jesus, universal realization of brotherly love, can occur – if we can return to the unalloyed Truth of his message.

Chapter Six
True Servants

s had happened in Hinduism, Egypt's devotion to Ma'at, Judaism and Buddhism, dogma and doctrine replaced Truth in Christianity and the people fell into reliance upon idol and image worship, ritual, and the authority of a power-hungry clergy, all of which rested upon mistranslated, edited scripture as its foundation. In order to continue its development unhampered by human misunderstanding, the Southern Stream used successive spiritual innovations to carry its mission forward. Egypt's loss of Ma'at elicited a return to the Formless which manifested as the God of the Israelites. The multitudinous, stern laws which sprang up in Judaism necessitated the compassionate wisdom of Jesus. The later Northern Stream corruption of Jesus' Southern Stream concepts and the suffering this caused called forth another visit by Archangel Gabriel, bringing Islam, the Southern Stream's next flowering, which would cleanse it of Christianity's idolatrous leanings.[23] Islam would also unite people through religion rather than through 'blood' and fulfill the concept of 'hallowed action,' brought to the Southern Stream by Judaism, through the introduction of commerce conducted under the aegis of religion. Rather than asking Muslims to adhere to a large number of rules and regulations, Islam limited its prohibitions, focusing instead on the 'Five Pillars of the Faith' (testimony to the truth of Allah and His prophets, worship five times a day, almsgiving, observance of the holy days of Ramadan through fasting, and hajj or pilgrimage to Mecca at least once in a lifetime).

---

23 • *Unlike the early Northern Stream Greco-Roman pantheon and later Christianity, Islam considered human or natural representations of the Divine to be idolatrous. This gave rise in Islam to a rich and varied use of geometric patterns rather than the human form, in architecture, art and calligraphy very similar to Hindu yantras and Tibetan mandalas.*

Around 610 A.D. Muhammed, a shepherd and trader, began to receive transmissions from Gabriel, the same angel who had visited Abraham so long ago. These teachings, which he continued to receive for the rest of his life, later became the Koran, a manifestation of the Southern Stream power of oratory. After years of exile in Medina, under nearly constant attack by surrounding Arab tribes, Muhammed and an army of ten thousand followers defeated Mecca, ending worship of Al and Uzza, the god and goddess of the Arabs.

Muhammed lived in a world teeming with a variety of religious ideas. From Nestorian Christians Islam adopted the rejection of celibacy, as well as abhorrence of saint, image, and relic worship, relying upon worship of the Formless. From Arabian Jews Muhammed learned that Hebrew Abraham fathered Ishmael, the patriarch of the Arabs, as well as Jacob, who later became Israel, father of the Jews. In Muhammed's eyes, Abraham's complete surrender to God made him the first Muslim, which means submission to God. The theme of devotional surrender was common to the ancient Goddess religions of that region, as well as in India, whose merchants had long ago established trade routes in Yemen, not far from Mecca, enroute to East Africa. This concept is clearly exemplified in Eastern Stream Krishna's statement, "Abandon all dharmas, offer everything to Me; take refuge in Me," which is also echoed in Jesus,' "No one comes to the Father but through me," and again in Southern Stream Muhammed's proclamation, "If you love God, follow me and God will love you."

Muhammed also reintroduced the age-old Southern Stream view that the world itself is a Divine epiphany. To one who is surrendered to God, a Muslim, the world is real, a manifestation of the Divine. This idea is exemplified in one of the Koran's names of Allah, "Zahir," which means "the outward God is the manifest universe." Another name, "Batin," means "the inward or unmanifest essence of God," which, when not well understood, can make "Zahir" appear unreal.

The Koran (The Speech of God) was intended to be ritually recited aloud in Arabic, engaging the Southern Stream Power of the Word just as the Egyptians revered the oratory power of Ma'at or the Roman Catholic Mass invokes the ecstasy of God's descent into the Logos. Much like the mantras used in Hindu worship, these rituals transform the psyche through sound, meaning and symbol.

Koranic recitations and Torah readings in ritual worship of the One God merge the use of language with the spiritual heart. Worship in this way unites the worshipper with the image/concept of God in his heart and during worship in a sacred language with coherent numerical values, such as Hebrew or Sanskrit, deeper, mystical knowledge is imparted which transcends ordinary time and literal mind.

The coherence between spiritual Truths, language, and everyday life in Jewish society was carried forward through Islam, bringing the Divine into Form through applying spiritual principles in the development of their empire. The One God without a Second merged into letter, word, language, number, calendar, commerce, and worship. All aspects of life in their non-secular society were touched– commerce, art, science, community.

Islam's unifying influence first brought together the nomadic Arab tribes, then Christians in Byzantium, Syria and Palestine, Coptics in Egypt and later, Roman Catholics in North Africa welcomed Muslim liberation from the austere yoke of the Church. The people in these Christian territories found the untampered Southern Stream message of Islam more appropriate for them than the Northern Stream's patchwork presentation of Jesus' work and around 655, Christianity almost completely disappeared in Cyprus, Rhodes, Turkey, Corsica, Sardinia and North Africa, replaced by Islam.

More inclusive than Christianity and far less isolated than Judaism, tolerant Islam initially had no compulsion to convert others. Under Islam's tolerant rule those who retained their faith prospered. The Jews, who along with the Greeks and Armenians had conducted trade between Europe and India since Roman times, were protected from persecution in Islamic areas, resulting in justice, equality and a fair distribution of wealth. Many Christians and Jews were hired as administrators by Muslim rulers and Jewish scribes were employed to translate Greek, Persian and Hindu treatises.

Between 700-900 A.D., a thriving Muslim-controlled trade stretched from Spain and North Africa to Peking and Indonesia, promoting the great cultural exchange that assimilated the best of Greek and Persian culture. Merchant caravans, sailing ships and armies carried the message of Allah from Mecca via the Mosque, which served not only as a place of worship, but also as a haven for beggars, travelers, the sick and the stranded, creating a massive religious fraternity which crossed cultural barriers.

The great humanizing and harmonizing influence of Islam arose from the fact that to the Muslims, there was no such thing as a secular world; commerce and religion, traders and teachers were all manifestations of one and the same Force. The spiritual and ethical principles that were taught in the Mosque were applied throughout every aspect of Muslim life. This led to the outworking of the original intention behind the "people of priests" founded in Abraham's lineage.

Islam brought the hope of a better life to many downtrodden peoples by spiritually liberating them from whatever class or caste system held them in bondage. For Muslims, racism and classism was subordinate to religion, commerce and trade. Those who traded with Muslims found that actually living according to God's will in equality, brotherhood and tolerance was a great innovation over caste and class systems such as those of Hindu India or feudal Christian Europe.

Through Christianity, authority was transferred from the Roman Empire to a "Christian Empire." This appealed to the ruling class which often used forced Christian conversion as an arm of their political authority. Islam, on the other hand, appealed to the common man seeking to break free from oppressive forces and many voluntary conversions were made among the poor and dispossessed. In a very short span of time, relatively speaking, Islam spread like wildfire throughout Spain, North Africa, the Middle East and India.

One group, however, did not benefit from Islam's promise of freedom. Even though the Koran places women in perfectly equal spiritual status with men, the cultural traditions of the Middle East, which repress women, prevailed in Islamic countries and still do today. In the Koran's 33 Sura (chapter) women are clearly given spiritual parity with men, "Verily the Muslims of either sex, and the true believer of either sex.... either sex who remembers Allah frequently for (him/her) hath Allah prepared forgiveness and a great reward." Even on his deathbed Muhammed told his daughter Fatima and his aunt Safiya, "Work ye out that which shall gain acceptance for you with the Lord, for verily I have no power with Him to save you in any wise." Here the prophet clearly indicates that a woman's spiritual salvation relied on her own relationship with Allah and not in her reliance on her husband or male relatives. Although this was a definite improvement over the Mithraic exclusion of women from esoteric mysteries, this spiritual equality did not extend into everyday life. As usually happens, people continue to rely upon custom and tradition and spiritual truths are interpreted and applied according to a people's temperament, development and ability to understand.

Like Christianity, and its other spiritual predecessors, Islam experienced the fragmentation which occurs in all institutions during their expansionist phase. Around 670 A.D., Islam split into Sunni and Shi'ite Sects at the death of Mohammed's heir, son in law, Ali. Semi-autonomous dynasties called Caliphates (political governors) and Emirites (spiritual rulers) formed along ethnic and geographical lines. Doctrinal differences also surfaced along those same lines, separating the Shi'ites of Iran from the Sunnis in Turkey, Arabia and Iraq. Over the centuries numerous Islamic sects split off from the Shi'ite and Sunni divisions: the Ismailis, Assassins, Druzes, Yazidis, Zaydites, Kwarij and the Alawis.

Unlike what occurred in early Christianity, doctrinal differences among Muslims did not result in a sculpting of the image of Muhammed or a doctrine pieced together from mistranslated, edited texts written long after the master had left. Christianity is an intentional creation of the men who came long after Jesus left. It is a conglomeration of lore, ritual and belief from many different sources, often put together in order to gain conversions in regions that were earmarked for conquest or to prevent destabilization of society. Islam, however, is an intentional flowering of the Southern Sacred Stream, a direct response to the Northern Stream's appropriation and twisting of Southern Stream concepts.

∞

While Europe was steeped in the conflict and superstition of the Dark and Medieval Ages, the Islamic Empire (711-1250), which extended from Spain, across north Africa and through Persia (present day Iraq and Iran) enjoyed a Golden Age which predated the European Renaissance by over 500 years. Muslims considered faith, logic, metaphysics and the sciences complementary to Islam, unlike the Church's perception of a literate populace as a threat to its authority. The Islamic Golden Age produced works of art and literature which rivaled those later produced by the European Renaissance. For example, the Shahnamot is an epic story on par with Greece's Illiad and India's Bhagavad Gita or Shakespeare's brilliant theatrical enactments of the comedy and tragedy inherent in humanity's conditioned mind.

In stark contrast to the apparent insanity that gripped Christian Europe, the rationality of Muslim scientific study and inquiry seemed most attractive to Europe's medieval scholars and students. Christians from all over Europe flocked to Moorish Spain to study philosophy, mathematics, science, architecture and medicine. During this time Arabic became the language of learning and a Southern Stream partnership developed between Muslims, Jews and Nestonian Christians who kept the wisdom of classical Greece alive by translating Greek texts into Arabic. For instance, the combined texts of Razi (844-925 A.D.) and Ibn Sina (known to Europeans as Avicenna (980 -1057), both Islamic philosophers, physicians and scientists, served as the basis for European medicine for 500 years. The rediscovery of Aristotle in Europe was due to the work of another devout Muslim, Ibn Rushd Avorres (1126 -1198), who gave all glory to Indian ayurveda as the source of Hippocrates' medicinal philosophy, theories and treatments. Avorres' disciple, Rabbi Moses Maimonides, (d. 1204) a Jewish scholar, physician and author of *Guide to the Perplexed*, introduced Aristotelian thought to European philosophy and profoundly influenced Thomas Aquinas' (d. 1274) treatises which brought Artistotle's rationalism into Christian doctrine.

∞

In the 9th century, Sufism, a mystical movement with ties to early Christian asceticism, arose in Islam. Al Basri and Rabia, Muslim mystics and father and mother of Sufism (the mystical arm of Islam) said one must approach God and please Him as you would a lover, sacrificing one's own desires for your lover's pleasure and becoming One with Him. This leads to annihilation of ego.

Later Sufi Kwajagans (Masters), such as al Junayd of Bagdad, in addition to spiritual liberation, saw the practical application of wisdom for the good of an evolving society was an even greater use of one's realization. They felt that a balanced development of all parts of man's nature and culture was important and saw philosophy, theology and even spiritual ecstasies as useless.

Unfortunately, Muslim tolerance for religious difference did not extend to mystics who reported on their experiences of high spiritual states. Sufi saints, such as al Hallaj (d. 922), were martyred by the Muslim orthodoxy for making proclamations such as, "I am He whom I love and I am the Truth." A statement very similar to Jesus,' *"I am the Way and the Truth and the Light."*

Sufi mysticism was brought into the ordinary world of the devout Muslim through the works of Persian al Ghazali (1065-1111) and Spanish Muslim, Ibn al Arabi (1165-1240) and by the middle of the 13th century Sufi orders were commonplace in the Islamic world.

For al Ghazali, philosophy, logic and science couldn't prove the existence of the soul or God. In his 'Tahafut al Filasifa' (Destruction of Philosophy) he asserted that reason alone (the very motive for Europe's strong interest in Islamic Spain) leads to "moral decay and social collapse." Unfortunately, most European students clung to the intellectual side of Muslim teaching and ignored the more mystical.

Al Arabi, who was frequently referred to as Sheikh al Akbah (the Great Master), offered perhaps the most profound spiritual realizations ever written, relating to every human being, regardless of Sacred Stream or religion. Predictably, it was Arabi's work which was overlooked by European Northern Stream scholars.

Arabi's 'Futuhat' and 'Fusu al Hikan' (Meccan Revelations), state that the cornerstone of Islamic tradition is Tawhid (the Oneness of God's Being), yet affirms the reality of the many in relationship to the One. In Himself God is One, the Real, (Haqq) incomparable, and in His self- disclosure, His divinity in Creation (Khalq), He takes the form of many names, attributes, beings and their many ways of approaching Him, through belief, consciously or unconsciously, through understanding and suffering and faith. For Arabi, all supposed 'duality' or in the case of Tawhid, 'Divinity' and its properties or entities are signs of Oneness in Essence. In other words, Tawhid is both infinitely beyond all things (Tanzih) and simultaneously present in all things (Tashbih). In Islam, the deeper understanding of Truth is present in the very names of God and hard to miss for a devout Muslim. For Christians, such knowledge is much more difficult to come by. Except for the writings of often discounted Christian mystics, the only place the Northern Stream expresses this Truth is in the Catholic *Tome of Leo* where it is restricted to a description of the divinity of Jesus.

Arabi believed that every person is unique, for God never self-discloses knowledge in the same way twice, whether in a snowflake or a human being. This individual expression plays out its uniqueness first through building an ego-identity and later through the emptying out of that identity, as the Divine discloses Itself to Itself through the egobuilding/emptying process. Arabi's clear exposition on the nature of uniqueness does not suggest we abandon laws, authority and teachers but that we fully receive them into ourselves to do as they will, rather than to parrot them. By receiving and not following the leaders, the groupist imitation that plagues mankind is eliminated. This understanding is the single most valuable contribution of Ibn al Arabi. Grasping it reveals the age old human pastimes of intolerance, persecution and exclusivity as foolish and irrelevant.

Arabi also saw that the Divine ties Itself in a knot, fitting Itself into the beliefs of man. Al Arabi brought this point home when he wrote, "When man performs ritual prayer, man lags behind and follows God. When God performs His prayers for man, God lags behind man by following man's beliefs." The Divine restricts and constricts Itself to create, to emanate and also to disclose Itself to Its creation, otherwise it could not know Him. In Truth, God discloses or reveals Himself only to Himself, it can be no other way than this. People imagine they believe in God; that belief is itself a knot, a binding in the heart which sets the soul on a path suitable to its nature. In actuality, what people believe in is really God's Self-disclosure to themselves, always in accordance with the changing shape and preparation of His untying of the knot. As the untying occurs, God makes Himself known by virtue of bestowing awareness itself on us and later, knowledge of Him comes through following His laws, being His servant and receiving His blessings and bestowals, which in Islam are revealed as mystical stations or states of consciousness.

No one worships or is one with God as God is to Himself. One is only in relation to God as he perceives, experiences and believes or is at one with Him in her/himself. In this sense, one also worships no one but oneself. Muhammed's saying, "He who knows Himself of his soul knows his Lord," clearly bears the same message, as does ancient Egypt's "Know Thyself," and Lord Krishna's "the Lord of His Self resides in the silent chamber of one's own Heart." When the servant knows his true self, then he knows God; not as God knows God but he knows God as his (man's) own Lord. This unveiling is verification of faith, law, belief and study. Arabi saw that each being has as his God only his specific Lord, this is a blessing of his imagination and not the Totality of Allah. From this mature view, it is blasphemous to profess the medieval Christian belief that only one unique, holy son of God incarnated the totality of God, which is infinite.

During the time of the Crusades Sufism became a bridge between Southern and Western Stream peoples through the mysticism common to both Sufism and Shamanism. Through this medium, Arabi's contemporary, Rumi, and other Sufi masters such as Azizan spread the influence of Sufism from Turkey, through Turkestan, to the borders of China and Northern India. Influenced by Sufi Kwajagans, fierce Mongols adopted Islam in Persia and fifty years later the Russian Khans did the same. This brought millions under Islam's wing, from the Caucasus Mountains to the Great Wall of China. Islamic conversion of these nomadic warriors took place within only 100 years, while Christianity required some 500 years to saturate Europe.

Through Islam the Southern Stream brought Spirit Source into practicality. Islam's Sufis carried this breath of God to the Northern Stream through the timeless contributions of masters such as Rumi, Kabir, Hafiz and much later, Gibran. Although unable to appreciate the beauty of Islam itself, the contemporary Northern Stream world marvels at the practical, yet mystical, wisdom of these Sufi greats.

The second 600 years of Islamic history involved massive conversions among Western Stream ethnic peoples, such as Turks and Mongols, who relied upon study, teachers, reason, faith, and the law to prepare an opening for the Divine. These Muslims, however, did not treasure refinement and academic excellence with the same fervor as their Middle Eastern brethren. Unlike the earlier Caliphates of Arabia, Persia or Moorish Spain, the Turks discouraged intellectual pursuits outside of study of the Koran and enforced a rigid dogma. In fact, the Mongol and Turkish hold on Islam was very similar in effect to the European hold on Aramaic Christianity during the time of the Crusades. Unlike the laissez-faire attitude of Hindus and Jews, who abhorred proselytizing, Islam, like its cousin, Christianity, eventually fell into the use of military, missionary, authoritarian conversion after adoption by the Turks and Mongols.

Muslim converts swept into northern India towards the end of the 12th century, bringing military and political conflict. By 1191, they had taken Delhi and went on their own religious crusade, destroying most Buddhist monasteries and throwing the Hindu kingdoms into turmoil.

As this wave of Islam flooded into India, voluntary Indian conversions to Islam became relatively common, with nearly 90% of those converts coming from the so-called lower castes. Islam's Southern Stream emphasis on egalitarianism held a strong appeal to those shut out of equal participation in their own society because of the caste system. Originally designed to regulate the social order in ancient times, India's caste system had degenerated into bigotry and segregation by class and color. Those of lower caste seeking to participate in the equality that was sweeping the Southern Stream world through Islam at that time found a safe harbor and hope for a better life in converting to Islam.

The 12th century invasion of India was just the beginning of massive invasions of Mongolian warriors. From the late 13th century through the 14th century, successive waves of Mongolian tribesmen disrupted older, more settled societies. Just as nature's predators feed upon the weak and infirm, the more "civilized" peoples, made too comfortable by their civilization, fell prey to Mongolian invasion. China, India, Russia, Eastern Europe, and Persia all suffered under the onslaught, each forever altered by their conquest. Under the leadership of Genghis ("world encompassing") Khan, Mongol hordes engineered the fall of Peking in 1211. In just 20 yrs he had extended his rule from the Pacific Ocean to the Caspian Sea.

While defeating Mongol armies in Palestine Egyptian Muslims also put an end to the last Crusader state stronghold in the Holy Land, Acre. In comparison to the social and economic upheaval caused by the Mongol disruption of the Persian empire, the Crusades were a rather minor episode to the Muslims.

Chapter Seven
False Masters

slam's integration of study/worship and commerce/ trade reached deeply into every facet of life in Muslim culture. The breadth of the accomplishments of this society, coupled with those achieved by Muslim partnership with the Jews in scholarly and economic pursuits, dwarfed the petty squabbles, land grabbing and jockeying for position which dominated Europe's illiterate Dark Ages, superstitious Medieval Age and the literalism of the Christian Reformations. During the flowering of the Islamic empire, destruction, disease and death ruled Europe for centuries.

During the latter days of the Roman Empire, civil unrest sparked by religious differences was common. Radical Christian monks burned synagogues in Persia, barbarians burned the sanctuary of Eleusinian mysteries in Greece in 396 A.D., and in 415 A.D., Hypatia, the high priestess of the greatest mystery school of its time in Alexandria, Egypt was made a public spectacle and murdered by a Christian mob.

Around the same time, wave after wave of warring nomadic tribes swept into the Roman Empire, bringing death, destruction and eventually collapse seventy-six years later. The Church, however insured its own survival by securing its autonomy from Rome in 461 A.D. In the East, the Byzantine church remained subordinate to the emperor of the Byzantine Empire as head of Christendom.

After the fall of Rome, the Church became the European repository of knowledge with Irish bishops and Italian Benedictine abbeys preserving what little education remained. The ensuing chaos in Europe did not however, prevent Christianity from establishing a stronghold within the European psyche. Indeed, humanity's immaturity and the vacuum created by the demise of the Roman Empire, as well as the threat of barbarian invaders, provided a perfect medium for the growth of the moralistic and dogmatic Christianity of Paul and Augustine. However, with its tainted Holy Scripture, focus on suffering and Mary iconography, post-empire Christianity could only express the Northern Stream's oppression of life by ego-driven mind.

In Europe from 711 A.D. up to the time of the Crusades, the Frankish and German Holy Roman Empire (Roman principalities that became their own little kingdoms after the fall of Rome) were constantly under attack from all directions; from the north, Vikings; from the East, the Magyars (formerly Hungarian Huns) and Spanish Muslims from the Mediterranean sea in the south. Coinciding with Charlemagne's rule over the Holy Roman Empire, Norse/Danish attacks extended into Ireland, England, Spain, Italy and Russia. Due to the nearly constant vying for wealth and power, the people of Europe lived with war and the threat of war for centuries.

During his rule, Charlemagne prevented the Muslim Moors from infiltrating Western Europe, and subsequently forced his subjects to accept Christianity by imperial edict, in the same manner as Constantine had done much earlier. With this, the Northern Stream tendency toward oppression was further grafted onto Christianity and oddy enough, Christianity, once oppressed by Rome, became a tool of oppression.

Just as in Constantine's time, Christian conversion often took place by coercion, and very few of these people (Franks, Lombards, Saxons, Britons, Goths, Celts) genuinely converted to Christianity, unlike the original Jewish apostles. Those who wanted to survive had to become 'believers' in order to appease the power-hungry Church and stay out of trouble by remaining under the protection of nobility. Becoming a Christian became a survival move, but not with the salvation of the soul in mind. No real effect or inner change in the nature of the people occurred. Unlike the early Christians of the Middle East who had access to the teachings of Jesus in their original language, most Europeans were poor and illiterate. Access to biblical scripture was allowed only to clergy and scribes hidden away in the cloistered abbeys and monasteries of Europe. Along with accused witches and members of heretical sects, European Christians were burned alive for attempting translations or even possessing unauthorized biblical texts. For European peasants, Christian belief was whatever the head of the local parish and the nobility said it was.

$$\infty$$

The Romanization of the Southern Stream Truths taught by Christ prevented the Northern Stream from fully grasping them. Instead, a gap was created between the two Streams, which manifested first as the split from the Byzantine Empire and then, during the Dark Ages of Europe, as the Crusades – a distortion of the deep desire to tap the true source of their spiritual inspiration: The Holy Land.

Europe's first great coordination of the Crusades to the Holy Land, financial considerations notwithstanding, was professed to be based upon the belief that the Jews and Muslims were enemies of God. In 1073 the pope at Cluny, France told the crusading knights, "The only sin is to kill another Christian."

By 1096, Church doctrine sanctified the murder of German Jews, Slavic Pagans and members of a heretic Christian sect called the Cathars enroute to "liberating the Holy Land from the infidel Muslims." By redirecting the ferocity of the Normans (Vikings) of Northern France toward a common "outside" enemy, the Church effectively halted the petty, internal wars plaguing Europe.

Although the Crusades did open Christian pilgrimage sites in the Muslim-dominated Holy Land, the real bonus was in establishing European trade routes to the Orient without having to pay tribute to the Muslim Turks or the Byzantines. Economically, this was quite a boon to the coffers of the Church and European aristocracy.

For adventurers, fortune seekers and the small number of the faithful, the Crusades provided a way to escape debt and to absolve themselves from all past sins. The Crusader's sword became the symbol for a crucifixion-fixated populace, who mixed an estranged piety with incredible brutality, all of which convinced Islamic people of the European/Christian tendency towards unquenchable aggression, hostility and violence. These professional soldiers, ostensibly in the service of God, were authorized by the Church to commit murder and were empowered before entering battle through magical war rituals called Christian masses.[24]

Although many Crusades were failures, the Crusaders pillaged the Holy Lands for 200 years, establishing the beginnings of wealthy trade/banking systems in Italy and fulfilling the economic aims of both the Church and European aristocracy. An elite group of financiers (Knights Templar) positioned themselves to profit from war itself and it was now no longer necessary to pick the winner in a military conflict in order to prosper. Italian Catholics from rich merchant families developed banking and insurance to finance papal and political military campaigns – the Crusades – despite the condemnation of 'usury' by Aristotle, Jesus, and early Church fathers.

The Crusader city/states of Edessa, Antioch, Tripoli and Jerusalem served as warehouses for merchandise brought back from the Orient after trade opened up with Middle Eastern merchants. (Ironically, these places were the first areas in which the apostle Paul preached the Gospel to gentiles centuries before.) Competition was fierce and the city-states of Genoa and Venice battled each other for 100 years over the privilege to control the spice/silk trade route through Muslim territory to the Orient.

In keeping with the theme of mercantile consideration, the Church refused to allow anyone to put forward or promote ideas or spiritual practice without church approval, control and tithes. The Roman Catholic Church had 'cornered the market' on spirituality, franchising religion in much the same way as McDonald's franchises its hamburgers. However, in medieval Europe, starting your own 'spiritual burger stand,' outside the auspices of the Church had more than just legal consequences and could result in your torture and execution. Even Francis of Assisi, later canonized by the Church, was not immune. In 1210 the model of piety, purity and poverty found it necessary to seek permission to pursue his spiritual goals. Had he not done so, he would have been branded a heretic, like those who came after him.

Seventeen years later, the Church reacted to the huge numbers of religious nonconformers, not by reevaluating Church doctrine and dogma, but by calling for Inquisitions. In 1323, within 100 years

---

24 • *The original purpose of the mass, which was to merge people with the spirit of Christ, became contaminated by the hysteria of the times and was subverted in these cases to malific purposes.*

of St. Francis' death, pious zealots renouncing church property and leading lives based upon the life of Christ, as St. Francis did, were burned as heretics by Pope John XXII. Devout Christians such as the Bogomils of Bulgaria, Humiliati of Italy, the Waldenses, Cathars and Albigenses of France were murdered by the hundreds of thousands.

Ironically, during the persecution of millions of heretics and other outcasts, an equal number of Christian pilgrims were crisscrossing Europe, visiting holy shrines which contained relics of apostles and saints, praying in thousands of gothic cathedrals built in honor of the Virgin Mary. A trade in relics (both real and fake) sprang up around these pilgrims, providing a financial bonanza for sharp (yet unscrupulous) merchants and clergy. Apparently, for the Northern Stream, even spiritual matters were not immune from the 'bottom line.'

Having effectively controlled the dissenting views of the heretic Christian sects, the Church turned to stamp out the remnants of the popular Western Stream folk religion of Europe, which was earth-centered and woman-friendly. Followers of this tradition honored nature, both the feminine and masculine principles, and sexuality. Practitioners had and used the gift of prophecy, provided comfort for the dying, herbal/folk remedies for the sick, birth control, and when needed, abortion. Church inquisitors accused female herbalists, spiritual healers and midwives of being witches,[25] in league with the devil. These women became scapegoats for difficult times, blighted harvests, war and even the Black Plague.[26]

In the late 1400s, Pope Innocent VIII commissioned two Dominican monks to write an instructional manual on interrogation and torture of witches to extract confessions. Sadly, the manual they produced was used extensively over the next 250 years. Later, through the mass distribution of that book, the *Malius Malifasorum*, via the newly invented printing press, non-Christians became

---

25 • *The words "witch" or "wizard", which mean wise woman and wise man, come from the Gaelic verb "wett" – to know. Wett is derived from an earlier Welsh term Gwed, much like (Hebrew) Yed or (Sanskrit) Ved, meaning knowledge. Similar terms in Anglo Saxon, wicce (witch), wicca (wizard), come from the word "wit," an obvious variant of "wett." The word "wicked," which originally meant "under the influence of knowledge," later came to mean "evil."*

26 • *Starting in 1347 the Black Plague lasted 200 years and killed roughly one third of the European population, approximately 20 million people.*

known as devil worshippers and those who espoused any trace of folk culture as witches. The nature god, Pan, and the horns of the bull, both symbols of untamed, natural fertility, became associated with the Evil One Himself.

Constructed primarily from misunderstood bits and pieces of older religions such as Mithraism, Judaism and Manichaeism which held deep fear and resentment toward woman and even Life itself, the pre-Reformation, patriarchal and highly superstitious Catholic church was permeated with the ideas that sexuality was sinful and women were a serious obstacle to man's holiness. A woman who was too independent, wealthy or powerful was considered a threat – spiritually, socially, and politically – and was dealt with severely.

The Church's witch hunt was not, however, restricted to followers of the "Old Religion." Targets of Church fury were often independent[27] female landowners of considerable wealth, but with no political protection. Their persecution actually amounted to a transfer of wealth, as their lands and other assets were confiscated by the Church, ostensibly to pay for the public spectacle of their capture, imprisonment, torture and execution.

The Christian exclusivity which led to the Crusades and Inquisitions was the result of an extreme form of ignorance. Intolerance, which stems from judgment, is antithetical to the teachings of Jesus and exhibits the inability to be consciously responsible for one's own behavior. Born out of entrenched reactivity, this kind of automatic reaction has no real choice in it and is an obvious sign of unconscious conditioning rather than the use of free will.

Both Crusaders and Inquisitors were people whose twisted individual instincts were enhanced by mass paranoia and supported by distorted scriptural authority. The intolerance so rampant during those times was a natural result of the strong faith of fearful, simple-minded people, under the guidance of unscrupulous religious and political leaders. The Crusades and the Inquisition gave grim testimony to European Christianity's misapplication of divine

---

27 • *One such independent woman, a visionary named Joan of Arc, led France to victory over England in 1429 during the Hundred Year's War. However, seen as an abomination by French clergy who sympathized with England, she was sold by them to the British and later condemned as a witch and burned at the stake. Ironically, the same institution that martyred her canonized her centuries later – without ever truly acknowledging their previous misdeed.*

energy; an error which repeated itself again and again in future holocausts in Africa, the Americas and once more in 20th century Europe. The world dominance of the culture which produced Christianity and its extremes have served to make clear the ego-mind distortions in humanity which need purging, as well as work them out through the process of exhaustion. This same mechanism is still in operation today, without respect to religious persuasion.

∞

Between the 11th and 17th centuries, during the double horror of the Crusades and the Inquisition (c. 1096-1650) extraordinary undercurrents of Divine energy flooded into humanity to offset the barbarous slaughter of millions of heretics, pagans, witches, knights, Jews, and Muslims. From 1096-1291, new infusions of spirituality were firmly established through a global surge in mysticism in the Southern and Eastern Streams. Persia, Turkey, India, Tibet, China and Japan were all receptive to this energy, as evidenced by the rise of Milarepa in Tibet, a resurgence of Confucian thought during the Sung dynasty in China, another flowering of Zen in Japan and through the Ramanuja devotional sect, a revival of Vaishnavism (worship of Vishnu) in India.

Europe, although generating an enormous amount of tribulation, also saw the effects of this grand influx of spiritual energy. Moses de Leon, a Spanish Jew, wrote the Zohar (The Book of Splendor), an interpretation of the mystical Kabbala. Eliezar of Worms in Germany preached a return to more basic Jewish principles, while Ashkenazic rabbis, influenced by St. Francis, preached that piety and purity were most pleasing to God.

The light of Christian mysticism was also at work to counterbalance the darkness generated by the Northern Stream's violent excesses. In Germany, the pronouncements of mystic Meister Eckhart (1260 -1327), another great Christian philosopher who was influenced by Maimonides, echoed the Sufi principle of 'emptiness' (fana) and the Kabbala's "nothingness" (ayin) with his declaration that God is 'nothing.' Concepts, imagery and theology were considered by Eckhart to be hindrances to spiritual attainment.

The Divine also made Its appearance in Europe through less intellectual avenues as well. First in Italy, then in France and Spain, Catholic saints known as "incorruptibles", whose bodies never decayed upon death, became evidence of miraculous powers at work. Through the immaculate faith of these mystics the adaptability of the Divine produced outward manifestations – despite the distortions of orthodox dogma. So permeated with Divine Presence were these saints that their mere physical presence was enough to heal others, and after death their bodies became holy and healing relics. The existence of these holy people during the barbarism of the Crusades and the Inquisition bears witness to the fact that healing grace is always accessible, even in the most dire of times and under the unholiest of circumstances.

Living acetic lives of malnutrition and suffering, some 50 Spanish and French[28] incorruptibles (1450-1650) maintained their high level of consciousness, bearing the light of Truth during times of extreme spiritual darkness. Acting as human lighthouses, they radiated Truth amidst the incredible suffering and death caused by religious and political wars and disease in Europe and genocidal abuse of other peoples abroad. Their steady maintenance of high levels of spiritual awareness throughout all kinds of adversity not only served as a reminder of Christ's suffering for all mankind, but also inspired faith and healing.

During the time of the French and Spanish incorruptibles another wave of spiritual benediction swept the planet. In India this energy manifested through holy people such as the Muslim mystic poet Kabir (1440 -1518), who welcomed and inspired all seekers of truth, regardless of religion, Chaitanya, who later became the inspiration for the devotional Hare Krishna movement and Mirabai, a Rajput princess who flaunted convention and took to the streets singing praises to her beloved Lord Krishna. Guru Nanak (1469 - 1538), inspired by Kabir, established the Sikh religion, dedicated to the One True God.

In Europe this energy gave rise to another group of Christian mystics, most notably St. John of the Cross, St. Teresa of Avila and St. Ignatius Loyola. St. Teresa, a "converso", or a Jew who converted to Catholicism, wrote *The Way to Perfection* and her autobiography, *Life of the Mother Teresa of Jesus* and founded a reformed Carmelite order.

---

28 • *Oddly enough, wherever the major political power was located in Europe, there the incorruptibles were also. Early on, when the seat of European power was in Rome, most of the Christian mystics were Italian. Later, one finds that French and Spanish incorruptibles made their appearance during the period when France and Spain controlled the European political scene.*

St. John, a Carmelite friar, was the author of *Dark Night of the Soul,* an exposition of the journey toward God through de-conditioning the mind without the use of religious imagery of any kind. For attempting to implement the reforms received by Teresa of Avila in her visions, St. John was imprisoned several times, then banished to a distant monastery until his death. One hundred and thirty years later he (like Joan of Arc and others) was canonized. St. Ignatius Loyola, originally a Spanish nobleman and leader of a contingent of counter-Reformation military forces, later founded the Jesuit Order. His spiritual practice used images such as the Stations of the Cross or imagined scenes from the life of Jesus.

Repeated inundations of Grace, matching and mitigating periods of seemingly overwhelming hardship, raise human beacons to shine spiritual light in times of darkness throughout human history. Like Noah's rainbow, they are a sign that humanity is not forgotten by the Divine during terrible times. Despite all appearances to the contrary, we are, indeed, loved and cared for.

While Northern Stream Christian Europe descended into chaos and the Southern Stream brought forth the flower of Islam, the Eastern Stream was embarking upon an era of spiritual revival and expansion through Advaita in India and by reaching out to Western Stream peoples in Asia. The compatibility of the Eastern and Western Streams made itself readily apparent as Indian Buddhism touched the more shamanic Chinese Taosim, Tibetan Bonpo and Japanese Shinto, demonstrating the inherent harmony between the qualities of Heaven (acceptance) and Earth (absorption).

Around 700 A.D., Western Stream Bonpo met Eastern Stream Buddhism. By special invitation of the King of Tibet, Padmasamhava, an Indian Siddha yogi, brought Buddhism to Tibet through pure transmissions, becoming the founder of Nyingmapa, the first of four lineages of Tibetan Buddhism. Tibet's Bonpo tradition and expansive landscape prepared her people to receive direct transmissions of Truth, without need for the normal means of preparation and purification through study, worship, etc. Different from Hinduism's darshan, Islam's baraka (spiritual presence), Christian purity or the holy resonance that radiates from a sage or saint, pure transmission is a direct transference of the Reality outside of causation, time or space to the recipient.

Hindu description of the Divine as absolute, consciousness, bliss (Sat, Chit, Ananda) took on a decisively Buddhist flavor even portrayed as "Buddha bodies" or Kayas. Absolute Truth (Sat) became emptiness. Clarity and compassion are the natural extensions of consciousness (Chit) and Bliss (Ananda) into the world or community.

By 1073 the cornerstone of the second wave of Tibetan Buddhism, the Kagyu School and the Karmappa lineage, was laid by Marpa and his student Milarepa with the aid of Indian Buddhists, Atisa and Naropa. These practical applications of realization reformatted through Buddhism became the foundation for the bodhisattva vow, Mahayana (the Great Vehicle) Buddhism, dedicated to the altruistic liberation of all sentient beings. Compassion, as a discipline, is a wedge that counteracts arrogance and aggression; but at a more advanced stage of development is a spontaneous outpouring of Bliss. Whether as a layperson or a monk/nun clarity promotes the integration of the various facets of life as emanations of the Buddha Field, as Awakened Truth, rather than negating the world as *illusory*. This innovation served to extend kindness into the suffering world, evolving the Eastern Stream idea of enlightenment to include giving assistance to others; no longer would one focus on nirvana just for oneself. The bodhisattva vow also serves as a refined form of ego purification, as one places the welfare of others above oneself.

For thirteen centuries, up until the time of the Chinese invasion in 1959, Tibetan culture remained somewhat isolated, unaffected by the Northern and Southern Sacred Streams. Those who dedicated themselves to spiritual development in Tibet were unhampered by outside influences for over a thousand years.

With the arrival of Sengtsan, the 3rd (Chinese) Zen patriarch some time in the late 6th century, China's Chuan (Zen) brought Buddhism to Shinto, the Western Stream nature religion of Japan. In the Hsin Hsin Ming, possibly the first Chinese Zen document, Sengstan states, "The Great Way is not difficult for those that have no preferences. If you wish to see the truth, hold no opinions for or against anything. ...When thought objects vanish, the thinking-subject vanishes. Don't waste time in doubts and arguments. Do not dislike even the world of the senses and ideas. Accept them fully.

Do not search for truth, only cease to cherish opinions. If there is even a trace of this and that or right or wrong, Essence will be lost in confusion." The sense of personal responsibility for one's own spiritual awakening found in Zen as described in the Hsin Hsin Ming is a far cry from the dependency that authored much of Christianity during the same time period.

Japanese seekers sculpted Buddhism, cutting away the weighty scripture chanting and ritual, fashioning Chinese Ch'an into the simplicity of Zen, incorporating some of the character of Shinto's sun goddess and nature spirits. Even though Japanese Zen got its start in the 6th century, it took another 600 years to really take root. During the Kamakura period (1185 -1333), the Japanese Rinzai school, made famous by its use of paradoxical statements (koans) to induce spontaneous enlightenment, was founded under the patronage of the Shogun Tokimune, who ruled from 1251-1284.[29]

In ninth century India, amidst a resurgence of devotional sects, Shankara, a child prodigy who became a celebrated sage, re-established Hindu Advaitism. A return to non-dualism which glorifies the Upanishads, Shankara's Advaitic Vedanta is best suited to mature souls with unconfused minds, ready for direct knowledge of Self. Shankara established the Shankaracharya, a council of Vedantic wisdom intended to rekindle and maintain the glory of Vedanta in the hearts of the people. To this day, only those determined by the people to be God-realized beings are allowed to hold those posts.[30]

Even though Eastern Stream India was experiencing a tremendous resurgence in spiritual energy at this time, in ninth century China all religious pursuits were under attack. Around 845 A.D.,

---

29 • *Divine intervention prevented Kublai Khan's (one of Genghis Khan's sons) attempted conquest of Japan, safeguarding the development of Zen. Two typhoons, one in 1274 and another in 1281 (called the Kami Kaze or "Divine Winds" by the Japanese) stopped the Mongolian navy, sinking hundreds of vessels, carrying 100,000 Mongol warriors. Had Mongolian rule established itself in 13th century Japan, Zen's full flowering may never have taken place.*

30 • *Indians who find themselves installed as Shankaracharyas generally don't want the job, but the people insist that they serve. Wouldn't it be wonderful if our political system was held to the same criteria? Paradoxically, those who really want to hold political posts are often the least qualified spiritually for the position, due to their ego-based motivation.*

Chinese emperor Wu-tsung, in an effort to regain control of his empire, persecuted all Buddhist sects, which had grown extremely powerful and had taken over printing, money-lending, public works projects and care of the needy. An estimated 250,000 Buddhist monks and nuns were forced into the streets as the emperor forcibly closed 40,000 temples and shrines. Lands and assets once owned by the monasteries were confiscated in order to replenish imperial coffers. Nestorian Christians and Zoroastrians were banished, removing all foreign influence from China. Ignoring the tradition of Confucian, Taoist and Buddhist beliefs, the emperor allowed his desire for wealth to override the good of the people, causing massive social dislocation and chaos which lasted for 50 years. Then, having survived a half century of internal conflict, China's Sung dynasty emerged as the Bagdad and Cordoba of the Orient, primarily due to the simultaneous reemergence of Buddhism, expressed through Chinese Ch'an (Zen), which initiated a Golden Age in China.

Unlike Northern Stream ego projection and reaction against others, Eastern Stream ego reacts against itself. This pattern has repeated itself periodically in China with the social 'reforms' of Chiang Kai-shek's Nationalist Movement, Mao Tse Tung's rise to power and the Great Leap Forward, during which 50 million people died of starvation, and the Cultural Revolution which also caused great misery and death.

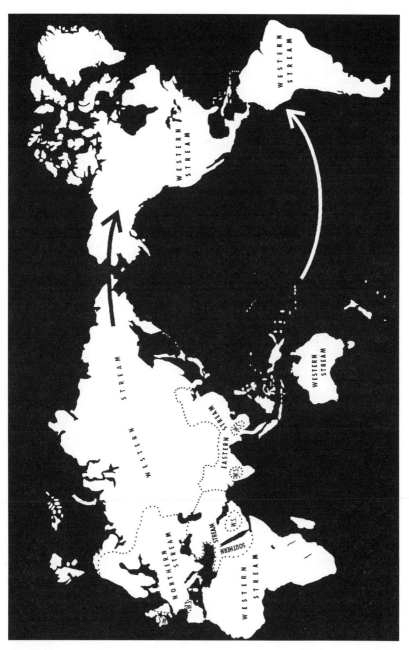

Map #1   *Geo-Sacred Loctations of Four Sacred Streams*

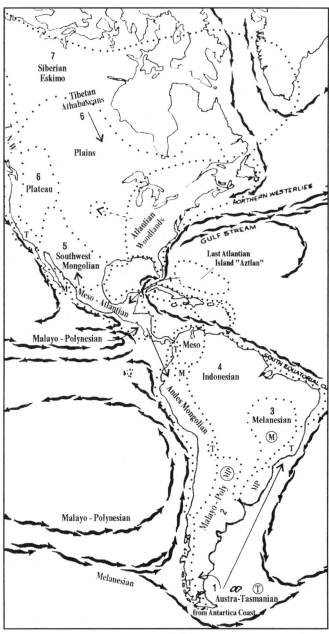

America's indigenous peoples parallel with Asian Ethno-Linguistic racial traits.

Earliest migrations 40,000 BC represented by #1.

Latest migrations 10,000 BC represented by #7.

Pacific sea migrations may be both post and pre Aztlan (10,000 BC)

Meso-Atlantian culture diffused with Mongolian Southwest, Andean and Atlantian Woodlands.

Map #2   *Amaruca - (Land of the Plumed Serpent).*

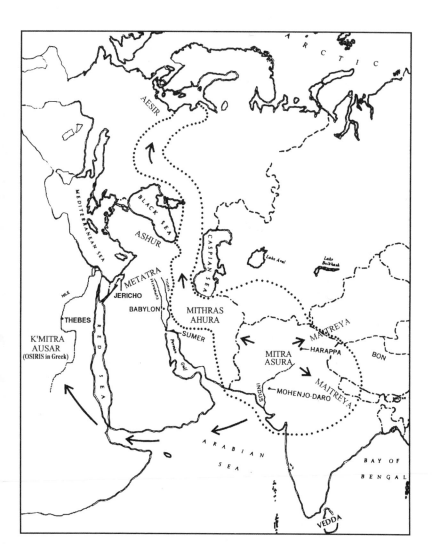

Map #3   *Cultural Diffusion or Series of Divine Revelations?*
Appearance of "The Lords or Solar Deities" along the Indo-
European Migration Belt from Vedic India to the Baltic Sea
and Egypt/Israel.

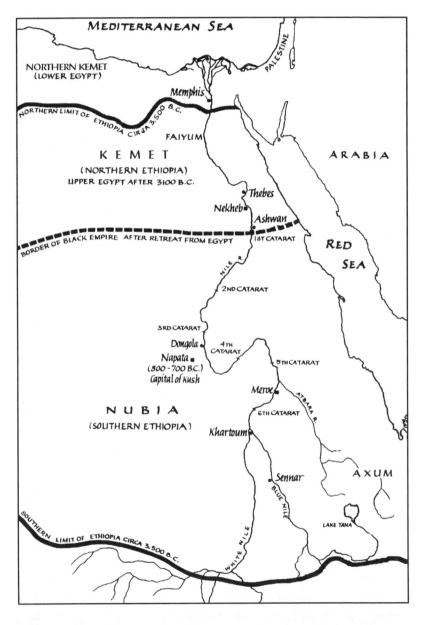

Map #4

Kemet. Ancient Afro-Egypt

Key: S=Spain, P=Portugal, F=France, B=Britain, D=Dutch, Be=Belgium, G=Germany, = I=Italy, R=Russia

Map #5 *Northern Stream remapping of the Earth. 1500-1950.* Colonialism, Imperialism, Industrialism and Investmentism.

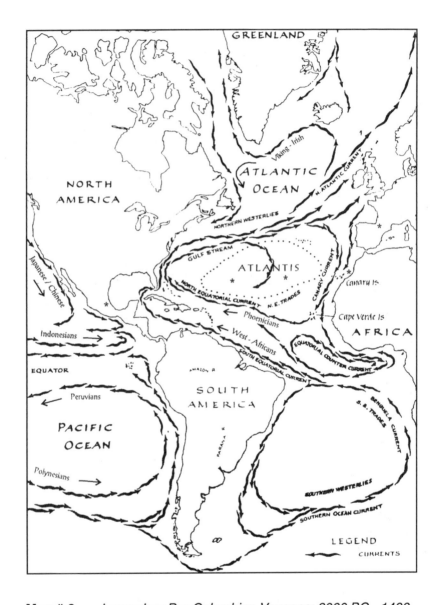

Map # 6   *Legendary Pre-Columbian Voyages: 3000 BC - 1400*

*Note: star symbol: similarity between Nahuati languages of Central Mexico with the indigenous Canary Islanders and Basque peoples on Spain-France border.

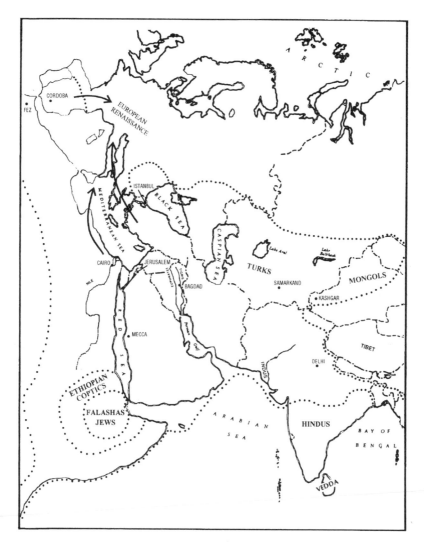

Map # 7   *The Southern Stream Contribution to the European Renassiance.*

Islam's Golden Age extended from Spain to the Philippines. Judeo-Greek-Islamic-Persian civilization (10th Century) entered Medieval Europe through Spain and Egypt, returning crusader knights (13th Century) from the Holy Land and by Greek evacuation (15th Century) during Turkish recapture of Constantinople.

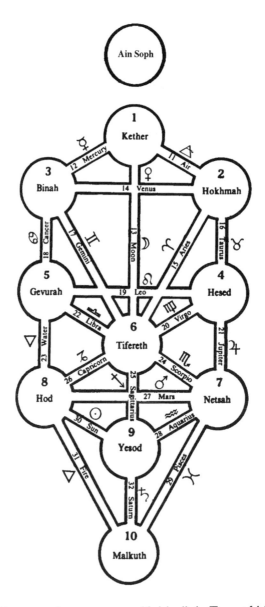

Diagram A *Kabballa's Tree of Life*

Ten Sephiroth (Divine Lights) emanating from the Source.
Note the pathways as a source of astrology, 22 letters, 10
numbers, 32 paths of wisdom and magical Tarot.

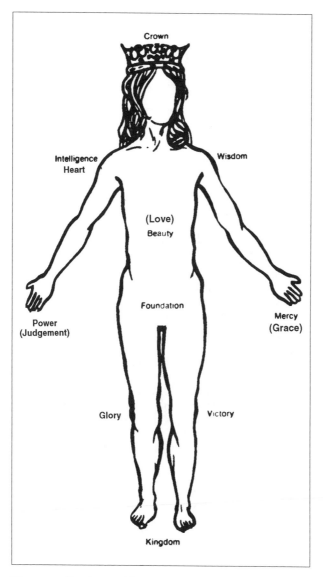

Diagram B *Adam Kadman – Son of Man – Logos*

The Divine Man holds all attributes/names of God superimposed over the Tree of Life. Note the positions of the sephiroth in the Christain prayer "for thine is the Kingdom, the Power and the Glory."

Great Pyramid and Sphinx in Egypt

Buddhist Temple

Mayan Astronomical Temples

Chapter Eight
A Quest for Fool's Gold

By 1453 Islamic Turks seized Greek Orthodox Constantinople, effectively closing the Italian trade route to the Orient. (See map #7). Once again, Northern Stream Europe was separated from the Southern Stream source of Christianity in the Middle East and the Eastern Stream in the Orient. Again forced to grow without reliance on other Streams, the Northern Stream with its material focus understood this loss of their spiritual rudder as the loss of access to the material wealth of the Far East. For them, this translated into the need to discover new trade routes and expressed itself as an explosion in maritime exploration.

On one level, Vasco de Gama's trade route around Africa, discovered in 1498, assured that European mercantile contact with the Orient would no longer be controlled by competing Italian merchants through Muslim middlemen. On another level, Italian/Roman control of the spiritual treasures of the Eastern and Southern Streams was starting to slip as Spain and Portugal took the lead in exploration and trade and made the 'treasure' of the Orient available to a larger portion of the European population, without first filtering through the control of the Roman Church. Northern Stream countries had now gained direct access to the wisdom of the Eastern Steam. But without Islamic tempering, Northern Stream Europe would inflict great harm upon itself and the other three Streams.

In 1452 the Doctrine of Discovery was issued, giving religious sanction for the enslavement of indigenous peoples and the theft of their lands in newly discovered territories. This papal decree demonstrated Northern Stream arrogance by declaring all lands not owned by Christians to be considered vacant and thereby claimable for the Church. In this way, Europeans used religion to justify their belief that those who are inferior (i.e. not the same) must be saved by them and/or can be exploited by them. This concept found its ultimate expression in Northern Stream colonialism, imperialism, religious 'missions' and the American idea of "Manifest Destiny." The world was soon carved up by Spanish, Portuguese, Dutch, French and British governments[31] while Europe's artists, musicians, scientists, religious reformers and mystics enjoyed the Renaissance. (See map #5.)

The first wave of explorers usurped the indigenous peoples already living in the 'newly discovered' lands, establishing European colonies in the Americas which eventually revolted against their own parental systems of government to become autonomous political entities. The second wave imposed imperial rule upon the peoples of Africa and Asia, making them economic pawns in a global competition for greater wealth and power. In most cases this eventually resulted in native revolt against foreign rule and the establishment of additional autonomous governments, but not before the indigenous cultures, traditions and religions of these peoples were either supplanted or severely contaminated by European influences, preparing fertile soil for further, subtler forms of exploitation.

Most of the history we're taught about the dramatic surge in maritime exploration during the 15th century centers around the voyages of European explorers. However, there is evidence that other cultures from earlier times fully explored our planet's oceans and it was from the maps drawn up by these previous maritime pioneers that European explorers planned their voyages. (See map #6.) Between 1362 and 1408 Icelandic sailors went to Greenland and left records of their visits. Almost seventy years later (in 1477), Columbus went to Iceland to study the maps and records of Viking Olaf Tryggresson which record five landings in the Americas between 985A.D. and 1011. Turkish sailor Piri Reis drew up a map in 1513 which indicated that the world is round. This map also

---

31 • *Italy and landlocked Germany, which later became the Axis powers, did not participate in the 15th century European rush to conquer the world. Five hundred years later, however, they attempted, through World War II to grab what the rest had cultivated.*

showed an accurate rendering of the land mass of Antarctica –
below the ice cap! On the map he states that he copied the
information from much, much older sources.

Spanish and Portuguese mariners got a head start to the New
World over Britain and France because of the Muslim contribution
of ship/sailcraft brought to Spain from China and Africa by Arab
traders. China's well-developed maritime skills are evidenced by the
fact that Chinese sailors used longitude and latitude coordinates
from as early as 100 BC; Europe didn't develop this necessary skill
until the 18th century. Between 1405 and 1433 Cheng Ho, a Chinese
Muslim sailor, made voyages to Indonesia, India, Arabia and Africa
with 60 ships, carrying a total of 28,000 men (compared to Vasco De
Gama's 1498 voyage with 4 Portuguese ships and 500 men). Arab
routes to the Azores, deep in the Atlantic, were already 300 years old
by the time the Portuguese made their trips in the 1400s. The work
of Nubian Muslim geographer Idrisi states that by 1157 Arab sailors
had reached the Canary Islands, Cape Verde, and the Azores. Long
before Europeans 'discovered' these routes, the islands had been
given Arab names, assigned by a Franciscan friar. And even more
amazing, twelfth century Arab cartographer, Abulfeda, was well
aware that the world is a sphere.

With the onset of Portuguese slave raids and gold trading on the
West African coast of Guinea in the mid-15th century, Europeans
learned of earlier African mariners who sailed to the New World.

Muslim traders in West Africa already knew of the Americas
from information gathered during earlier voyages by Africans. Later,
ship's logs of nearly all early voyages made by Columbus, Balboa
and Diaz remarked on the presence of marooned West African
sailors in the New World.

Mariners from Mali used the equatorial currents and trade
winds to reach the New World. One such journey was made in 1300
during the height of Timbuktu's Golden Age by the Mali King,
Abubakari. This trip was well-documented by his brother, Kankan
Musa, who later made a pilgrimage to Mecca. This could explain the
Aztec worship of Tezcatlipoco, a god with decidedly Negroid
features. Older archeological evidence, dating from 700 BC, points to
Olmec sculptures with Negroid features. This time period coincides
with the last Black Egyptian dynasty (Kush). There is some evidence
that the Kush dynasty's alliance with Phoenicia led to quite a few
maritime explorations. As further evidence of this contact, Mayan

jaguar societies, West African leopard societies and the lion gods of the Kush dynasty all share striking similarities. The same can be said for the worship of the Mayan plumed solar serpent and the cobra worship of ancient Egypt.

∞

During the beginnings of its maritime expansion, Europe existed in a state of feudal slavery in which corrupt religious and state authority abused the bodies and minds of the peasantry. Most Europeans were oppressed, illiterate and landless peasants and had been so for centuries. This was the condition, the cultural climate, in which the Spanish conquistadors, and other early settlers of the Americas, all members of the Northern Sacred Stream, found themselves when welcomed by the guardians of the Earth, the Western Sacred Stream. Their pent-up demand for land ownership and freedom found opportunity and unlimited resources in the Americas – lands poorly defended by indigenous peoples who practiced a form of spiritual communalism without written language, currency or private ownership. The shamanic cultures of the Western Sacred Stream had developed social structures that did not promote distorted ego values. Ironically, their lifeways exemplified the traits most treasured by the very scriptures the new explorers and conquerors forced on these peoples but could not themselves apply.

The early colonists were often the undesirables of Europe – religious fanatics, criminals and fortune hunters. These were the first to meet the medicine men and women and holy people of the Earth-based Western Sacred Stream in the Americas and West Africa and the Eastern Sacred Stream in India, China, and Japan. The Northern Sacred Stream, flowing through the White race, cut off from both their own Western Stream Celtic/Norse heritage and the Southern and Eastern Stream source of their treasured Christ figure, met the Western Sacred Stream, flowing through the Red race of the Americas, and the Black race of West Africa. The history of these encounters and what followed demonstrates what happens when the unprepared lower self meets the Sacred and cannot recognize It for what It is. The lower self seizes what it believes it can have and control, rather than focusing on what can be learned and shared. What might have happened had the colonists arrived on these shores as fellow students rather than conquerors?

When Cortez landed in the New World, he was mistakenly believed to be the bearded white god of Incan, Aztec and Mayan legends, Quetzalcoatl or Kukulcan. His 16th century arrival, predicted by the Mayan calendar, was greeted with great celebration and feasting by the native people. Some believe that Pizarro and Cortez were oblivious to the fact that their arrival was the fulfillment of the return of the great white gods of native peoples. However, what is more likely is that they took advantage of their misidentified status, using their influence to help weaken any resistance to conquest.

Eventually, Spanish military might and European diseases defeated the Yucatan Mayans, Mexican Aztecs and Peruvian Incas, reducing their population to 1/10 its original size (3 million by 1565) and even less by the turn of the 17th century. The number of human sacrifices made by the Toltec and Aztec civilizations was but a drop in the bucket compared to the decimation of the population brought about by European disease and warfare. By 1565 less than 10% of the population survived the onslaught, a far greater loss than that caused by the Black Plague that decimated possibly up to 30% of pre-Columbian Europe.

Long before the Europeans arrived, civilizations of Meso and South America such as Teotihuacan, Tiahuanaco and some 100 Mayan city-states thrived in their own Golden Ages during the time that the Roman Empire declined into the chaos of the Dark Ages. Information to that effect was destroyed or covered up by Northern Stream conquerors and historians. The European practice of destroying written evidence of ancient knowledge (the libraries of Alexandria and unauthorized writings of the Middle Ages are better known examples) carried over into the destruction of the Mayan Codices, ancient texts which may have contained unparalleled information about the history of our planet, previous civilizations and their ancient technologies. This incident exemplifies, once again, the Northern Stream need to control – in this case, information which may have controverted the 'party line' about the New World 'savages.' This practice is still in operation today, evidenced by Vatican control of unreleased information about the Dead Sea Scrolls, and prophecies made by the apparition of the Virgin Mary at Fatima and Lourdes. On a secular level, media control, censorship and government propaganda and disinformation are issues in every country in the world.

The Northern Stream's spiritual hunger, focused through the lens of secular materiality and unquenchable thirst for wealth, power, and adventure led to the loss of ancient wisdom teachings that revered and worked with the natural world and its laws; Western Stream cultures and values fell under the wheel of 'progress.' And, because of its success at colonialism and imperialism, the Northern Stream led the bulk of humanity deep into secular materialism.

Northern Stream Europe was incapable of holding the wisdom contained in the vast reservoir of Southern Stream stewardship. Unlike the Southern and Eastern Streams, the Northern Stream has no sacred language and no continuous, innate spiritual tradition. Their own Celtic/Norse traditions were destroyed, first by the Roman Empire, then by Roman Catholicism. Christianity, assembled from often misunderstood bits and pieces gathered from many Eastern, Southern and Western Stream traditions, was forced upon the European population. Without the understanding gained from their own tradition or a sacred language to support that understanding, the holy books of Europe, (the Geneva, and King James Bible and the Latin Vulgate) held no inherent power and the people could not truly engage that power in the symbolic initiations of their liturgy. Because of this, the Northern Stream, ego-mind/self, continued to express through a decrepit culture, devoid of depth.

The Christianization of Europe, and later, America, sidetracked the Northern Stream by preserving 1000 years of illiteracy, blind obedience to authority, and superstition through the Dark Ages, the Crusades and Inquisition; and another 500 years of arrogance and abuse through colonization, wars, revolutions, genocide and pollution. In essence, the darker recesses of the Northern Stream psyche were brought to the fore by the power of the Christ light, which it not only misunderstood and twisted, but also violently defended and imposed on the rest of the world. Paradoxically, it was the Northern Stream itself that needed saving, not the non-Christian peoples it later conquered.

Because the Northern Stream focus is on self and changing the outer world, rather than the inner, their natural inclination was to worship anthropocentric images of God, rather than to focus on the Transcendent. That focus translated into the images of Jesus, Mary and the saints with which we are all so familiar. Just like the other three Streams, the Northern Stream has the capacity to hold its own wisdom, not that of the Southern or Eastern Streams. Predictably, dissatisfaction with the patchwork, imported irrationality of Christianity led to the enshrinement of science as the religion of the Northern Stream.

Having evolved a parochial view of the world, the Northern Stream is characterized by a 'hive mentality,' a belief in their superiority to others and severe intolerance for differences. Its strict, shallow literalism spawned a new trinity of supremacy, salvationism and materialism, which they exported and enforced throughout the colonial world. As this new trinity effectively hid the secrets of God's inner workings within the convoluted dogma of Christianity, the Northern Stream borrowed Islam's deeply matured tools of inquiry to probe God's outer secrets through scientific investigation of the mysteries of nature. Rational science, which followed on the heels of biblical literalism, began to take hold of humankind, restricted at first, to Europe. Technical knowledge and skills began to replace the more ancient understanding and organic symbology found in following nature's cycles. The refinement of the rational faculties which occurred through scientific investigation, along with the later acceptance of science as the new religion, led to a disconnection from nature, mysticism and magic and the secularization of European culture. For some reason, the Northern Stream mind could not contain scientific information and mystical truth simultaneously. It could operate with only one at a time, discarding the other.

It is important to grasp the significance of the Northern Stream's incursion into science. In Europe during the Renaissance, Spirit and lower mind necessarily polarized themselves against one another with the collision of science and religion. The seeds of the present social decay of Western culture were sown with the creation of this deep schism in the human heart. With the advent of scientific inquiry, the Southern Stream reasserted its influence on the Northern Stream mind. However, the Northern Stream could not embrace Southern Stream science in a balanced way, any more than it could harmoniously absorb Southern Stream spirituality.

Science was born as both a reaction against the irrationality of Christianity and as part of the evolutionary path for the Northern Stream. Through science, questions left unanswered by the Church were finally addressed; the Northern Stream found the 'reasons' behind natural phenomena and stopped there, not looking to the 'reasons behind the reasons'; thus canceling out centuries of superstition... along with Truth. Religious reforms came along later to soften the effects of scientific reaction against religion. However, without a solid spiritual foundation these reforms did not create an alchemical change within those who took up religious study. Instead, they led to separation between church and state.

True spirituality is about alchemical transformation, uniquely suited to each personality's requirement. When Christianity restrained, stagnated and stultified instead of providing spiritual sustenance and growth, European science was born. Rising out of Southern Stream alchemy, much as early Christianity rose from Judaism, science emerged from a spiritual need for alchemical transformation. However, with its focus on materiality and lack of deeper understanding, the Northern Stream mistakenly used science to fill the spiritual void left by Northern Stream religion. True to its pattern, the Northern Stream substituted scientific discovery for the true alchemy of a spiritual life, something seriously lacking in European Christianity. Not surprisingly, much scientific inquiry for Europeans revolved around the belief (and misunderstanding) that non-precious metals (such as lead) could be changed into gold through the use of secret alchemical processes. Indeed, Italian Renaissance patron, de Medici, instructed Jewish scholars to translate Hermes Trismegistus' Corpus of Hermeticum before Plato's Republic – no doubt anxious to discover that secret.

The forerunner of modern science and chemistry, alchemy came to Europe with the Muslims and Jews. Although its origins are lost in antiquity, some clues can be found in the word itself, which is Arabic ('al Khemia') for Egypt. It was thought that through the study of alchemy one could glimpse the mystery of the solar deity, allegorically hidden in the metaphor of gold. Alchemical processes were originally intended to use nature's own laws and substances to awaken the golden, solar seed of divinity in man, liberating him from the hold of the base mentality (the 'base' metal lead) of his lower instincts in order to shine forth like the sun, giving sustenance and illumination to all.

Members of European mystical brotherhoods such as the Freemasons, Rosicrucians and Knights Templar, which had their beginnings in the ancient mystery schools of pre-Roman times, were often students of Arab and Jewish custodians of these wisdom teachings and many were well-versed in the sciences of alchemy and astrology. Their teachers' Southern Stream emphasis on balanced development and practical application of spiritual realization had a profound effect upon some who later became famous for their impact on Northern Stream culture. Mysterious personalities such as Sir Francis Bacon, Comte de St. Germain and Rosencranz were socio-political alchemists who influenced the leaders of European society. Their work energetically counteracted the distortions in fanatical Christian reforms and kept the flame of the deeper knowledge burning. By allowing the aristocracy to play out their excesses and exhaust their lower impulses, the gap between the classes was widened, finally erupting in the upheaval which led to the rise of democracy and greater personal freedom a century later.

With the advent of science as the new religion, God became an object, dethroned, absent from daily affairs and current history, relegated to a superstitious, unenlightened past. The Northern Stream's new-found emphasis on individualism and specialization of the mind was highlighted by the empiricism of Descartes, Spinoza's atheism, Hume's materialism and Newton's mechanical universe.

The almost overwhelming Northern Stream tendency towards over-intellectualization is a double-edged sword. Because it is the nature of the mind to misinterpret and distort what it encounters as long as it is servant to the ego, even when exposed to Spiritual Truths, the result of strictly mental probing into any subject is often less than desirable. Both the Eastern and Southern Streams, through Buddhism and Sufism, emphasized that mere acquisition of knowledge, other than for technical use, hinders human development and unleashes degenerative ego impulses which contaminate society. However, by using the most extreme intellectualism for the renaissance of inner consciousness, the Buddhists showed that logical proofs themselves were not destructive when through them the mind could be left at the doorway to the soul.

Roman Catholicism was dealt a serious blow by the rise of scientific inquiry. Investigation of many commonly held beliefs began to take place, usurping Church control over the minds of the people. Scientists such as Copernicus challenged the Church's heliocentric model of the solar system and Keppler identified the orbits of the planets and the axial tilt that gives rise to the seasons. The light of reason began to dawn, leading to a re-evaluation of the Church itself – and religious reform.

A thousand years of control by the Church produced a predictable reaction and some of those who chafed under Church rule dared to make their thoughts and feelings known. Martin Luther (1483-1546) denounced papal power and found himself the leader of a breakaway Christian movement in Northern Europe. He is believed to have been a Rosicrucian. Along with John Calvin's (1509-1564) Puritan movement, Luther's Protestant Reformation broke the medieval power of the Catholic Church and replaced it with the direct fear of God, without the intermediary role of the Church. For Northern Stream Protestants there was no longer any intermediary but conscience, prayer and the work ethic, all of which covered a growing denial of their own fragmentation and lack of spiritual foundation.

Luther was an Augustinian monk and professor of theology in Saxony. He believed that inner transformation occurred through God's mercy. This assured salvation without the intermediaries of church, priests, sacraments or saints, leading, of course, to rejection of papal authority and that of the early church councils that established canon and doctrine. German kingdoms tired of paying tribute to "Italy's papacy" shifted monetary support to German-born Luther. Action taken by the Catholics to put down the Reformation led to the 30 year war (1618-1648) in Bohemia that decimated the German population (from 14 million to 4 million).[32]

The ancients understood that the energy of a place can help mold human behavior. Certain areas radiate extraordinary amounts of energy which, when imprinted by human action and emotion, continue to affect inhabitants for centuries as each successive generation is motivated, partially by the energy, to repeat the same behavior, resulting in reinforcement of the initial imprint. This creates a cycle that is very difficult to break without extreme effort. In places where the imprint is one that supports spiritual growth,

---

32 • *The area in which Martin Luther lived, Bohemian Germany, was home to much fanaticism and resistance to authority from the time of the Crusades. Many heretical sects survived persecution by the Church in German Bohemia, preparing the soil for Luther's reform movement 300 years later. The association between the area and fanatical rejection of the norm became so inseparable that by the 20th century the word 'Bohemian' came to mean someone who lives an unconventional, if not somewhat dissipative, lifestyle. But what is the underlying cause for this?*

such as Tibet, this can be a positive thing. In places where the imprint is less than uplifting, such as Bohemian Germany, it can have devastating effects, such as those of the Reformation, World War I and Nazi Germany.

Another of the Church's detractors was Henry VIII, King of England, who, when refused a divorce by the Catholic Pope in 1533, closed all monasteries and established the Anglican Church of England which would allow him to do as he pleased. However, much like his Catholic predecessors, the king saw to it that failure to attend the Anglican Episcopalian Church meant fine or a jail term.

It seems, however, that the Christian reformation was more a political break from the control of Rome than a true reform of Christian doctrine or behavior. Unlike Hindu and Jewish reformers (the only two religions that never promoted conversion) who emphasized a God of Oneness and ecstatic bliss, Christian reformers, with few exceptions, remained focused on the Northern Stream concept of a wrathful God who can be found only through suffering and self denial, and who punished wrongdoers with eternal suffering and damnation. These ideas were not substantially different from those of Roman Catholicism. The Northern Stream affinity for harshness, suffering and death caused them – Catholics and Protestants alike – to choose death (the crucifixion) rather than the mystical nature of life (resurrection) as their symbol of holiness. The real change was that Europe, through the Reformation, finally threw off the yoke of Roman rule after 2,000 years of subjugation, first by the classical Roman Empire, then by the Catholic Church.

After the Reformation, the Doctrine of Discovery, which gave spiritual 'carte blanche' to European plunder of the New Worid, still served as justification to missionaries, conquistadors and colonists, both Catholic and Protestant, centuries later. Unbelievable as it may seem, those who operated under this pseudo-religious concept actually believed they were doing God's work. This irrational seed of religion-backed racism, economic exploitation and religious oppression planted so long ago was later sown and cultivated in South Africa in the form of Dutch Apartheid, resurfaced in the diabolical behavior of German Nazis and still later (in the 20th century) sprouted in the fundamentalist Christians' attempt to evangelize all nations, and more sadly, still grows in the ranks of the Ku Klux Klan and other white supremacy groups.

Chapter Nine
Rights without Responsibility

n the 17th and 18th centuries, global energies pushed humanity towards personal liberty and freedom. But the expression of this unprecedented innovation was limited by the immaturity of the dominant Northern Stream which took drastic measures to insure its own success and freedom at the expense of others.

The spiritual forces that drove the establishment of the 13 American colonies began an experiment in bringing together the Four Streams to explore liberty, justice and freedom on a continent unspoiled by thousands of years of human opposition to nature. The human forces that participated in this grand experiment were driven partly by fanatical religious idealism, found unacceptable in Europe, and partly by the need to protect the commercial interests of wealthy New World merchants. Their desire for liberty was based upon wanting to cut out the imperial middleman from what was correctly perceived as an incredible financial opportunity. Their success was assured due to African slave labor and acquisition of virgin lands stolen from the Native Americans.

A strange American alliance formed between Protestants, Baptists, Puritans and commercial magnates who, through the American Revolution, dismantled the monopoly on colonial wealth held by the Anglican Church and British Parliament in much the same way as Henry VIII broke Roman Catholicism's hold on England.

The Northern Stream's immature understanding of the use of wealth and power, as well as its expertise in devising clever disguises, is well illustrated by the apparent demise of the old style aristocracy/monarchy, thought to have been erradicated by various forms of democracy in the United States and Europe, and its surreptitious resurrection in banking institutions and industry... and the families that control them. Now the free individual could amass concentrated wealth, like the kings and popes of empires past. All lipservice to government "by the people" aside; whoever controls the money, controls the government.

In pre-Colombian North America, the 14th century spiritual benediction which swept the planet and produced the Spanish and French incorruptibles in Europe, manifested in a Western Stream reform which eventually affected people everywhere. Deganawida, a Huron Indian, introduced Wampam, the Great Law of Peace that unified the Iroquois Nation in fairness and justice. The American Indians safeguarded Wampam by relying on a council of spiritual elders (with women) as the only people empowered to impeach their representatives. This system was later used as a template by the authors of the American Constitution.

The philosophy upon which Wampam was based, known as Ne Gayaneshagowa or the Great Law of Equity, Righteousness and Well- being, consisted of Ne Skenno, peace between groups and individuals and Ne Gaiihwiyo, peace in thought and conduct and justice in human rights. Ne Gashedenza was the maintenance of "orienda" – the sacred power of the people and institutions. Extending these concepts into the secular, technical world and all Four Sacred Streams is part of the American experiment which so far we have failed to fully accomplish.

As before, with the construction of Christianity, the people of the Northern Stream had no solid spiritual foundation from which to develop its own version of this Western Stream innovation, and they could neither fully embrace the undistorted wisdom of those they deemed 'inferior,' nor truly implement it.

Although inspired by both the Greek patriarchal ideal of democracy and the Iroquois Sacred Law of Peace and League of Nations, (similar to our Congress), our forefathers chose to overlook the elements of checks and balances considered by the Iroquois to be essential – election of representatives by the female elders, the input of both male and female elders, and spiritual principles. Despite that oversight, Divine Providence guided American release from colonial rule and America came to serve as an example for the liberation of all peoples from the yoke of oppression. For example, with Napoleon's invasion of Spain and Portugal in 1808, the power of the aristocracy was broken and the puppet colonies of Argentina, Peru, Mexico, Venezuela and Ecuador soon declared their independence, following America's example. Ironically, the United States had already taken the the role of oppressor in its own land.

The constitution of the United States, the first document of its kind, was adopted in order to replace corrupt religious rule with government based upon natural, inherent, human rights, which placed sovereignty with the individual. The original version of the Declaration of Independence clearly had a decidedly spiritual flavor, focusing on the fact that human rights were God-given. The first draft read, "We hold these truths to be sacred," not "self evident" as it now reads; a more secular approach replaced a blatant religious reference. By separating church from state, freedom of religion and individual God-given human rights were to be assured, at least in principle. Paradoxically, the seeds of constitutional freedom were planted in the soil of the oppression of Native Americans, the enslavement of Africans and the exploitation of the new land's resources. Because the secular idealism which formed the foundation of America was no less subject to the ego afflictions of its own Northern Stream Christian population than any other system, it would take hundreds of years for the new nation to begin to legally enforce and adapt socially to the high ideals set forth by its constitution. In its rebellious establishment of freedom from English monarchy, accompanied by the thoughtless exploitation of others and resources, the American branch of the Northern Stream exhibited its immaturity, very much like the behavior of a poorly raised teenager left to his own devices.

Rights and freedom for a select few evolved into a system which eventually enslaved the populace with countless laws and regulations, resulting from the people's refusal to manage their own affairs in alignment with the freedom of a spiritually-based lifestyle. American government, which was originally designed to protect citizens from outside invasion, grew into a tax-hungry, regulation-generating machine, bent on maintaining and increasing its power over citizens in order to perpetuate itself. This is the natural result of attempting to apply an external solution (legislation, religion, etc.) to an internal problem. An immature people left to their own devices (spiritually) in a materialistic atmosphere will over time sink more deeply into materialism, abandoning ethics in favor of self interest as a yardstick for decision making. The answer lies in deepening cultural support for spirituality, not more legislation of either a secular or religious nature.

Dependant upon a falsely inspired sense of patriotism (another version of the 'us versus them' script) and public opinion molded by media propaganda, government continues to extend its control over the populace, promising security in exchange for freedom. Without strong personal understanding and spiritual foundation, Americans have gotten into the habit of using government as a substitute for Father God, never moving out of spiritual adolescence. Rather than appeasing a pantheon, one must now appease the many-armed god of government by paying one's taxes, obeying the multitudinous laws, not questioning authority and not rocking the boat.

The natural outcome of such abdication of personal responsibility and the reliance upon external authoritarian systems to assume that responsibility, is the rise of rebellion in the form of diverse factions clammering for attention and citizens 'sticking up for their rights,' followed by greater authoritarian repression. Eventually, as the cycle continues, the adolescent-minded populace must revolt to regain autonomy. Revolution occurs, a new 'system' is installed and the wheel goes 'round again. There has always been, with colonialism and imperialism, the opportunity for everyone to genuinely rise out of oppression, and step completely out of the victim/villain cycle. However, unless a true shift in consciousness takes place, history will merely repeat itself with a change in names and faces; the oppressed become the oppressor; yin becomes yang, and back again.

The Northern Stream's rudderless adventure mimics Southern Stream evolution first by equating God in Form with monarchy, then equating the formless nature of God with the amorphous power of The Government. Today the all-powerful Government seems as unfathomable and is just as feared by us as the Old Testament God was feared by early Hebrews. Patriotism and consumerism have become the American liturgy; credit cards, the holy sacrament. Financial success ("Making It") and Comfortable Retirement are our salvation; however, in the scientific religion of secular materialism, the salvation of financial success is something to be achieved in this life, there's no need to await the Hereafter. All means of exercising our "freedoms" are now funneled into supporting our media-sculpted, consumer-oriented reality.

∞

In 18th century Europe, the energy moving toward individual freedoms found expression in the French Enlightenment, which paved the way for Napoleon Bonaparte's ascendancy. This introduction could, however, have been more accurately named the French Idealism. True to its Northern Stream origins, it was an awakening to the idea of social betterment, not spiritual realization. Distinguished writers such as Rousseau and Voltaire criticized the Church and called for the overthrow of absolute monarchy which would be replaced with just, responsible, humane and rational government. Works such as these deeply influenced the philosophy of Jefferson, Madison, Adams and Franklin, sculptors of the United States' constitution.

Napoleon Bonaparte, a great soul who acted as a tool of Existence to destroy the outdated aristocracy, was originally driven by the intention to work in alignment with the ideals of the French Enlightenment, but his own character flaws got in the way. Giving in to his impulses, he declared himself emperor. His loss at Waterloo in 1815 ended the aristocracy and established a partial democracy, free of the slave labor economy upon which the Americas depended. The new European equality gave rise to a business (middle) class, secured property ownership for commoners, legal justice, a market economy without overt government intervention and opportunity in education. With this socio-political reform of Europe, the old order of feudal aristocrats completely disintegrated.

∞

While the French Revolution and later reforms antidoted the European aristocracy and signaled the end of European slave trade, the American Revolution threw off the yoke of British colonialism. But in America, the revolution resulted in only pseudo-freedoms with quasi-liberties. Here, the founding fathers of this country excluded Whites who didn't own property, women, Indians, free Blacks and slaves from the protection given by the Constitution.

Unbeknownst to most Americans, slave labor built the colonial wealth of the Americas and provided the foundation for its financial and industrial centers, including Wall Street. The feudal system and persecution of the Jews found in old Europe was simply transferred to American soil in the form of oppression of Native Americans and kidnapped Africans forced into slavery. Because they were darker-skinned (and not as well-armed), they were considered to be more savage, primitive races, barely, if at all, human, and therefore, fair game.

Boston rum was used to buy West African people for torturous export to Caribbean sugar cane plantations. Sugar cane was shipped to Boston where it was used in the manufacture of rum. It was the molasses tax on rum (pre-dating the stamp and tea taxes) that resulted in the Boston call to arms against the British. The ensuing revolution united the northern and southern American colonies into a viable agri-commercial market, insuring the accumulation of wealth outside the grasp of European taxation and the longevity of the institutions that made that wealth possible – slavery and land grabbing.

One of our founding fathers, Thomas Jefferson, himself a slave owner, originally wished to abolish slavery. However, financial considerations won out over the moral rectitude of abolition, deemed untenable because the planned tax revolt and secession from Britain depended almost entirely upon commercial freedom and slave labor to succeed.

Two hundred and fifty years of slave trading had caused perhaps as many as 30 million Africans to be seized from their native lands, the majority of whom died at the hands of African slave traders, European shippers and American plantation owners. By 1800, 10 million African men, women and children had made it to port to be sold into slavery in the Americas. Seven years later, while it became illegal to import African slaves into the United States, plantation owners could still legally own, buy, sell, trade and force them to produce offspring for sale on American soil.

When massive African slave raids began in the fifteenth century, slavery was a still a universal fact of life, having been common since pre-biblical times among nearly all people in most parts of the world. Women and children of defeated tribes/societies/cultures were often taken as slaves by the victors as spoils of war. The Old Testament encouraged servitude or slavery as a punishment for crimes. Girls and young women of low social status were often sold by their families into slavery as concubines (sex slaves).[33] But the

---

33 • *This practice continues today in some Third World countries.*

15th century Portuguese slave raids on the West African coast ushered in a new era in the buying and selling of human beings. The focus shifted almost entirely to the 'harvesting' of Africans to be used as slave labor in the New World. This idea has become so ingrained that today the word 'slave' conjures up pictures of Africans or people of African descent.

Abraham Lincoln, remembered as the president who ended American slavery, was not a religious man, but was a great political strategist and social engineer. His reasons for the civil war and freeing the slaves, contrary to popular opinion, had more to do with promoting national economic unity than carrying the torch of human rights. Proof of this lay in the fact that even though the slaves were freed, Black Americans still suffered unbelievable discrimination, and 150 years of Indian genocide went completely ignored as the government continued to deny the Indians their treaty rights. Since there was no political or economic advantage to ethical behavior in either case, the government chose to eschew it. Ironically, without black troops, the North may have lost the Civil War. And just as ironically, without Black slaves and confiscated Indian territory, there would not have been much economic superiority for the North and South to fight over.

After the 1862 Emancipation Proclamation was made, "Jim Crow" laws allowed the continued denial of civil rights for Americans of African descent. Thirty-four years later the Supreme Court upheld segregation, giving legal sanction to unequal treatment. In other words, the law was used to justify the continued humiliation and harrassment of Blacks at the hands of Whites. This state of affairs continued unquestioned until the birth of the Civil Rights Movement in the 1950s. Despite later legal victories over racism, African Americans have never been offered assimilation into American society. White America preferred to either quietly (and sometimes not so quietly) persecute Blacks or ignore them – but never fully accept them. An American with both European and African blood (virtually 95% of African Americans have European or American Indian blood) is considered Black because Whites had (and still have) no desire to assimilate Black people, even their own children of mixed parentage. That's why we have "light-skinned Blacks" instead of "dark-skinned Whites."

In the Americas, those we now call Black are actually a people of mixed racial ancestry and Sacred Streams. Out of necessity, these people have developed the capacity to endure tremendous suffering of all kinds. Some carry the entire rainbow of human colors within their own genetic coding and encompass all Four Sacred Streams. This genetic intermixing represents in physical form the evolving unity of the human species.

In addition to the merging and harmonizing of these Four Great Streams in the cauldron of human interaction, those who incarnate into bodies of mixed racial heritage accomplish this great work within themselves by personally undoing the ego distortions of the Streams they each carry in their genetic makeup. This is both a rare privilege and tremendous contribution. When they can fully step out of the victim/villain cycle their passionate understanding and embodiment of Truth and Justice will be as strong, powerful and effective as their suffering has been long and torturous. Their lives can be seen as magnificent altars of sacrifice for the common good, and stunning examples and reminders of the invincibility of the human spirit. It is only after each Stream reconciles and heals its own internal wounds that all will walk as brothers and sisters in the bright rainbow light of Truth.

American hypocrisy didn't stop with the institution of slavery. The concept of Manifest Destiny, a government-sanctioned philosophical excuse for genocide and land-grabbing, claimed that the American People, meaning White people, were superior to the native peoples and therefore it was their destiny to own this land and do with it whatever they willed. Certainly this was just an extension of the assumptions made and enforced by all royalty in the past. However, once free of their own monarchy, White Americans, rather than extending the same freedoms to the native inhabitants of this continent, chose instead to graft the curious arrogance of royalty onto their own common status.

The establishment of the hard-won individual liberties for which the Amercian revolution was fought led not only to a loss of liberty for those who already lived in North America, it almost resulted in their annihilation. As an unprecedented number of immigrants from many nations fueled the westward expansion of the Northern Stream, the United States government enacted deliberately genocidal policies which resulted in Native American death tolls rivaling those which later occured in Nazi Germany's

Holocaust, destroying the culture of those who had once welcomed them as brothers. The estimated 5 million North American Native peoples who thrived in the 1500s were reduced by imported disease and government policies to less than 500,000 by 1890. On one level, the Western Stream was sacrificed on the altar of racism and greed. On another, it gave up its freedom and stewardship of a pristine land in order that a merging of all Four Streams could occur.

Racist propaganda and outright lies were used to encourage White settlements in Indian territory. In many instances, government armies were used to aid the pioneers in their quest for land, minerals, etc. In the 1830s the U. S. military forced native peoples off their treaty-guaranteed lands against Supreme Court rulings that favored the Indians. Cherokee, Choctaw and Chicasaw tribes were made to walk the Trail of Tears from their ancestral homes in Georgia (where gold had been discovered) to settle worthless land in Oklahoma...until oil was discovered there. Every one of the 389 U. S. Government treaties with the American Indians were broken by the American government. This pattern of betrayal repeated itself in forced relocations, deliberate inoculation with disease (smallpox-infected blankets) and wars with noncompliant Indians until the tragic battle at Wounded Knee in 1890.

Even though this country was supposedly founded to establish and guarantee freedom of religion, predictably, the same right was not extended to others. As had been done to kidnapped Africans living in slavery on American soil, Native Americans were legally prohibited from performing their own religious ceremonies and replacement with Christianity was attempted through missionary work and enforced boarding school education, which separated Indian children from their families and sent them off to schools that were not part of American Indian society. There they were not allowed to speak their native language or practice any of their traditional ways under pain of severe physical punishment.

Apparently, their Northern Stream tormentors understood enough about Native American culture to know that their connection to the land was what sustained them. Native people were forced to live in "camps" away from their ancestral lands. On those reservations they were not allowed to live in their traditional ways. They were put into a null zone; not part of White American culture and forcibly separated from their own traditions, much as African slaves had been. The result, deliberately sought by government officials, has been an almost complete destruction of Native American culture and people.

America was not alone in its racist persecution of dark-skinned peoples. Like the early settlers of the Americas, and later the British in Australia, the Dutch in Africa found a people spiritually tied to the land, living a subsistence lifestyle with no concept of personal ownership of the land that provided for them. At their arrival in Africa, White Dutch cattlemen met Black Bantus with the same occupation. Even though the Dutch Boers and African Bantus were both cattle farmers, their motivation and therefore the scope of their activities was different. The Protestant work ethic ("More is better; therefore work harder to have more") contrasted sharply with the Bantu idea that such ambitious striving for wealth was at best some form of mental illness and a character flaw at worst. While we don't know what, if any, judgments the Bantu may have made about the 'character flaws' of the newcomers, we do know what the Dutch thought, based upon their actions. Viewing the Bantu cattlemen as inferior, and themselves as some sort of 'chosen people,' the Dutch usurped native use of the land. Around the same time as the British freed their slaves in 1834, the Dutch withdrew to the interior of Africa to preserve their religious doctrines and racist way of life, keeping the native people captive in their own land and later legally formalizing their oppression in a type of modern day slavery – Apartheid.

The Boer Great Trek to the interior and the resulting Zulu wars took place in areas which fifty years later would give the Boers reason to "relocate" the native people once again – gold. Strangely enough, this coincided with the American Cherokee Trail of Tears caused by the discovery of gold in Georgia. The Northern Stream ancestral memory of the legend of the Holy Grail found immature expression in the incessant search for wealth and gold – the material correlates of spiritual realization. Without the light of deeper understanding, the Northern Stream continued its neverending search for God in the form of money.

Even though Europeans considered Africa the "dark continent", the people of Africa had already discovered some of the brightest simple truths, such as, "A man who strives for possessions does not deserve respect." This view was shared by the Amercian Indians who believed one could not really own anything – neither land nor sky nor river. Being simply caretakers, they believed we must potlatch it away. This is contrary to the whole thrust of the Northern Stream's domination of all with which it comes into contact, be it people, resources, products, services or information.

Africans, Indians and other so-called primitive peoples lived for millenia in successful communal (as opposed to communist) societies, based upon the curtailment of individual material ambitions which, when left unchecked by deeply matured wisdom as they are in Northern Stream cultures, tend to reinforce ego, but when guided by wise group approaches, can develop the individual in less egocentric, more generous ways. Western Stream social systems worked because spiritual wisdom was recognized and applied. The absence of spiritual wisdom will cause the failure of any system, regardless of how well thought out or 'perfect' it may seem to be. The wisdom of Western Stream peoples, written off as primitive or backward by the Northern Stream, holds the key to successful fulfillment of the Northern Stream's deepest aspirations.

Initially, tropical disease limited colonization of Africa, but by the late 1880s medical technology had made access to the rest of the continent possible, and much of it was divided up between European political powers. (See map #5.) The infiltration of European culture into Africa, searching for riches, trade, religious converts and later, wealth by providing economic aid (and encouraging debt), basically destroyed African cultures.

By the time African peoples formed nations independent of European government, the influence of economic aid and cultural domination had replaced the traditional community and its values with the ills of urbanization – the crime, poverty and disease that plague most cities today. The basic marketing principle which states, 'Create a need, then fill it,' was employed. Convincing people that more is better and that they can only get 'more' from you (government, religion, etc.), creates dependency. Greed-based trade follows, depleting resources, shifting agricultural priorities (encouraging people to produce cash crops rather than feed themselves) and disturbing communal lifestyles, undermining traditional values and support systems. The resulting depletion of all types of resources creates the need for future economic aid and continued dependence, perpetuating the cycle.

In Africa, the European Christianity foisted upon African people by well-meaning European missionaries served to support the sabotage of their culture by convincing them to accept their inferior status and oppression as mandated by God. Backed up with all the trappings of technological superiority and, if all else failed, greater firepower, this "logic" was unassailable. The irony is that they were force-fed a very distorted version of ancient African Southern Stream Truth. Unwittingly, Northern Stream religion became a means to destroy the hearts and cultures of Western Stream peoples.

Bolstered by the false belief that they are superior and driven by their fear and need to control what they don't understand, members of the Northern Stream attempted to wipe out Western Stream Earth-connected consciousness wherever they found it. Unlike the virtually untouchable, ethereal Spirit of the Eastern Stream, the immanent Divine in nature which flowed through the Western Stream could be manipulated controled, destroyed. The arrogance inherent in the immature lower self leads one first to tell a lie, believe it, then to live it. In this case, the Northern Stream, believing the lie of their superior status and hampered by their distorted spirituality, tries to ascend to the Godhead on earth by stepping on their brothers and sisters and ignoring their cries.

Today, peoples of all continents find themselves at the mercy of thoughtless industrialization and dehumanizing exploitation of one kind or another. The compulsive need to dominate and control which leads to such misery is actually the misapplied projection of humanity's deep, instinctive, spiritual desire to take command of their own faculties, both material and spiritual. Unfortunately, dominated by our own tyrannical egos, this drive is mistakenly translated into the need to take command of everything – and everyone – around us. Eventually, all must realize that what really needs to be conquered is the ego's misguided urge to acquire the bliss of spiritual attainment through the domination of others and accumulation of wealth.

Chapter Ten
Emissaries of Grace

s the energies of liberty and freedom continued to increase, an explosion in technological breakthroughs began with the Industrial Revolution. Simultaneously, a flowering of spirituality took place, finding expression through Christian-based, metaphysical spirituality, occultism and mysticism. Religious groups such as Shakers, Quakers, Christian Scientists and mediums and spiritualists helped to counterbalance society's overemphasis on industrial materialism as part the maturing of the the American psyche. Later, the Theosophical Society, under the guidance of Russian Helena Blavatsky and certain hidden Masters, surfaced to revitalize Western occult traditions.

Around 1823, new Christian revelations, brought to visionary Joseph Smith by an angel, once again brought to the fore the Jewish prophet Abraham's idea of a priestly people, promising that common people (Mormons) will become saints in the "latter days," just prior to the second coming of Christ.

Followers of Joseph Smith's vision called themselves Latter Day Saints in keeping with the original revelation. With its Old Testament-style polygamy, Mormonism professed, among other things, to train men to father a new humanity by fathering children from multiple wives. This was seen as a preparation for an afterlife in which they would become, in spirit, creators of new peoples and planets. Mormonism, maybe the first American-born Christian religion, is, according to them, the only revelation with any validity since the time of Jesus.[34]

---

34 • *The U. S. government saw an opportunity in Mormonism and used Mormons to hold onto territory won in the Mexican-American war (1848) by granting them large parcels of land; thereby fending off Mexican recapture and insuring a California Gold rush (1849) for America. Originally called Deseret, their land bonanza covered areas now known as the states of Utah, Nevada and Arizona.*

Along with the rise of interest in spiritual matters, many challenges to contemporary views of the nature of God and religion made their appearance, calling narrow-minded religious literalism into question. Around the turn of the century, Nietzsche (d. 1882) pronounced that God is Dead. Ten years later American literary figure and social critic Robert Ingersoll, ridiculed the narrow prejudices of Christianity, pointing to state anti-blasphemy laws (shades of medieval Europe!) that made it a crime to directly question the Bible or God. And twenty years after Nietzsche's pronouncement, Mark Twain, American poet and master satirist, spoke of the Bible as a mixture of clever fables, blood-drenched history and a few good morals with lots of incest.

In the first half of the 20th century the Northern Stream's secular orientation led to the channeling of mystical energies into and through its writers, poets, philosophers, artists and musicians, who broke through the limitations of literal reason, traditional dogma and conceptualization. American philosopher Alfred Whitehead saw the Divine as a process interwoven into the world as a sacred interconnectedness, very similar in concept to Sioux Indian elder Black Elk's 1945 vision of the Sacred Circle of Life. Artistic movements such as Impressionism, Expressionism, Surrealism, Cubism and Dadaism stretched the boundaries of realism and rationalism to their limits, investigating perception, light, color, shape and dream imagery, as well as delivering social commentaries on subjects such as war and the mechanization of civilization.

The increasing momentum of industrial materialism provoked an even stronger response from the energy of spiritual awakening which made its appearance during the mid-1800s. Secular society was ready for the experience of an Absolute nature to counterbalance the developing overemphasis on materialism. Ideals brought forth by the poets, romantics, mystical philosphers and free thinkers of the 18th and 19th centuries and the humanistic, mystical scientists, social seers and artists of the early 1900s were realized in the arrival of 20th century sages, seers, prophets and master servants from India during the time of the two world wars. One might say their presence was a timed release antibiotic against the spiritual disease of secular materialism. Only the living example of spiritual masters who lived beyond the hopes, ideals and illusions of the Northern Stream ego-mind could provide the needed antibodies.

The spiritual wealth of the Eastern Stream would be drawn into the Northern Stream to the same degree that material wealth had been extracted from Eastern Stream countries. This vital exchange began with the arrival in 1893 of Vivekenanda, a spiritual ambassador sent by the great Bengali saint Ramakrishna, first to London and then to the World Congress of Religions in Chicago.[35]

Vivekenanda opened the door for other Indian masters such as Paramahansa Yogananda, who arrived in America around 1920. Part of the Kriya Yoga lineage established by the immortal Babaji and Sri Yukteswar, Yogananda succeeded in harmonizing the principles of Indian yoga with the cryptic message of Christianity. Yogananda understood and conveyed the unity in the message of Jesus ("The kingdom of Heaven is within," and, "I and my Father are one") and the timeless purpose of all yogas – union with God.

The spiritual stance of J. R. Krishnamurti (d. 1985), an Indian groomed by the Theosophical Society to become a world teacher/leader, appealed to the secular man by breaking the bonds of dependence on authority or reliance on external teachers or organizations. He demonstrated this by doing exactly what Annie Besant (English socialist, feminist and Theosophist) professed a world teacher would do – he renounced the very principle, organization and even the very role for which he had been prepared. By disbanding the Order of the Star and walking alone into humanity as a common man with a great inherent capacity to question our conditioned modes of thinking, behaving and living, he became a living example of a true world teacher/leader.

Some Eastern Stream messengers never left their homeland but their message not only penetrated the Northern Stream but was received around the globe. One of these was Sri Ramana Maharshi, a poor, uneducated Indian boy who realized the Supreme Self through the death of the mind, a dissolving of the ego into the Ground of Being. Until his passing in 1950, his direct approach to Truth and immense presence embodied the ancient Truths of nondualism[36] as professed in the Upanishads – the Self is All, and All is the Self; this is the only shining reality.

---

35 • *In the same year as Vivekenanda arrived in the Eastern U.S., Soyen Shaku, the first Japanese Zen Roshi to set foot on American soil, arrived in the western United States, symbolically outflanking Northern Stream America with Eastern Stream wisdom.*

36 • *Schelling, Schopenhauer, Emerson and Thoreau, all regarded as great western thinkers, revered the nondualism of the Upanishads.*

Coming up in quite different circumstances, we have another great Indian spiritual pioneer, Sri Aurobindo, (d. 1950). Highly educated in Britain, speaking seven languages, politically active in India's drive for independence, even before Gandhi arrived on the scene, Aurobindo was a divine renaissance man – prolific writer, poet and publisher, mystic, historian and visionary, all in one. Recognized in India for his greatness, his birthday was chosen as India's Independence Day. Ironically, this proponent of Indian independence found himself supporting Great Britain during World War II, countering, in the subtle realms, the forces of negativity which used Hitler as their pawn.

With no inclination toward traditional Indian spirituality, nor the old-style yogas which focused on an ascetic lifestyle geared to escape from the suffering and illusions of the world, Aurobindo's uniqueness was used by the Divine to Self-disclose in a manner quite different from India's previous spiritual traditions, bringing the Eastern Stream out of its lofty, spiritual aloofness, back into the physical world.

In collaboration with a spiritual companion, a French woman of Jewish/Muslim descent whom he called The Mother, their immense visionary example and collective writings served as the foundation for the South Indian international community of Auroville, and as the inspiration for the founding of the psycho-spiritual explorations of Esalen in Big Sur, California. After his death in 1950, The Mother carried on Aurobindo's work towards the spiritual liberation of humanity until her own death in 1973, freely[37] conversing with India's political dignitaries.

According to Sri Aurobindo, humanity is being prepared for its next evolutionary step. In contrast to the belief that the mind, emotions and body are merely karmic or conditioned hindrances to realizing the Self, he saw these vehicles as actually evolving toward conscious recognition of their divinity. Aurobindo indicated that Ramana Maharshi's concept of Impersonal Being is the only foundation for a Divine Becoming that could divinize all human expression. He also saw the development of new divine faculties coming as an expression of the energy of unity flooding the planet.

---

37 • *To date no American President has met with the 1989 Nobel Peace Prize recipient - the Dalai Llama*

As humankind moves towards Oneness on all fronts, one of these new faculties, the Superheart, is beginning to emerge. In the same way as new intellectual capacities were added to the older emotional mind associated with group or tribal societies during humankind's individuation process, the Superheart is an evolutionary innovation associated with the greater spiritual challenges of a unified humanity.

The cognitions on human evolution professed by Sri Aurobindo and The Mother were shared by many great philosophers and mystics of the 19th and 20th centuries. Frederick Schelling, a Berlin philosopher of the 1840s, felt that reason is not the final development and that Source is in a continual process of expressing oneness through the many in a successive series of unfolding and increasing wholenesses, integrated through the many towards a final Summit. Schelling profoundly influenced Kierkegaard, Heidegger, Goethe, Nietzsche and later, Whitehead. French paleontologist and Jesuit priest, Pierre Teilhard de Chardin, also shared the same views on human evolution as those expressed by Aurobindo. Unfortunately, but not surprisingly, Chardin's work was not published until after his death in 1955, due to prohibition by the Roman Catholic Church.

Evolutionary themes were also supported by the occult genius of German-born Rudolf Steiner (d. 1925), who devised an educational system based upon the developmental stages of the soul, in contrast to the socialization stages of the personality. Known as the Waldorf schools, this is the fastest growing school in the U.S. and its curriculum incorporates the deeper mysteries of the Christ: the advent of integrated, mature and evolved humanity.

The work of Alice Bailey, (d. 1949) another Northern Stream occultist and mystic, echoed the idea of human evolution. Her occult philosophy, said to have been received from certain hidden masters, professed that as primitive man was a prototype for modern man, we are the protoype for a future species that will acquire 2 more senses. She believed that humans were first projected from higher semi-divine beings who actually extend into man to become his "higher vehicles," bringing the light of consciousness to the mind.

An Islamic saint, Mohammed Iqbal (d. 1939), saw the evolution of mankind culminating in the Sufi concept of the perfect man in which one is not only freed from personal conditioning, but is divinized or transfigured, becoming a value to his society.

Many of these views share a belief in an evolving humanity through the descent of what what Sri Aurobindo and the Mother referred to as a "supramental, transformative Light and Force" which is no different in principle than the power that evolved the eternal becoming of matter into simple life forms, plants and animals, then humanity, but in this instance the purpose is to evolve the human mind from animal/human to divine/human. The same natural, regenerative power which fosters renewal following winter's slumber will actually occur in the mind of man and in society. Rather than through the slow, awkward struggle of ego-generated systems such as religion and politics, the supramental manifestation will burst forth with the same unstoppable, delightful budding that takes place in springtime.

The last great incursion of Eastern Stream energy into the Northern Stream came with Meher Baba, a spiritual master who maintained silence from 1925 until his death in 1969. Proclaimed an avatar by both his Hindu and Muslim master mentors, Meher Baba's discourses represent a compilation of practical wisdom that the world would do well to incorporate into the educational system of the future. He furthered the harmonizing work of Kabir, Vivekenanda and Yogananda by showing the parallels between Islam, Hinduism and Christianity. Meher Baba's universal message of love and obedience to God, through whatever religion served one's unique character, recommended first eliminating all selfishness and then serving all beings. This is the basis for the true New World Order. Without this foundation, suffering, both personal and global, would continue to escalate, serving to purge humankind of its excesses and deficiences.

In addition to the arrival of physical masters to help light the way, apparitions of religious figures, particularly the Virgin Mary, which have been recorded since the 13th century,[38] have occurred in the 20th century with increasing frequency, especially just before, during or after natural disasters or armed conflicts.

Twentieth century appearances of the Virgin Mary are full of spiritual warnings for humanity. During these events, people are admonished to pray, to love one another and love her son, Jesus. In Fatima, Portugal, near the end of World War I in 1917, Our Lady of Fatima appeared, asking the world to pray the rosary for world peace. In 1932 the Immaculate Virgin appeared in Belgium, and one year later, reappeared as the Virgin of the Poor after Hitler took power. Just prior to the Spanish Civil War and World War II, the Virgin of Revelation made her appearance in Tre Fontane, Italy. In Garabandal, Spain from 1961 to1964 Our Lady of Mount Carmel appeared and in 1968 after the war with Israel, in Zeitun, Egypt thousands witnessed her appearance as the Lady of Light. 1980 saw her appear as the Mother of Jesus in Nicaragua during heavy CIA involvement in Central American conflicts, and starting in 1981, as the Queen of Peace in Medjugorie, Bosnia.

Miraculous occurrences, apparitions and healings are not the sole province of Catholicism, however. (They just get more air time.) In 1995, the Ganesha Milk Miracle in which all statues of Ganesha (one of the Hindu pantheon who specializes in removal of obstacles) all over the world started drinking the milk traditionally offered by devotees. This miracle united Hindus worldwide as do the appearances of the Virgin Mary for Christians. Sai Baba, an Indian guru said by many to be an avatar, heals devotees, materializes objects, and produces vibhuti (sacred ash) out of thin air – actions that defy the cause/effect understanding of science and are a testament to laws of nature outside the realm of current scientific understanding.

Miracles, apparitions and certain paranormal occurrences inspire hope and awaken and unify the faithful en mass, usually according to their religious persuasion. People steeped in materiality often require miracles to activate their faith. Such events are a form of communication from other, unseen worlds that interpenetrate ours, just the other side of our self-imposed mental limits on perception.

---

38 • *In Orleans, France in 1219 the Queen of Heaven appeared; 230 years later she showed herself in Belgium as Dame de Grace. In the 16th century she appeared in Mexico as Our Lady of Guadalupe in 1531, and as the Black Virgin to Aztec Indians on a site traditionally held by pre-Colombian indigenous people as sacred to the Mother of all Gods, and as Our lady of Kazan in Russia. In the 17th century she made seven appearances – in the Dominican Republic as Nuestra Senora de Altagracia (1600), as Nuestra Senora, Virgen del Cobre, in Cuba (1604), as Our lady of Conquest in Sante Fe, New Mexico (1625), in Naples, Italy, announcing the eruption of Vesuvius (1631), in Costa Rica as Our Lady of the Angels (1635), and in Ecuador as Queen of Heaven (1696). In the 19th century there were three apparitions in France – as Our Lady of the Immaculate Conception in Paris (1830), as Our lady of Tears in La Salette France (1846), and once again as Our Lady of the Immaculate Conception in in Lourdes (1858), she also made one appearance in Knock, Ireland as Rose of Ireland in 1879.*

Events appear miraculous due to our partial understanding of the laws governing manifestation. Masters such as Jesus or Sai Baba know and understand this and use miraculous events to "shake us up" and open the doors of perception. Jesus, however, never gave the impression that such works were limited to 'special' people such as himself; he said, "He that believeth on me, the works that I do shall he do also, and greater works than these shall he do, because I go unto my Father," John, 14:12.

The similarity in messages from the Divine crosses the human barriers of time and culture, for the Infinite does not acknowledge such things. During a visitation from Jesus in Madrid (1922), Sister Josefa Menendez received this message, "Have no fear, all is arranged by My Love. Your misery attracts Me. Love transforms and divinizes all. When a soul loves truly, she neither measures what she does, nor weighs what she suffers. I will seek you in your nothingness to unite you to Myself. For all you give me, I give you my Heart. I want you to be all Mine." This statement strongly resembles the final instruction given by Lord Krishna in the ancient Bhagavad Gita, "Do not grieve. I will deliver thee from all sin and evil. Abandon all dharmas (paths, effort), take refuge only in Me alone. Become my Minded, my lover, a sacrifice to Me, My Hearted. This is My supreme secret, that I give to the most beloved of souls." When one looks closely at the deepest, simplest Truths in any faith or tradition, one finds they are all essentially the same – One.

Chapter Eleven
Ego Terrorism

Despite supernatural warnings and admonitions from the "other side," the world descended into an era of ever-escalating armed conflict. War and all its accouterments became very big business worldwide. Man-made disasters of tragic proportions characterize the 20th century. World War I claimed more than two million lives. Stalin's industrialization program starved 10 million Ukrainian farmers. Under Francisco Franco's fascist Catholic Regime in Spain (1936), 1 million people lost their lives. Over 40 million people died in World War II. In 1948, the partitioning of India and Pakistan into separate Hindu and Mulsim states, after the British dismantled the nation's infrastructure, left 14 million dead. The economic and social reforms instigated by Chairman Mao's Great Leap Forward (c. 1959) starved 50 million Chinese citizens to death (similiar to Stalin's earlier Ukrainian fiasco) and were responsible for the deaths of 1.5 million land owners at the hands of angry peasants. And, despite the drain in manpower and resources enlisted in her pogrom against the past, China still managed to carry out the genocide of 1 million Tibetans in their own land. Add to these casualties the deaths in the Korean war, the Vietnam war, the Khmer Rouge pograms in Cambodia and the multitudinous ethnic conflicts all over the globe and the total is staggering. Even the deaths that took place during the Crusades, the Black Plague and the Inquisition (which took place over several hundred years) are dwarfed by these figures.

The high man-made death toll of the 20th century is the result of human misunderstanding and misapplication of the continued increase in energy simultaneously pushing humanity towards both freedom and unity. Unable to recognize the inherent oneness of all peoples, the immature ego-mind, steeped in fearful dualism, juxtaposes these two concepts, pitting one against the other. This prompts the mass of humanity to seek out like-minded others in order to band together in a lower form of unity to revolt against an 'oppressor/enemy' producing a lower form of (temporary) freedom, easily usurped by yet another 'enemy.'

When the Northern Stream (the immature self) through its explorers and exploiters ravaged Southern Stream Jews and Muslims (Divine in Form/Body), decimated Western Stream shamanic, indigenous populations (Immanent Divine in Nature) and was unable to penetrate the Eastern Stream Indian and Asian populations (Spirit), except for material profit; then the only remaining outlet for its internal frustration was to react to itself, to implode. Ego-mind's belief in death rather than renewal as a problem solver leads to war. World Wars I and II were the predictable result of the Northern Stream's pattern, as seen repeatedly throughout history, to flip-flop between fighting itself and attacking "others."

Sadly, unless a higher level of consciousness begins to guide this process, the cycle will merely repeat itself. There is, however, one major difference between the cycles occurring in this century and all those that have gone before. Technology has made the stakes higher and communication faster and more complete. More people are now aware of the horror taking place at an accelerated pace all over the globe, making it easier to see the patterns and grasp opportunities to uplevel consciousness.

In addition to a global surge toward freedom, the late 19th century was also earmarked by a drive toward unity,[38] manifested in such movements as the push for a Jewish homeland, the rise of Marxism and the appearance of the Baha'i faith; all of which polarized war into existence, just as Christ's love brought about the dark side of Christianity. Germany's attempt to annex the world

---

38 • *Even in the isolated roof top of the world, this universal impulse towards unity sweeping the planet didn't go unnoticed in Tibet. Towards the end of the 19th century a a synthesis of all four Tibetan Buddhist lineages came to be recognized as the Rime tradition. Harmonizing the strict sectarianism of the past, the most illustrious example of this high quality of leadership is the late Dilgo Khyentse Rinpoche (d. 1991), who served as a mentor for the universal messages of the current Dalai Llama.*

during WWI and WWII was another misapplication of both the global impulse towards unification and the Northern Stream's deep desire for self mastery, polluted by illusions of superiority, fear of dissolution by outside contamination from "inferior" elements and lots of projection of faults onto others. These components, coupled with the geologically stored energy of more than a thousand years of sometimes violent fanaticism in Germany, later gave birth to the horror of World Wars I and II.

Humanity could only express the global drive for unity as a merging of sameness which often manifested more as consolidation along ethnic, religious, geographical or ideological lines in order to establish national identity for reasons of protection rather than true unification. This found expression in the consolidation of many European city-states as Germany, Italy, Bulgaria, Serbia and Rumania became sovereign nations. In Asia, Japan responded to the unification energy by abolishing feudalism and taking up modernization in order to avoid the fate suffered by India and China which had been colonized by foreign powers.

Riding the wave of national and ethnic identity, Theodor Herzl, a successful Jewish playwright and social commentator living in Austria, put forward the idea of a homeland for the Jews through the Zionist movement of the 1890s. This sparked massive Jewish immigration to the Holy Land, which continued until World War II was declared in 1939.[39]

Rallying around an ideology was also a cause for unification, as the rise of Europe's merchant middle class was challenged by the socialism of Karl Marx's Communist Manifesto (1844). Intending to protect the lower class poor and the collective good, worker unity under Marxism/Leninism became a substitute among communists for the spiritual unity spoken of in all mystical writings of every religion and exemplified by Great Souls from India. Dubbing religion the "opiate of the masses," communism confused spirituality with religion and jettisoned both.

Fueled by Marxist fervor, Russian feudalism was abolished in 1862, just after the American Emancipation Proclamation, freeing

---

39 • *Eastern European Jews (Ashkenazic) unlike their mediterranean (Sephardic) may be descendants of Persian Jews and the Khazars, a Turkish people that converted to Judaism (740 A.D.). They were subsequently displaced from the Black Sea region into the Ukraine and Eastern Europe with the rise of the Russian Tzar and the invading Mongol hordes.*

millions of serfs and setting off an enormous explosion in population and economic expansion. Pushed by the pressures of phenomenal growth, the Northern Stream's Russian branch expanded east into the territories of decaying central Asian Tartar and Turkish dynasties and into Siberia. Unfortunately, Western Stream Siberian tribes and Southern Stream Jews shared the same fate at the hands of Northern Stream Russians as Native Americans did in America – persecution in the form of forced relocation and extermination.

In the realm of religion, the birth of the Baha'i religion from Islamic roots in 1844 (the same year as the anti-religious Communist Manifesto appeared) made efforts to unite all religions and all people for the common welfare and the evolution of mankind. The Baha'i's trace their origins from a John the Baptist-like prophet named 'The Bab,' (meaning "gateway"), who paved the way for the prophet Baha'u'llah, who founded the Baha'i faith.

Baha'i's emphasize the coming era of unity of mankind, equality of the sexes and individual worship without the authority of clergy. To the Baha'i's, clergy and liturgy is renounced in deference to the individual's own inner authority and spiritual seeking, to interpret and bring the fruits of religion into the community of mankind through, among other things, practical, humanitarian programs for the poor, underprivileged and uneducated, without the kind of proselytizing found in other socially active religions that creates separation and exclusion.

This mild, yet powerful teaching polarized a vehement reaction from Islamic clergy, sparking persecution, imprisonment and execution of Baha'i faithful which continues today in parts of the Middle East. Ironically, despite the fact that Muslims developed the highly rational outlook of the Shari'a (law) and during Europe's Dark Ages kept scientific exploration, discovery and invention alive and well, by the 19th century the balance between religious belief and rationality had been seriously compromised. Even though Jewish prophets, including Jesus, were accepted by early Muslims as part of a continuing lineage leading up to Muhammed, Islam rejects the possibility that any other messengers of God could appear after Muhammed. Baha'u'llah was soundly denounced by Muslim orthodoxy, despite the fact that he was a descendent of Muhammed. Even stranger still, the teachings of the Baha'i stress all the major points of the Southern Stream, including tolerance, equality and bringing the spiritual and secular world together in harmony through service.

An interesting quirk of the Southern Stream is that the status quo cannot recognize its next innovation. With the exception of the ancient Egyptians, all Southern Stream religions have rejected their offspring. The Jews rejected the innovations of Jesus and Muhammed. Islam rejected the Baha'i because physicality itself is a collection of the thoughts, feelings, attitudes and experiences that have gone before, it is the nature of the Southern Stream (Form/Body) to cling to the past. Form is more comfortably oriented to the past than to the present or future. The challenge of the Southern Stream is to understand their 'law of referral to the past,' and move forward into its next flowering without 'throwing out the baby with the bathwater.' The very nature of the Southern Stream Baha'i faith will make this much easier in the future. Their all-inclusive acceptance and understanding of human spiritual evolution make rejection of spiritual innovation nearly impossible for them. Not surprisingly, the other three streams must also overcome the same challenge.

Due to the fact that it is the nature of institutions to perpetuate themselves, the doctrines and dogmas of all great religious and political forces often fail to adapt appropriately to changing cultural eras, and to the world's tendency towards unification. Only eternal Truths require no such adaptation to the times. The cosmically inspired urge toward unification, if thwarted by the ego's fear of oneness, often leads to war, which also, eventually, leads to a lesser type of unification. The Cosmos will not, in any case, be denied; unification occurs either through suffering or cooperation; the choice is ours.

The energy of liberty and unity which began to sweep the planet during the 18th century did not go unnoticed (or unused) by the aristocracy which replaced the kings and queens of old 100 years later. Hidden among the families in control of banking and the new Industrial Age, the descendants of Northern Stream medieval adepts, known to some as the Elite, began to guide the course of world history from behind the scenes. Riding the cosmic wave of freedom, Northern Stream monarchies, sometimes difficult to predict and control, were replaced by the rule of "democracies" run by often poorly educated, misinformed citizens, whose labor, currencies and votes could be more easily manipulated through careful management of their economies.

The seeds of this New World Order were sown in Europe's distant past, in the age of knights and kings and emperor-popes. During those times, semi-religious societies such as the highly prosperous Orders of Knights were formed by those privy to ancient esoteric knowledge, yet still under the spell of ego. The most renowned of these, the Order of Knights Templar, began as brokers and armed escorts during the Crusades, taking their share of the massive amount of wealth extracted from the Holy Land. They also helped set the stage for introducing pre-Renaissance, Judeo-Islamic thought into European culture by bringing innovations in medicine, banking, arts and sciences back with them to Europe.

Providing military protection for merchant class transactions from Spain to the Middle East, the Knights Templar learned about bank drafts, money lending and other banking procedures from their Middle Eastern counterparts, eventually making loans to monarchs and bishops bankrupted by their crusading escapades. With no allegiance to any pope or king, they functioned much like today's international bankers, many of whom can trace their ancestry to Templar commercial dynasties. Even though these Orders lost control of their interest in the Holy Land at the close of the 13th century, their prosperity and notoriety grew as they turned the focus of their financial transactions to Europe. This was, of course seen as a challenge by the Church which wished to eliminate competitive influences (both spiritual and temporal) and did so by inquisiting the dissident.

By the middle of the 14th century, Knights Templar suffered the same fate as all heretics or treasoners. Many were arrested, tortured and killed. Those who survived either went underground, disappearing into Freemason guilds, joining the Portuguese Knights of Christ (still favored by the Church), or infiltrating similar Orders of Knights in Germany which, because of their fealty to a king, were not subject to persecution. Later, the Knights of Christ pursued maritime adventures as the greatest New World explorers under the protection of Catholic kings. The German Knights gave both monetary and military support to Martin Luther against Rome's bid to squelch the Reformation, preventing his execution by Counter-Reformation forces.

Over the centuries, certain Freemason guilds and reassembled secret Orders of Knights would craft the future societies of the world through economic and political manipulations, operating outside, but fully utilizing, the jurisdiction of religious and governmental institutions.

As economic power was shifted from agriculture to industry, beginning in the 17th century, people were encouraged to move from rural areas to the cities to seek work rather than to grow their own food. Manufacturing began to provide more things to buy, more reasons to have a more substantial income. Slowly, over time, the agrarian-based foundation upon which humanity built civilizations for thousands of years, was replaced with a new order based upon industry, urbanization, and consumerism – no less dependent upon nature, but certainly more disconnected from it.

The advent of urbanization and industrialization and the shrinking of our agrarian base began to remove the last vestiges of Western Stream influence from our societal ferment. Man-made inventions and enterprise – industry and manufacturing – replaced agriculture as the basis for Euro-American civilization, taking Nature out of the cultural loop. As the bulk of the Northern Stream's population moved into cities and lost contact with natural cycles, its penchant for intellectual, technical development was given free rein and humanity accelerated into the Industrial Age. Scientific discoveries and industrial power were used to further harness Nature, wage war and promote world-wide consumerism. The days of agrarian-based cultures were over and the seeds of our decline were sown.

Without the balancing, Western Stream-like energy of pre-industrial agriculture, an individually autonomous, interdependent society such as ours easily falls prey to widespread shortsightedness, arrogance, selfishness, and alienation, leading to corruption, cultural and social passivity, mediocrity and greater susceptibility to authoritarian control. Humanity's move away from acknowledging the importance of its connection to Nature was a pivotal point – as important as the discovery of fire and the invention of the wheel. Without the deep understanding that we are sustained by Nature, and through Nature are connected to everything and everyone, all our clever technology goes toward killing – each other, ourselves, the very planet that gives us life. Our ability to deal appropriately with this false step on our evolutionary path will mean the difference between life and death for our civilization.

The final shift from the Old Order to the New was heralded by the creation of the American Federal Reserve, a privately owned banking organization, brought into existence on the eve of World War I in 1913.[40] The printing of American money (and therefore the management of the American economy), originally controlled by elected representatives in Congress, was now in the hands of a group of private foreign bankers. This destabilized the original triune design of our government's structure (legislative, judicial and presidential) by introducing another element, destroying the alchemical balance of our metaphysically inspired American heritage.

The esoteric origins of American government can be traced to the Rosicrucian and Masonic membership of founding fathers such as Thomas Jefferson and Benjamin Franklin and are still visible in the alchemical symbology found on our currency. Based upon one of the principles of alchemy – the self-regulating, alchemical interaction of salt, mercury and sulphur – our government was designed as an analog to that transformative process. The free interaction of the three branches of government was to provide a system of fair governance and protection for the citizenry under the aegis of metaphysical principles. Allowing the non-elected Federal Reserve to captain our economic ship destroyed the alchemically balanced triune nature of our system. Rather than the regenerative alchemy found in the power of three, with four elements in the socio-political crucible (one of them essentially hidden) our government began to play out the adversarial energy of two's.

Around the same time as America lost control of its money supply to the Federal Reserve, governments around the world (ours included) stopped applying the full gold standard to their currencies and 23 years later, no single currency was fully backed by gold. After only eighty years of private control, today's currencies are no longer backed by gold at all. Gold (spiritual essence), so sought after by the Northern Stream, has disappeared as a foundation for its societies.

The fact that there is nothing of any inherent value backing our money is a reflection of the ego-generated mirage of our culture; it no longer has any real basis. We have at last unmasked the terrible truth that our teetering, Northern Stream civilization is precariously balanced on a perceptual "soap bubble" held together

---

40 • *Today, the United States government owes the Federal Reserve more than 5 trillion dollars.*

by the thinnest membrane of consensus reality. Our current socio-economic situation mirrors beautifully both the latest scientific discoveries in the world of physics and the timeless wisdom of countless mystics: the world we perceive is not what it appears to be.

Circumstances were carefully guided by those who control banking and industrial interests in order to produce the "balance of power" under which we all live today. During the first half of the 20th century, a massive transfer of wealth and power took place through the use of a carefully orchestrated worldwide economic depression, world-engulfing wars and smaller "armed conflicts." Large tracts of land, resources, etc. were reapportioned all over the globe – except in North America. The seat of world wealth, power and domination was shifted to the United States, reinforced by the threat of total annihilation by nuclear and other weapons. A drastic reduction of the world's population was engineered as Jews, Gypsies and other Europeans, Russians, Chinese and others lost their lives by the tens of millions in wars and ill-fated social restructuring schemes financed by the Elite. The "Cold War" that followed this great shift was the challenge of Northern Stream's Eastern branch (Soviet) to the Western branch's (United States) world supremacy.

Around the globe Elite footholds in international affairs and vital systems were secured at the start of the 20th century using war as a tool. As it was during the Crusades so long ago, fomenting conflict, supplying arms, then rebuilding war-ravaged countries was still very big business. In order to control the commercial shipping interests between the Atlantic and Pacific, a revolt was instigated in Columbia (1903) and a puppet government was established in Panama through the United States. World War I, while providing financial bonanzas to the families that funded and supplied both sides of the conflict (mostly the Rockefellers and Morgans),[41] also served to destabilize Russia's Tzarist regime, making it easier to topple by funding Lenin and Trotsky during the Russian Revolution. The British seizure of Iran and Iraq from Turkey after World War I secured Elite control of the oil fields of the Middle East.

---

41 • *The Elite's ability to finance war is a product of the American Dream. Home and business mortgage interest is the foundation for the wealth of the eight international banking families that finance war and post-war reconstruction worldwide.*

After WWI Elite families such as the Rockefellers (Standard, and now Chevron Oil), Morgans (General Electric), Fords (automotive giant), and Rothschilds (I.G. Farbin, producers of explosives) sculpted American foreign policy through the formation of such non-elected bodies as the Council on Foreign Relations (CFR)[42] and later, the Trilateral Commission (est. 1972), ensuring a nearly perpetual source of income, political power and influence. Over the years, CFR membership figured prominently in U.S. foreign policymaking and "intelligence gathering," with 14 of the last 18 Secretaries of State and and the last 8 CIA directors (including George Bush) being CFR members.

Elite family members were (and still are) tied to political officials through marriage, business and Freemason membership. Averell Harriman, whose family helped the Rockefellers to finance the Russian Revolution, was a close advisor to Roosevelt. As the Henry Kissinger of the 20s, 30s and 40s, Harriman fostered Elite-friendly negotiations between war-torn nations and helped George Bush's father make his fortune through depression and wartime business transactions in oil and banking. Allen Dulles, cousin to the Rockefellers, aided Hitler's Nazi regime by providing legal assistance for funds transfers from American sources to Hitler's forces in Germany. Appointed 1st director of the CIA in 1948, Dulles was later fired by president John F. Kennedy. Those connected by more esoteric bonds included Great Britain's Winston Churchill, who shared masonic brotherhood with President Franklin Roosevelt, CIA director Allen Dulles, Supreme Court Justice Earl Warren and President Gerald Ford, all of whom were 33rd degree Freemasons, the highest level of Freemasonry.

In the United States after the worldwide economic depression laid America's once thriving agrarian society to rest, the Elite's New Deal, put forth through Roosevelt, came along to put America back to work in the cities and over the next four decades corporate agriculture swallowed up the American family farm, bringing food production under Elite control.

---

42 • *The same members of the CFR, set up in 1921, under the guise of keeping government out of industry would later give birth to the United Nations. The U.N.'s laudable ideals of humanitarian relief would later erode into cultural indoctrination and the distribution of (patented) genetically engineered foods; its World Health Organization's international regulations would override on an national level vetoed laws that would not have given governmental control over U.S. citizen's health. Finally, U.N. military forces would be converted into a global police.*

Although much economic and political maneuvering and manipulation has taken place throughout the 20th century, World War II and the restructurings that followed it were critical to the solid establishment of the New World Order. The rabid dogs of fear, bigotry, greed and violence were goaded into action by radical economic manipulation and allowed to run free due to human spiritual slumber. Nazi Germany and Japan, the two villains in WWII's morality play, cannot be excused for their cruel excesses, but with a broader look at the circumstances surrounding their participation, their actions can be understood in another light.

Suffering from massive financial burdens imposed by the victors of World War I, the German economy collapsed, providing enough fear and discomfort to reawaken the energy of violent fanaticism sleeping in Bohemian Germany's geomantic memory. Once more the Southern Stream became the focus of Northern Stream cruelty as the Jews were again singled out as scapegoats for Germany's distress. The massive Zionist-inspired immigration of European and Russian Jews to British-controlled Palestine, begun in the late 1800s, was stopped by Britain with Hitler's rise to power in Germany. Those who might have escaped the Third Reich's pogrom were prevented by Hitler's foe from leaving.

The Roman Catholic Church, often the self-proclaimed keeper of moral rectitude for the civilized world, helped elect Hitler in1933, supported the Nazi march into Austria and later cheered Hitler's 'holy war' against Stalin's 'godless communism.' No outcry was raised by the Church when Hitler diabolically coalesced latent German anti-Semitism in the slaughter of the Jews.

Like the Roman Catholic Church, America's president Roosevelt was not overly concerned about the slaughter of millions of Jews and Gypsies. He viewed this war in much the same way as Lincoln viewed the American Civil War – as an excellent opportunity to bolster the American economy, in this case taking over a global market previously dominated by Britain and Spain. American industrialists supplied the Nazis with money and products through discreet Swiss and South American avenues, similar to the way in which American funds were funneled through Iran to CIA-supported guerrillas in El Salvador in the Iran/Contra affair decades later.

On the Eastern front, Chiang Kai Shek's nationalist army received aid from U.S. sources in their fight against invasions by both Mao's Communist army and the Japanese. America cut off

Japan's oil supplies in the Philippines, thereby forcing Japan into the anticipated retalitive strike on Pearl Harbor. While Hitler harried the allies, Japan took advantage of this diversion, searching Europe's Pacific colonies for a source of oil.

Without the Navajo code talkers stationed throughout the Pacific islands, the Japanese might have succeeded in defeating America and capturing the allied imperialists' Asian colonies. During World War II Northern Stream America used the Navajos and then discarded them in much the same way as Northern Stream Europe had used the Jews centuries earlier.

The dropping of the atomic bomb was both a shrewd (and ruthless) business move and a sinister scientific experiment. (No one knew for sure the long-term effects of such radiation upon the target population.) To insure the Japanese would surrender to American capitalism and not Russian communism and to justify two atomic production plants, two bombs were dropped, even though one would have been more than adequate. This merciless demonstration of military supremacy, while ending WWII, also ended Japanese hopes of maintaining their culture unsullied by Western influence. It also curtailed Russian expansion into Asia; but it did nothing to protect Eastern Europe from Russian advances. Oddly enough, what the Northern Stream couldn't do in Japan with Christian missionaries in the 16th century was accomplished by secular brute force in the 20th century.

In order to create the geo-political tensions necessary to "divide and conquer" the world, the unseen forces that govern the Allies' political machine came into play after the end of WWII. Despite General Patton and General MacArthur's best military advise to the contrary , proposed anti-Stalinist military advances into Russia and anti-Maoist aid to Nationalist China would not support a profitable post WWII Cold War economy .

The horror of Nagasaki and Auschwitz, both Northern Stream examples of glorified ends justifying extreme means, was a cruel reminder of Nietzsche's proclamation, albeit with a new proviso – God is dead – and economics is alive.

∞

After the war, nuclear weapons in the hands of the United States secured a massive wealth-building machine for the Elite, making it possible to rebuild Germany and Japan to their liking. Forty years later, after proving their loyalty to the new system, both Germany and Japan joined the Trilateral Commission, a Northern Stream-run international organization which orchestrates the political and financial lives of nations worldwide, thereby controlling the fortunes of people all over the globe.

The reshuffling of the world's financial and political deck which took place after WWII, ensured that the reins of human economics and society were placed firmly in the grip of techno-industry and banking under Elite supervision. In post WWII Iran, the Shah (groomed by Britain to hold the post) was placed in power, establishing a puppet government. Palestine was divided up by the Allies between Jews and Arabs, interjecting a lasting source of conflict that would destabilize the Middle East for decades, increasing the need for arms, foreign aid and diplomatic and military intervention (a proven source of income and political influence) and precluding the possibility of unified Middle Eastern control of the oil fields. India shared a similar fate, being divided by outsiders to form the new Muslim nation of Pakistan.

The Cold War paranoia that followed WWII led to McCarthyism and later, the erection of the Berlin Wall in '61 and the American/Soviet arms race was not completely unfounded. On the surface, the perceived threat to "the American Way" was overreacted to, ostensibly because Russia was strengthening its hold over its puppet governments in Eastern Europe and the Muslim provinces of Soviet Central Asia. The truth, however, is that the Cold War was a Northern Stream battle for the right to control others – the U.S. through so-called democratic puppet governments, the U.S.S.R through Soviet satellite governments. Both capitalist imperialism and communist oppression were just variations on a Northern Stream theme. Both used the same strategies, erecting puppet governments, controlling public opinion in their own countries through propaganda – all with the threat of total annihilation hanging over the heads of the populations of all nations; it was just a matter of who could outspend and out-wait the other.

In Southeast Asia, North Vietnamese leader Ho Chi Minh asked the United States for assistance in establishing a united Indochina (Vietnam) shortly after WWII, but allegiance to France took precedence, so North Vietnam was forced to go to China and the Soviet Union for help. The U.S. found itself fighting communist forces in Vietnam because it chose to back a former ally rather than further the cause of freedom. After the French pulled out of Vietnam, U.S. forces were used to protect Elite interests (and furnish more economic grist for the Elite money mill). Assuring access to China Sea oil and creating and maintaining a business monopoly in Indochina was the main concern.

In addition, the growing apartheid-like subjugation of the 80% Buddhist population by the U.S. backed, South Vietnamese Catholic President was another massive coverup that never reached public attention. According to radio messages intercepted prior to his assassination (one month before U.S. President Kennedy was silenced) South Vietnam was perched on declaring a religious war of independence which would have effectively destabilized the war efforts against the Communist North VietCong, jeopardizing the future of massive military defense spending.

As the Vietnam war came to a close in 1973, the slow pullout of U.S. troops from Laos, Cambodia and Vietnam masked the milking of the vast wealth generated by Golden Triangle drug trade in order to fund covert CIA operations abroad. Simultaneously, Nixon's Watergate disclosures exposed the corrupt action taken in the name of "national security," throughout the 50s & 60s. One such scheme destabilized Chile's Marxist government, chosen over American-style democracy by the Chilean people in free elections. The current flap over CIA involvement in crack cocaine distribution among low income African American neighborhoods reveals another instance of CIA misdeeds,[43] this time taken against U.S. citizens in order to finance protection for Elite interests abroad.

---

43 • *Given the CIA's history for amoral coverups, their sponsorship of biological espionage is an even more convincing chapter that has yet to unfold in its entirety. Originally funded through the efforts of Henry Kissinger in 1969, the AIDS and Ebola virus may actually be the by-product of government biological research developed under the guise of an alternative to nuclear defense in the Cold War. Stemming from the fear of contaminating "American purity" the government backed eugenics programs of the 1920s-1940s aimed at sterilizing undesireables (criminals), or those deemed mentally or racially inferior or incompetent (retarded or insane). Unlike all prior health risks to American citizens, (and usually government researched and sanctioned) involving nerve gas in the Gulf War, Agent Orange in Vietnam or the toxic pesticides, preservatives, and pollutants in our food, soils and drinking waters of 50s and 60s (DDT) ; it would be difficult to blame the deliberate and diabolical use of biological weapons on homosexuals and Black Africans as an amoral testing ground for population control devices. The culprit can now be scientifically and psychologically explained away as nature's mutations and immoral behavior.*

U.S. foreign policies (guided by the CFR and the Trilateral Commission) created foreign aid programs acceptable to the American people in order to fund and control puppet governments. Taking over the function previously relegated to Christian missionaries, these "social improvement" programs were a way to indoctrinate the people in those countries to adopt the Northern Stream capitalist paradigm, buy the ideological loyalty of their leaders and provide the avenues through which corporate arms sales to U.S. puppet governments could be made. "National security" and "democratic freedom" were the excuses used to establish, protect and promote Elite business interests in Chile, the Phillipines, Panama, Africa, Nicaragua, El Salvador, Korea, Vietnam, Puerto Rico, Cuba, Zaire, Indonesia, and eventually, Kuwait.[44]

The Elite's New World Order continues to sculpt the lives of people all over the globe into the Northern Stream image. Through the Northern Stream "dream" we are offered a distorted version of the energy of liberty and unity. We are free to unite under the banner of secular consumerism and seamless uniformity. No other option is available. Those who refuse to comply are subject to either military or economic obliteration or both.

Some may argue that it is unfair to single out any one group as being overly aggressive when indeed all humanity shares this unwelcome trait. The tragedy wrought by hypocrisy, inequity, and the need to dominate and control are part and parcel of all human culture and is not restricted to any one people or era. However, the more blatant transgressions represented by the Northern Stream's Inquisition and Crusades, deliberate, systematic genocide of indigenous peoples and civil, ethnic and world wars tower in scope above actions of the same sort undertaken by other Streams. Until mankind ends the war going on inside its collective psyche, it will remain vulnerable to manipulation of its psycho-emotional conditioning and death's shadow will continue to fall on human history in the name of God, country, survival, security and personal profit.

---

44 • *The Gulf War could have been more accurately referred to as the "God save the Queen" War because it was Queen Elizabeth's ownership of the Kuwaiti oil fields which the United States was protecting.*

∞

"When the bird of iron shall fly, when ponies move on wheels, and carriages upon lines, the Dharma (Buddha's wisdom) will flower in the land of the Red Man." – Ancient Tibetan Prophecy.

During the deadly machinations of the power elite – the frantic race among Northern Stream peoples for more control and more things – there were others groping for Light in the darkness of secular cultural conditioning. This yearning for Truth and spiritual depth expressed itself in forms both religious and secular in the decades following World War II, flowing through the worlds of theology, philosophy, music, art, literature and film. Leaders in religious and psychological thought such as Jewish scholar/ philosopher Martin Buber (d. 1965),[45] Thomas Merton (an American Trappist monk/scholar who harmonized the Eastern Stream wisdom traditions of Taoism and Tibetan Buddhism and Northern Stream Christianity. d. 1968), American theologian Paul Tillich (d. 1967)[46] and Carl Jung (d. 1961)[47] bore witness to the shallow spirituality and deep fragmentation in Northern Stream America's psyche.

---

45 • *Buber insisted that only on meeting another human being in an I-thou, rather than the typical Northern Stream I-it relationship, could one encounter a personal God. I-thou bridges the gap of separation between people and nations and de-emphasizes the "itness" of an "other." Taking Buber's I-thou relationship to its next level – Thou/Thou – would dissolve the mind-born distinctions of I-thou or I-it consciousness into unity consciousness.*

46 • *Tillich felt that the concept of a personal God in our secular society is a dangerous one because our artificial culture lacks the depth to support true spirituality.*

47 • *Much of Carl Jung's (d. 1961) pioneering psychological work on archetypes, synchronicity (or divination) and the "shadow self" is derived not only from his Freudian apprenticeship but through his fascination with the experientially based eastern teachings of the Orient. Jung concluded that the old order of religious beliefs and its pious Christian images, could not adapt or even survive in a secular society whose immediate short term demands for subjective experience, material pleasures and scientific proofs far outweighed the long term hope for rewards in an ethereal afterlife or fear of punishments in a fiery hell. Essentially, all of life, whether religious , secular or psychological is spontaneously conspiring on the surface, to reveal, retrieve and re-integrate those disowned shadow parts of ourself and our society. By embracing the ideology of superficial gain and its insidious focus on bandaging symptoms (whether in health, vocation, politics or relationships) without investigating the underlying causes and more essentially, the wisdom that is inherent in that illusive mystery which is even found underneath our shadow world, then unspeakable personal, social, environmental, and economic disasters can and do befall humankind.*

Artists, writers and musicians once again came to the fore as the Northern Stream's social conscience, reflecting the spirit of the times for a culture that lacked its own true prophets. Music and film became powerful media for awakening the masses to new possibilities and paradigms, not always toeing the line as support for unquestioned cultural standards, government-generated disinformation or legislation used to maintain mass mediocrity.

The repressive atmosphere of the McCarthy era polarized a response in the form of the massive revolt of Northern Stream youth against "the Establishment." Great Britain and America, the last two great imperialists, gave birth to the rebellion of the rock and roll music counterculture during the anti-communist hysteria of the 50s and 60s. A product of blues, jazz and gospel music, the Rock and Roll hysteria brought on by Elvis, Buddy Holly and the Beatles, had some of its origins in the rhythms of African Voodoo, brought to the Northern Stream by the people they abducted into slavery centuries earlier. Ironically, the music of those they oppressed became the battlecry for the rebellion of the 60s. Calling the "old guard" to task for its injustice and excesses, the 60s Rock beat also heralded the advent of a Western Stream tradition: sacred use of drugs.

Mind-altering substances and music have been the tools of initiation into Western Stream adulthood for eons. Natural and chemically induced states of higher consciousness, absent in our materialistic, secular society, were celebrated in all sacred cultures of the past as doorways to other realities which held deeper meaning and greater spiritual clarity. Deprived by their own culture of meaningful rites of passage and access to their own mystical heritage, Northern Stream youth rediscovered the use of hallucinogens which grew into a fascination with the mystical traditions of other Streams. It took LSD to awaken, en mass, American youth out of the collective somnambulance of the "Cold War" generation.

The very thing serving as a wakening agent to the flaws and abuses of "the Establishment" was (not surprisingly) made illegal by that same Establishment. The drugs that are socially unacceptable and illegal include those that can actually expand consciousness, if properly used. Oddly enough, substances (natural hallucinogens such as peyote, ayahuasca and pscilocyben mushrooms) over which our government has the most legal control actually have the greatest potential for creative good; whereas those which are the most dangerous to physical health and the most soul-numbing (cocaine, heroin, crack, etc.) are those over which our government professes to have the least control. There is even evidence to suggest that certain government agencies (the CIA) have been involved in actively promoting drug use by aiding in its distribution among low income (mostly Black) neighborhoods.

Certain modes of "numbing out" are deemed acceptable and are actually subsidized by our government, mostly because powerful political factions ensure this through media advertising and lobbying. Legal drugs such as alcohol, tobacco, caffeine and prescription drugs pose no threat to the established order; they support it by providing blessed anesthesia, allowing people to continue living under spiritually untenable conditions.

Use of hallucinogenic drugs cracked the armor of Northern Stream authority in the 60s by giving some a peek into other realities. But as the years passed and the cynicism of secular materialism strengthened its stranglehold on the Northern Stream, spiritual seeking was replaced by entertainment, recreation and escapism as reasons for most of today's drug use.

Ironically, as the flower children of the 60s were experimenting with the highs of "inner space," the heights of "outer space" were heralded by the synchronistic 1969 landing on the moon. Eventually inner mystical exploration of consciousness and the outer astrophysical investigation of the universe will simultaneously point us to the scientific discovery of the divinity behind and within all matter and mind.

Infiltrations of the other Streams began to open the eyes of the children of the 60s to other possibilities, offering alternative world views and paradigms, some of which invalidated the Northern Stream's perceived right to dominate. Immigrants to Northern Stream countries brought gifts of such treasures as the martial arts, acupuncture and Oriental medicine, psychic healing, ayurvedic medicine and herbology. The Southern Stream mysteries of Egypt and forgotten Biblical texts were reintroduced by new archeological discoveries. Cultural anthropologists, biologists and later, ecotourists, marvelled at the shamanic and botanical healing arts and non-ordinary modes of perception common among Western Stream peoples. Pushed by the energies of liberty and unity, the exposure to the wealth of wisdom from other Streams, coupled with the deep dissatisfaction wrought by the Northern Stream's spiritual void led to the birth of the so-called New Age and Back-to-the-Land movements, and the rise in interest in such subjects as holistic health, sustainable agriculture, renewable energy sources and deep ecology.

Some Northern Stream youth, awakened by altered states (either natural or substance-induced), were drawn to the living spiritual heritage in India and began to explore, in earnest, Eastern Stream traditions. Spiritual masters/teachers such as Muktananda, Amrit Desai, Chogyam Trungpa, Kalu Rinpoche, Maharishi Mahesh Yogi[48] and others found Northern Stream people hungry for spiritual sustenance. Famous people such as the Beatles and later, charismatic speaker Deepak Chopra, brought the Vedic truths of the Shankara tradition into mainstream culture through the Maharishi's Transcendental Meditation (TM). This also incorporated an obscure, yet powerful form of devotional worship to the Divine Mother (Sri Vidya) rarely found today even in India, directly into western society.

This was made acceptable to Northern Stream people by scientific research on the effects of Transcendental Meditation on stress management and optimum health. Made attractive by the promise of scientifically validated benefits to health and well-being, TM brought consciousness-expanding techniques associated with Raja Yoga and Vedanta into mainstream western culture and made meditation not only a familiar word in many households, but also a common practice.

Bhagwan Sri Rajneesh, later known as Osho, was another Eastern Stream spiritual teacher/master whose impact on Northern Stream youth is still felt worldwide. Although shunned in his own country for his flaunting of tradition, his unconventional therapies and Tantric philosophy were a necessary counteraction to the

---

48 • *With slightly different motives than the material elitists, the spiritual visionaries of our century counselled among themselves for the spiritual advancement of the race. The most pertinent meetings of recent times (that we know of) are Maharishi Mahesh Yogi with Swami Muktananda, Upasni Maharaj (one of Meher Baba's masters) with the Shankaracharya Brahmananda Saraswati (the Maharishi' master), Yogananda with Ramana Maharshi, the Dalai Llama with Thomas Merton, The Mother of Pondicherry with the Baha'i Prophet, and even Ramakrishna appearing to Sri Aurobindo while he continued his sadhana (spiritual openings) in jail as a political prisoner during Britain's stranglehold over India.*

insanity of the hypocritical values systems and gluttonous consumerism which control our world. To Rajneesh, every system of authority was suspect. He spoke out against the shortcomings of every political and religious persuasion, leaving no stone unturned. His work unified descendants of the WWII Axis and Allied countries (Italy, Germany, Japan, United States and the rest of Europe) by going beyond the boundaries of conventional thought and morality regarding sexuality, spirituality and money. Encouraging his followers to question the prevailing values, mores, assumptions and precepts of Western society, he and his devotees presented a threat to the status quo which could not be ignored. Predictably, it was the system he mocked that confiscated Osho's Oregon property and poisoned him during his long stint in a U.S. jail.

The nearly simultaneous rise of such Northern Stream self development systems as L. Ron Hubbard's Dianetics and Werner Erhard's EST demonstrate once again how great spiritual teachings of other Streams can be reformatted to the mentality of the Northern Stream. Often feeding upon the consumer mentality of dissatisfied members of the Northern Stream, their teachings are based upon fulfillment of desire and ego gratification rather than spiritual principles that transform the ego mechanism into a tool for the Divine. Even though they have some value in providing ego stability and removing internal conflict, such human potential seminars masquerade as a spiritual panacea, promising fulfillment on levels on which they cannot deliver. All advertising aside, they are not THE answer.

∞

In the midst of the counterculture rebellion of the 50s and 60s, three men rose to call attention to the deceit, manipulation and injustice of the New World Order. John and Robert Kennedy and Martin Luther King, Jr. paid the ultimate price for their attempts to change the status quo. Born into a family that had been playing the Elite game for decades, John Kennedy resolved to put a stop to it in America. His plan to disempower the Federal Reserve and expose the government corruption which allowed the CIA to do its dirty deeds abroad, was derailed with his assassination. His death, and that of his brother, Robert, effectively ended the influence of any noncompliant political factions. The Nixon years, in complete juxtaposition to the Kennedy plan continued the governmental corruption they had attempted to end a decade earlier.

The global energy prodding humanity toward freedom and unity found another channel in the Southern Stream genius of Martin Luther King, Jr. Even though his approach to securing equal rights for African Americans was nonviolent, even Gandhi-like, he was seen as a threat to national security, and was put under FBI surveillance. It was feared that his approach might turn towards the Black nationalism that had swept African colonies from European rule to independence over the previous decade. This fear of losing control was the same fear that resulted in the crucifixion of Jesus and other challengers of the status quo who preached unity, liberty and independence based upon personal responsibility.

Like John Kennedy, King was killed when it was discovered that he intended to publicly introduce his plan to merge the civil rights and antiwar movements. A multi-racial, politically active populace, truly united around the causes of peace and justice would have presented an even greater threat to the Elite military/industrial money machine.

The tempered Southern Stream strength of African-Americans has a role in exposing the hypocrisy of Northern Stream racist Christianity and the Southern Stream oppression of women, as well as leading the modern world in a spiritual crusade to eradicate social injustice and establish equality based on the inherent divinity of all humanity. As part of their contribution to the divinization of humankind, using the oratory power of the ancient principle of Ma'at – they must speak out against injustice and falsehood, bringing to others the understanding that harmony cannot occur in a society or an individual lacking the foundations of truth and justice.

Justice is the seeking of that which is True. Truth is the same as Love. Just application of law, according to the principles of Ma'at, is meant to turn the people towards Truth and Love. When wisdom guides the administration of law, justice will will be a purificatory rehabilitation, an act of love.

Legislation intended to right social wrongs such as racism and discrimination (affirmative action, for instance), although helpful, is merely a crutch. Ignorance, bigotry and prejudice cannot be legislated away. Core beliefs at the root of these problems must be exposed and/or exhausted in order to make room for a more enlightened view and mode of living. As the light of Truth infiltrates mass consciousness, eventually even the concept of race will become outdated, without validity in human affairs. There'll be just one race, the human race. All else will be secondary to the all-encompassing recognition that we are all here together, as spirits, on physical earth.

As a groundswell of yearning for liberty, unity, truth and justice continued to grow at home, for the Elite it was business as usual. U.S. foreign policy regarding Iran is a case in point. The 1979 Iranian revolution was provoked by the CIA sponsored de-throning of the Shah of Iran, whom they had helped Britain put in power 25 years earlier. The Shah's doubling of oil prices and the end of a 15-year sweet deal for British and American oil concerns no longer supported Elite interests. Almost overnight, the Shah, once a political friend of the United States, became an evil fiend. Suddenly the Shah had a host of human rights violations (which apparently either didn't exist or didn't matter while he allowed his country to be fleeced by the West) that led to his portrayal as a vicious despot. This was not because the Shah was a horrible person; we really don't know one way or the other. It was because he would no longer allow British and American concerns to be partners in Iran's oil business – he took back ownership of Iran's oil fields for Iran.

Elite businessmen on both sides of the Atlantic found themselves in the ignominious position of being simply customers, no longer able to call the shots. The Shah had learned to play the game to his own advantage and was using his new-found revenues to improve the lot of his people and restore Persian dignity by bringing Iran into the 20th century through education and modernization. This situation was untenable to Northern Stream interests because the leader's independent attitude rendered him (and Iranian oil supply and prices) no longer controllable. Using typically Northern Stream logic, Khomeini was installed as the Shah's successor because it was thought that a fundamentalist Islamic regime would be a good buffer against Soviet expansion and a pious, religious man such as he would be more easily controlled.

Later, the U.S. fueled a religious conflagration, arming both Iraqi Sunnis and Iranian Shi'ites, resulting in the deaths of over 700,000 Iranians and 150,000 Iraqis over 10 years' time. Not missing an opportunity to kill two birds with one redirected stone, arms intended by Congress to go to Iran found their way (with a little illegal help from the CIA) to Central America to aid the Contras in protecting U.S. business interests. [49]

---

[49] • *The Iran Contra scandal which erupted in 1986 brought to light one more example of CIA meddling in international political affairs in order to extract greater profits for the Elite.*

The current Northern Stream policy of economic isolation and threatened military aggression toward Iran and Iraq repeats the same strategy used against Germany after WWI and Japan before WWII, and is most likely to produce the same type of violent reaction. Like Germany, this region has a geomantically imprinted history of extreme, radical and fanatical outbursts that will probably erupt in war – further lining the pockets of the Elite.

The wildcard of Islamic radicalism, played without success by U.S. intelligence agencies, actually turned the tide against further Western inside intervention in Iranian affairs. The CIA was correct in their assumption that Khomeini would be welcomed by the people of Iran. But they totally misjudged the mettle of the man they sought to use as a puppet and in their spiritual ignorance they could not understand Islam.

The back-firing of clever manipulations such as these is explained by the fact that, unlike the apolitical stance of holy men in other cultures and times who focused on individual purification and salvation, it is the duty of Islam's Iman (in this case, Khomeini) to enter directly into the arena of hypocrisy, such as the false humanism found in the world of international business and politics, and root it out. Khomeini, a modern Muslim holy man, was the perfect foil to the cultural terrorism of our secular society. From his point of view, ours is an indulgent and hedonistic capitalism, divorced from the sacred, spiritual affairs of daily life as described in the Koran and must be denounced.

Afghanistan also harbors the geomantic memory of internal strife: warriors of Vedic India, exiled lost tribes of Israel , Alexander's Greek army, Genghis Khan's ruthless Mongols and most recent, Russia's own version of the Vietnam debacle. Subsequent to the U.S. installation of Khomeni and the engineering of the Iranian/Iraqi conflict, America's efforts to thwart the communist takeover of Afghanistan, (amounting to over 500 million dollars of military aid) ended up not only in defeating the Russians but in arming and training a worldwide terrorist network.

This unexpected turn of events is so typical a reaction to Northern Stream problem solving mentalities in their quest for world domination, which is in fact, a misinterpretation of the biblical tenant to have dominion over nature. True dominion is to be a steward or caretaker of a recognized owner, or in this instance a representative of God. This is understood in Islam as, al-tashabbuh bi'l-ilah, or "gaining similarity to God." It is accomplished through becoming His "abd or servant." Only by assuming His traits and names can one be qualified to represent God on earth. Serving one's own self interests is a sign that a person has abdicated "their likeness, their sonship, their similarity "to God. This translates into the languages of our litigious society as "what's in it for me and how do I cover my ass?"

With this enculturated attitude one is incapable of having responsible dominion over nature, the destiny of other human beings or for that matter over oneself. All human, social, ecological or economic problems will remain disconnected from the true solutions, until the cart of ego dominancy is no longer placed before the horse of servanthood to God. This is the true application of the New Testament saying "to live and die daily in the Lord." Vivekenanda echoes this eternal pastime of the supremacy of submissionìn and servitude and then representation or dominion, in that order ("doing God's will in the Christian sense, righteous acts in Jewish sense or compassionate acts in Buddhist sense," Vivekenanda says "God is present in all beings. They are his multiple forms. There is no other God to seek. He alone serves God who serves all other beings." Of course, terrorism is not sanctioned in the Koran as a means to serve God nor is the consumerism or ideological indoctrination by capitalism or communism an accurate representation of the biblical mandate to have dominion over nature.

Through Muslim fundamentalists, and yes, even Arab terrorists, the voice of the Southern Stream subconscious cries out through the violent few. In reaction to the godlessness of our society, it rails against the Northern Stream abandonment of the inherent holiness in everyday life.

Ego-run capitalism's violations of Islamic society resulted in Arab terrorism against Northern Stream countries, while the violation of secular society by that same egotism has resulted in the urban terrorism (increased violent crime and gang activity) which all city dwellers fear. While violent crime rates continue to escalate at home, American concerns about human rights violations abroad illustrate the ironic myopia of the Northern Stream's projections onto others.

∞

"If communism ever reestablishes itself successfully, it must be on a foundation of soul's brotherhood and the death of the ego. Vedanta realized is the only practical basis of a communistic society." – Sri Aurobindo

In the Soviet Union, the pressure brought to bear by the energies of liberty and unity finally manifested in the policy of Glasnost, or openness, adopted in 1986. Censorship of all kinds came to an end and freedom of the press came into being. Along with the new openness at home, the Soviet people were also allowed to receive information from abroad, exposing them to the brave new world of capitalism, without the paternalistic filter of the government. This eastern branch of the same Northern Stream that flows through Europe and America, was also attempting to create a perfect, just society. Better connected to its Western Stream roots than its western brothers, it did away with private property, giving everyone an equal share in the wealth. The dissolution of the Soviet Union, begun in 1991, was often wrongly attributed to the inferiority of communist ideology. In truth, the lack of spiritual wisdom they share with their Euro-American brothers doomed the Soviet attempt at a fair, just society to failure.

Predictably, the "free world" misinterpreted the Soviet's unsuccessful social experiment as proof of democratic capitalism's superiority. However, the danger in capitalist democracy lies in its masquerade as "the way, the truth and the light." This insidious distortion is difficult to recognize when dressed up in the half-truths of capitalism's promise of personal desire fulfillment. Actually, there is no ideology, no system, no military coup that can end the misery caused by ego's monarchy. Since all economic, political and military solutions are based upon the same faulty ego-driven values, none will solve the problem. As long as the ego is king, every revolution will eventually result in misery.

Egocentrism is built up through conflict-generating activities common to nearly all cultures, but particularly enhanced in the Northern Stream. Through this often painful process, a sense of identity is created with positive as well as negative traits, weighted by the cultural context in which it develops. The unconscious evolution of the individual soul takes place through identification with certain physical, national, racial and religious classifications. Cultures and nations also evolve through the same process and this development of collective identity is the underlying cause of ethnic and civil conflicts. Such a manifestation is a maladaptive response to the energy of unity and is part of the evolutionary process necessary to humanity's unification on a global (and sacred) scale. Serbs and Croats, Sikhs and Hindus, Indians and Mexicans, Tutsi and Hutu, Catholic and Protestant, French and British Canadians, White and Black Americans, Jews and Arabs, Kurds and Iraqis – these and more struggle to find liberty and unity without spiritual understanding – often with horrifying results. Until something happens to break the cycle of unconscious evolution through the friction of pain and conflict, it will continue.

Often in the awakening of one's true being, there is a period of "going inward" in which one may feel the need to withdraw from others in order to solidify oneself in the evolution brought about by one's experiences to date. This same process occurs within the group consciousness of a people, often manifesting through a move towards separation from the larger society or from other identifiable groups just before a collective shift occurs. The human tendency to identify with and cling to people of like race, ethnicity, nationality or 'causes' is a dress rehearsal, a preparation for the soul's final unity to which all religions point. Everyone is in their perfect place, according to their evolutionary development. Those who seek truth, uphold dogma, or gratify the senses, those who try to "fix" everyone else, even those who are seen by others as diabolical or evil are part of evolutionary perfection – all are acting out their perfect role. This is why, despite appearances to the contrary, all is well.

American involvement in the resolution of foreign conflicts is simply a distraction, pulling our attention away from our own socio-spiritual woes. Putting out ethnic fires in places such as Liberia, Haiti, Somalia and Bosnia, points a finger at "lesser" others who "need our help" with their problems, while simultaneously and subtly reminding us how good we have it here. In this way we avoid fully acknowledging and addressing our own domestic problems and allow carefully structured media coverage to control public opinion and thereby maintain the status quo.[50]

---

50 • *The media's blackouts or obsessions (such as O.J. Simpson), governmental censorship and disinformation is the equivalent in effect to the destruction of timeless records/book burnings in Alexandria, Granada, Rome, and the Yucatan. This is why the unregulated information superhighway of the internet is so threatening to the establishment media.*

The U.S. government's reaction to the Oklahoma City bombing is a reminder that Americans do indeed have problems at home that need their attention. The architects of our nation intended that government would use its power to protect its citizens from outside attack. Today, now that communism has been soundly defeated and is no longer a threat, we are told the enemy is within and government must spy on its own citizens to protect them from domestic attacks. Under such conditions our democratic process has already begun to degenerate into adoption of totalitarian methods, and may eventually impose marshal law to "protect" the populace against a domestic threat, whether it be anti-government militias, evil drug smugglers, or maybe even the victims of a horrible, communicable disease. Allowing fear to rule us, a domestic cold war could ensue and we could become a nation besieged by our own government "for our own good."

The equilibrium we all seek in order to stave off insecurity, is played upon in the extreme in Northern Stream consumer-culture, leading to an unconscious desire to control and standardize things. From election campaigns to the purchase of breath mints, human insecurity is used to prompt human behavior in our society. One of our biggest bugaboos, fear of the unknown, when coupled with the misunderstood and misapplied energy of unity, leads to intolerance and suspicion of difference. Confusing oneness with sameness, we attempt to alleviate our anxiety by making everyone and everything the same as we are. Our tendency to supplant the universes unity in diversity with our own unity in conformity stamps out uniqueness and replaces shining, individuated divinity with blind, seamless, mediocrity. Rather than growing secure in appreciation for the infinite variety in humanity and the rest of creation we grow afraid that difference will be our downfall. In our attempt to feel safe and secure we move in unknowing opposition to the unfolding, individualizing process of unification. Sadly, pandering to ego's fear, we eventually surrender liberty, along with our uniqueness, in exchange for a mistaken security.

Northern Stream Christianity is too weak in its collective mythological power to counter the egocentrism of the modern world it helped create. Actually, it is part of the problem – Christianity can't cure its own secular disease. "Family values" movements of the new conservative Right, corporate social conscience, idealistic New Age, ecumenical and humanistic movements of the liberal Left are only the very beginnings of the deep changes required to get at the root of the spiritual crisis in our society. In addition to the awakening of true caring on a massive scale in the Northern Stream, the modern fundamentalist Christian movement, bent on evangelizing the world, must admit the truth about its edited and mistranslated Bible. They must welcome back the dissident Eastern Churches which preserve the original Aramaic language of Christ and honor the Black Egyptian as the source and center of European civilization. They must, in short, reclaim all that they've disowned. And they must come to understand that much of modern Christianity has become a 'game show religion' – a by-product of modern consumerism with great packaging (tune in to nearly any television evangelist) and the promise of instant gratification (salvation) masquerading as spiritual awakening.

Although necessary to counteract the abusiveness of both institutions, the American invented separation of Church and State led to the fragmentation of self found in modern culture, resulting in spiritual bankruptcy. There has rarely been a time when spiritual values held sway for the Northern Stream – there has always been much superstition, dogma and doctrine. This has held true for the Secular Age, except without the window dressing of religion; we have merely substituted the doctrine and dogma of science and materialism for that of religion. In the Secular Age (whether in democratic, socialist or communist societies) the Northern Stream has divorced itself not only from religion, but from spiritual truths inherent in all areas of life. For this reason, the American system, based on the noble idea of individual liberty, has degenerated into the same greed-ridden, self-absorbed, narcissistic corruption that has crippled other attempts to order society in a just, respectful and fulfilling way. The very freedom designed to save us – separation of church from state and almost unlimited opportunity to make and spend money – has now locked us into a collision course with destiny.

Secular democracy, flawed with Northern Stream immaturity, has given license to unrestrained selfishness and greed, completely out of step with the eternal truths that point humanity to the Divine. As long as they're based in selfishness, our democratic rights and duties can never result in a just and equal society. A true democracy must be based upon the Eastern Stream concept of dharma, in which love, truth, justice and duty are all interrelated. Sri Aurobindo's definition of dharma clearly illustrates this point: "Dharma is the Indian conception in which rights and duties lose the artificial antagonism created by a view of the world which makes selfishness the root of action and regain their deep and eternal unity."

The freedom of the individual found in secular democracy only mimics spiritual freedom. Nothing in the material world can bring man the freedom he longs for; it can only provide the leisure and health to question what true freedom really is. Blessed as most of us are with material comfort and leisure time, we are not encouraged by our culture to use these blessings to gain our spiritual freedom. Instead, we are urged to engage in activities that further the continuance of the consumer machine. However, democracy's political analog to a spiritual reality has served well to bring greater individualization to the human race as part of its long journey to divinization.

The Secular Materialist's Creed
Having brings happiness.
Doing is a means to having.
Doing and having is what gives meaning to life.
Doing and having more is better.
No one and nothing is more important than getting my needs met.
Those who don't play by these rules are less than those who do.

Monopolized by a few very wealthy families with no national allegiances, today's industry and international business and banking are off shoots of the kingly family, giving rise to the new economic monarchy. The overt tyranny of feudal clergy and aristocracy have been replaced with a much subtler form of abuse, control and manipulation. For most of the Northern Stream, military control of people and resources has given way to the less obvious method of manipulation of information. Citizens have become the pawns and worker drones of government and big business through economic and media manipulation. Brainwashed into believing the insane premise of infinite economic expansion with limited resources, we have twisted the work ethic into the need to work more in order to have more "stuff." Our media supports this system by promoting consumerism and wage slavery as "the American Way" to "the

American Dream."[51] Twentieth century prophet Edgar Cayce summed up our situation aptly in one of his readings (#3976-29), "What is the spirit of America? Most individuals proudly boast 'freedom.' Freedom of what? When yea bind men hearts and minds through various ways and manners, does it give them freedom of speech? Freedom of worship? Freedom from want? Not unless these basic principles (in God we trust) are applicable ... for God meant man to be free. "

The root of ego-dominated capitalism and the foundation of the American Dream, the Northern Stream invention of the nuclear family took place with the demise of agrarian-based culture, which triggered the slow dissolution of the extended family along with the family farm. The wisdom of experience and tradition is no longer acknowledged or transferred through family connections from generation to generation. Now, each individual is more or less left to fend for him/herself, socialized and guided through the medium of television and the educational system. Lasting bonds and stable communities in which neighbors know one another are fast becoming things of the past as our youth are no longer guided by their community elders but by the toxic images created by our consumer-producing, media-based institutionalism. Not only are the youth unconsciously acting out societal distortions and hypocrisy, but they sense an impending crisis. Through isolating architecture and city planning, mobile lifestyles, our birthing, childrearing, educational and employment practices and television viewing (no one talks to anyone anymore) we design alienation into our society. The isolation we endure and are encouraged to support sparks more insecurity, fear and violence, leading to a greater willingness to give up sovereignty for security – all of which are used to grease the Elite money machine through massive consumerism and wage slavery.

With the rise of the nuclear family, Northern Stream society has broken itself down into smaller and smaller units. Today, more people live alone in Northern Stream countries than at any other time in recorded history. This distortion of the energy of liberty,

---

51 • *Misuse of power goes far beyond the covert manipulation of world economies and currencies by a select few. Television is an overt display of the power of mass suggestion (hypnosis) where the magical incantations of an assortments of polished politicians, evangelists, experts, news caster personalities, super models, film and rock stars all subvert our own autonomy and freedom.*

encouraged by nearly every aspect of our culture, is a financial bonanza for Elite interests. More single person households mean more housing, cars, tv's, stereos, refrigerators, lawnmowers, washing machines, coffeemakers, (you get the picture) can be sold. The cost in human misery and lives lost because of the rampant alienation and inability to relate to one another spawned in this atmosphere goes unnoticed, much less accounted for. As long as we each can work and spend in relative safety, no one cares.

Most don't even know they are suffering a cruelty far more hideous than that perpetrated by any dictators of past regimes, because it has been programmed into the Northern Stream cultural psyche. The insidious "brainwashing" which clouds our sensibilities, we take for granted as "our culture." Like a fish in water, we do not notice the medium in which we exist. We're not taught to see reality clearly. The cruelty lies in that even when one can see clearly what is taking place, there is no cultural mechanism for fundamental change in the system. Even more cruelly, the resulting apathy and despair only serve to feed the machine by stimulating greater desire for instant gratification and escape from reality into sensation. The rise in addictive behavior of all kinds gives grim testimony to our culturally-generated need for anesthesia.

Hypnotized by the system in which we live and our own ego-desires, most of us still believe in the illusory freedom of the American Dream, with its prospects for leisure and the comfort of a hi-tech, sense-gratifying lifestyle, despite the obvious increased moral decay, overcrowded prisons, escalating street and domestic violence, government and police corruption, crime and drug abuse.

Our social emphasis on government subsidy (Republicans subsidize the rich, Democrats the poor, and both subsidize the Federal Reserve) and our media emphasis on crime (both through drama and reportage of criminal activity) and sporting events is reminiscent of the Roman "bread and circuses" approach to cultural/social engineering. The Roman Empire provided a stipend or "dole" to some of its citizens and went so far as denuding North Africa and hunting some animals to extinction by "harvesting" trees, wildlife (and people!) in order to provide entertainment for its citizens and keep them "happy" and disinterested in governing themselves.

Today in our society individuals take less and less responsibility for themselves and their own needs, expecting government to make decisions and "handle things." We expect government and other social institutions to educate our children, preserve the environment, take care of our health, feed the hungry and clothe and house the poor. "They" (choose your favorite "inferior" group of people) are the cause of increased violence, drug abuse, soaring national debt, pollution, "dirty politics," etc. – none of which, of course, has anything to do with "us," and is certainly not our responsibility. Government should "fix it." "That's what we pay taxes for." This immature "buck passing" inevitably manifests corrupt political systems, putting into motion the oppressor/oppressed game. We must take our power back from the institutions and systems that hold us hostage without falling into the trap of ego-mind which will merely produce another replay of previous events.[52]

The proliferation of NGO's – non-governmental organizations which provide humanitarian aid – without affiliation to religious or philosophical institutions – is a sign that some are willing to take responsibility for society and not leave everything up to government. Without a sacred science, however, their efforts are still based on dysfunctional paradigms that tend to increase belief in separation and self interest and avoid focusing on the multiplicity of the One, or the Many within the One.

Our lack of spiritual moorings has given birth to a superficial definition of "quality of life" which in turn produced reliance upon "quick fix" technological advancements, legislation and money to cure our social ills. Because our spiritual problem won't yield to a material solution the result has been increasing mental illness, violence, degenerative disease and ecological disaster. Our weakness lies in our inability to establish Truth-based standards from which we individually and collectively can make intelligent decisions in any arena, whether politics, diet, relationships, or child-rearing. With such a foundation, appropriate choices become self-evident, in much the same way we know when music is played in key or off.

---

52 • *With only 49% of Americans accounted for in the 1996 Presidential election, we have a country run, in effect, by complacency that is even unable to hear the constructive truths from the third party underdogs. The media blackout of Ross Perot's "economic meltdown," the Libertarians Party's plea "that government doesn't work" or Taxpayers Party's revelation that government doesn't belong where its not needed;" are cries that are too down-to-earth for a special interest controlled society which is crippled in its discriminative capabilities, mal-nourished in its education, and mal-adapted by political doubletalk.*

Our deification of the limited intelligence of the human intellect brought with it the misuse of reason, and the abuse of will power. Our cleverness gave birth to the religion of materialism with its enshrinement of the dollar and worship of industrialization, technical science, capitalist economics and unchecked consumerism. In a speech given not long before his assassination, Robert Kennedy made a scathing assessment of our money-driven society, "the gross national product includes air pollution and advertising for cigarettes, and ambulances to clear our highways of carnage. It counts special locks for our doors, and jails for the people who break them. The gross national product includes the destruction of the redwoods and the death of Lake Superior. It grows with the production of napalm and missiles and nuclear warheads.

"And if the gross national product includes all this, there is much that it does not comprehend. It does not allow for the health of our families, the quality of their education, or the joy of their play. It is indifferent to the decency of our factories and the safety of our streets alike. It does not include the beauty of our poetry or the strength of our marriages, the intelligence of our public debate or the integrity of our public officials. The gross national product measures neither our wit nor our courage, neither our wisdom nor our learning, neither our compassion nor our devotion to country. it measures everything, in short, except that which makes life worthwhile; and it can tell us everything about America- except whether we are proud to be Americans."

Without denouncing our overspecialized workforce[53] resulting in the overall improvement in our standard of living, we must understand that what we call modern civilization is deeply flawed, and can only reach its next phase of development through an

---

53 • *When over-specialization infiltrates a society, it's citizens run the risk of contracting a serious cultural disease. This can best be described as a type of mental inbreeding which is further complicated by the effects of electromagnetic (or ELF) waves, pollutants in the food, water and air and anxiety ridden lifestlyes. As a result we have a culture that is mentally handicapped and incapable of synthetic thinking and problem solving, or displaying moral and selfless behavior. All the desire/fear based attitudes and behaviors feed equally dysfunctional institutions in an endless tape loop where bandaging the symptoms simply causes more problems to be later re-diagnosed and then of course, re-dressed again. This is the equivalent of the age old snare of Hinduism's illusory Maya, but given a secular twist and ironically named the "American Dream."*

unprecedented revolution of consciousness within each person. Neither technical innovations, marketing strategies, humanitarian relief, ideological shifts nor military revolt or diplomacy will save the day. No new invention of the mind can ever solve the problems created by the old inventions of the mind. They only further complicate matters, postponing true resolution of the problem.

The Northern Stream's manifestation of self serves the Divine, even through the arrogant, greedy use of its gifts. It was part of the Divine Plan that the Northern Stream would connect all peoples in order to develop a network for the evolution of humanity. That this happened through an exploitative twist on exploration and trade (colonization, imperialism and globalism) is a regrettable, yet apparently necessary part of our growth as human beings. Eventually, as all religions must, our secular materialism must bind us back to the Source. Through the results of our flawed way of life we will come to acknowledge our vulnerability to Life's need for balance.

$$\infty$$

"We owe the progress in the field of outer material culture entirely to this separation of capacities (sense and spiritual). What is already able to show its beginnings at present is the discovery of the link that unites the two impulses in the human breast: material culture and life in the world of the spirit. ...What he (man) there produces in the inmost depths of his soul is finally itself to become the outer world." – Rudolf Steiner, philosopher, occultist, founder of Waldorf Schools

Science, at first a direct reaction to the ignorance of religion, was originally meant to investigate nature. Stumbling under the weight of Northern Stream arrogance, ignorance and greed, science is destroying the natural environment it was intended to study. The fault in modern technology's attempt to best nature is that it assumes it can do the same thing nature does, only better, *without giving thought to the consequences.* Our dysfunctional, ego-driven technology uses fossil fuels, nuclear power, toxic chemicals and genetically altered bacteria to enhance convenience, comfort, pleasure and wealth, without regard for the destructive impact on ourselves or the environment. This insane behavior rests on the subconscious desire to play God. The Truth is that one can only attune to Source, become at one with It, never become It. We are

Source, but not in Its totality; just as drops of water in the ocean are the same substance as the ocean but a drop of seawater is not the ocean. Through science, humanity is like a drop of water believing it is the ocean.

Due to the pace and scale of human alterations to the environment in the last 50 years, we have come dangerously close to exceeding the carrying capacity of the earth, in terms of supporting the Northern Stream 20th century lifestyle. Our formula for "success" which, among other things, forcibly enhances earth's yield while ignoring the need for replenishment, diminishes earth's ability to sustain life in general, and human life in particular. We are witnessing Earth's adaptation to the human intrusions of overpopulation and pollution through a revolt of Nature, manifested by severe weather and geological disturbances, bizarre animal behavior, extinction of many species and more – all a direct response to human mistreatment of each other and the earth.

Placing economic and political expediency above human life and environmental balance is part of man's futile attempt to challenge Divine authority and control Divine Intelligence as represented by the laws of Nature. In its continued attempt to play God, the Northern Stream was willing to risk all life on the planet with its foray into the realm of nuclear energy. With no understanding of the effects on human populations, the atmosphere, ozone layer, seismic activity, or radioactive contamination, 1200 (or 2 per month for the last 50 years!) nuclear devices have been detonated to date worldwide. (There was a very real possibility of collapsing our planet's atmosphere or incinerating the state of New Mexico in testing the atomic bomb.) The long term ramifications may never be fully known or understood. And, despite the media silence on the subject, no safe, effective, long term (tens of thousands of years are needed) solution has been found to radioactive waste disposal (tons of it are produced annually in our country alone). On the other hand, Nature in her wisdom placed our Sun, a nuclear power plant, 93 million miles away from us; a good indication that nuclear power plants, much less nuclear weapons, don't belong on the earth.

Modern technology always mimics either nature or human capacities. Now virtual reality technology mimics the play of mind in projecting images on the screen of consciousness. Technology now mirrors what really is; there really is no objective world. All reality is virtual. With the information accessible through media, cyberspace and transportation, experiences that in the past would have taken many lifetimes to gain can now occur in one; the evolution of consciousness is condensed and speeded up. All humanity has the technological capabilities to witness at the very same moment, world sporting or warring events (via satellite, T.V., Internet and Stock market fluctuations), together as one humanity. This is indicative of the external evidence, of an all-seeing presence that pervades all time, space and beings.

Science has served humanity paradoxically by improving the standard of living on one hand and producing weapons of total destruction on the other. Both the threat of annihilation and the promise of comfort draw us together in fear of an uncertain future, menaced by the ever-present danger of chemical, biological and nuclear warfare and with the hope of new leisure-giving technologies. Simultaneously, that same hope is crushed by our enslavement to the treadmill of a modern lifestyle. Willing slavery to the dollar with the hope of fulfillment in the here and now has proven to be no better than religious slavery to the hope of salvation in the hereafter, it's just, for the moment, more palatable.

In its rush to make life better, science, ironically enough, has produced all the elements necessary to eliminate the human species. At no time in recorded history has humanity lived amidst the abundance of poisons in the air, water and soil, weapons of mass destruction, iatrogenic diseases, radioactive waste and polluted environments as we do today. Human arrogance and selfishness has destroyed the harmony of nature. In our Eastern Stream Tibetan brothers' view,[55] our desire for immediate gratification, complicated by the fear of death, causes our already anxious seeking of short term solutions to problems to be further aggravated by ignoring the long term effects of our actions on health, relationships, community, economy and the environment.

---

55 • *The exiled Tibetan Rinpoches encircling the globe have brought with them time tested antidotes for the very mental illness that would even have allowed China (a former Cold War opponent) to slaughter 1 million Tibetans, or for the U.S. to even consider offering China a favored trade status. It would serve these two consumer giants well to adopt these advanced inner technologies/tantras (of Tibetan Maha yoga, Anu yoga, Ati yoga) to combat the virus of anger, desire/greed and ignorance infecting both totalitarian China and democratic America. In a like manner, the traditional methods of treating the increases in chronic and acute pyscho-disturbances that are plaguing civilized man could be augmented with shamanistic healing journeys into the patient's underworld.*

Northern Stream science's penetration into the core of materiality, to subatomic levels, brought some of us to acknowledge that matter is Divine. Through secular society's full embrace of addiction to sense objects and ego gratification we discover that body, senses and the environment are crystallized Divinity. In the destruction of the harmony of nature for the sake of comfort, leisure and economic supremacy, we are confronted, not with the death of the earth, for the earth will live on and adapt, but with our own extinction and we see finally that all things are related, interconnected, all is Divine.

The discontent created by our fragmented, materialistic, cultural psyche made it possible for the Northern Stream to search for its source and completion in the gifts of the other three Streams, albeit first disguised as the quest for material wealth. And although the Northern Stream appears to have entrenched itself in materialism by ignoring the sacred truths of the other three more spiritually illumined Sacred Streams, it brought all Streams together, releasing wisdom from the guardianship of the few to be communicated to the many through its technical know-how, transcending tribal, national, religious and racial barriers. Secular commercialism has brought the whole world together into a kind of "functional" unity through materialism.

Love of money for its own sake unifies us by way of a monstrous commercialism, simultaneously trapping us in the conflicting beliefs that money is inherently evil and that having it is the source of happiness. Traditionally, there has been a ban on accumulation of wealth by spiritual seekers; the faithful are encouraged to proclaim their poverty and renounce possessions. But the truth about wealth is spoken very clearly by Sri Aurobindo's companion, the Mother, who said, "Money is the visible sign of a universal force." It, like everything else, belongs to the Divine and we must recognize money as another expression of the Divine. We must also free ourselves from the mad belief that possessing enough of the evil stuff will make us happy and also release the idea that acetic withdrawal from the world is the means to spiritual liberation. The transformation of humankind, spurred on by evolutionary pressure, cannot occur through either the unchecked egocentrism of commercialism or the reclusive renunciations of aceticism, both of which are actually forms of escapism, but from conscious and responsible involvement in life.

In the absence of wisdom traditions, ego-mind (the Northern Stream) surrenders to Spirit only after it exhausts all alternatives, including its own destruction. It is part of the Northern Stream evolutionary strategy to exhaust itself, to taste everything, expose itself totally and thereby never have to repeat the mistakes of the past in order to discover and then develop its gifts. The resulting continued mental fragmentation is simply the seed of further distortion if ego-drives are left unchecked. The Northern Stream has reached the prophesied point of purposeful exhaustion by distorting both religious truth and scientific technology with the vagaries of the ego-mind. Following exhaustion, the next step is surrender to God, not from the struggling mind's usual rejection of pain and aspiration toward pleasure, but from the heart.

Surrender from the level of mind is still just imagination. When surrender is real, one is already moved and merged with Source. At that point, making efforts at rejection of and discrimination between perceived negatives and aspiration toward desired ends seems foolish. One enters a natural state in which all that arises is inherently One with one's own being. There is no longer anything to defend against or strive toward. The "velcro" of ego involvement has disappeared. Or in Koranic terms "everything is perishing except His Face." – 28:88

Throughout Sacred History, the other Streams have been in service, waiting for the Northern Stream to complete the exhaustion process. It is part of the spiritual initiation of the other Streams to forgive and be compassionate toward the spiritual ignorance of the Northern Stream. These three patient Streams will show by their living example what true Christian forgiveness really is.

The meeting of the Four Sacred Streams during this time in Sacred History can bring oneness into focus in a global culture of world citizenship, integrated international economics and shared inner and outer technologies, heralding the evolution of a Sacred Science of Life that will test the religious/political beliefs of the past.

∞

"Only when egoism dies and God in man governs his own universality can this earth support a happy and contented race of beings." – Sri Aurobindo.

The peace and prosperity of the people and the planet, which is the Realization of God in the world, is impossible without first realizing God transcendent to the world and as one with one's own self. In answer to humanity's needs in this area, there is an awakening gnosis in America and Europe manifesting as a trend toward nondualism or Advaita. This awakening is an individual endeavor, a unique disclosure of the Divine to Itself, the One to one of the many. It can't be legislated, workshopped, globalized, humanitarianized or institutionalized but it can be realized. As Sri Aurobindo reminds us in his *Hour of God*, "When we are absorbed in world, we miss God in Himself; when we see God, we miss Him in the world. Our business is to break down and dissolve mental ego and get back to our divine unity without losing our power of individual and multiple existence in the universe." This is the blueprint for oneness with the Divine which will take us all beyond our present use of exhaustion as a tool for transformation. This is the value of nondual Advaita to the Northern Stream.

Nondualism is simply a natural state of mind, beyond its movements or identifications with concepts, reactions, or the dualities of body and life circumstances. When the mind is allowed to rest in its Silent Source, away from its incessant activity (ideation, conceptualization, sensing, imaging, judging) or even coexisting with, it becomes possible for creation to arise as a new manifestation of Source-mind, rather than from the imaginings of ego-mind. This non-dual awareness exists before, beyond and outside of race, ethnicity, religion or nationality. The source of all, of the many, is the nondual One. The realization of this truth is not something that can be studied with the mind. It is transmitted by nondual Reality, Itself to Itself, in humanity. Sometimes this occurs through a human being, but it can happen through anything.

Although transplanted from Indian Vedanta and Japanese Zen, Advaita is not an exclusively Eastern Stream approach. Southern Stream Islam's great Sufi poets referred to it as Tawhid and in the Kabbala it is called Ain Sof or Kether.

There are at present many proponents of nondualism from various religious/spiritual traditions crisscrossing the globe. Some of the best known being Nisagardata (d. 1981), Anandamoyi Ma (d. 1982), Krishnamurti (d. 1986), Jean Klein, H.W.L. Poonjaji, Gangaji and Da Free John. Their observations appeal to Northern Stream members whose intellects have been ripened through gradual methods of purification and transformation in more traditional religious systems. The beauty of Advaita's flowering in the Northern Stream is that non-dualism, normally the last step in extensive spiritual study is making its appearance in a culture so identified with mind and so deeply secularized. In this atmosphere of freshness, outside of religious traditions, nondualism can serve as a Truth foundation if one can sidestep potential pitfalls.

There is the potential for a misstep for Advaitic adherents, a tendency to declare the world is a product of mind, illusory, a waking dream. Ramakrishna alluded to this when he said, "Certainly the world is unreal, as long as you imagine it to be a separate, substantial world." The non-dual approach to life is a methodology, useful as an aid to opening to the Reality by assisting one to de-identify with objects of the mind/body (so-called subjective reality) and its projection – the world (so-called objective reality). The ensuing relaxation of the mind allows it to hang loose on reality and inquire as to the nature of the Doer. The confusion lies in mistaking the methodology ("this is a dream") for the actual Reality Itself. This is like believing that a thought *about* a thing is the thing itself, when in fact the thing itself is neither the idea nor the thought about it. Slipping into Advaitic literalism will arrest the fullness of the divine disclosure and only create a mirage, a mere imitation.

The basic human paradigm of belief in separation, when added to the illusion of mistaking a methodology for the Reality to which it leads, merely spawns another illusion, leading to impracticality in life. Many sincere spiritual seekers who truly believe that "nothing is real" often find it difficult to make decisions in their lives. Others use this belief as justification for avoidance of unpleasant, "mundane" duties or even personal realizations. One must be very careful not to proclaim the first impersonal step onto the stairway of the Divine as the landing!

All proponents of Truth throughout Sacred History profess that, "All there is is God, Pure Consciousness, beyond distinction or separation, imagination, words, form or concepts. If the Divine is All, then Its manifestation cannot be considered unreal, a dream or an illusion. But to profess this Truth of the Unmanifest while ignoring the Manifest is to limit the Divine. This would be like saying that the formless, nameless God is only like the Space of the Sky; infinite, the backdrop of everything. But the Sky is not empty, there are the forces of air, water, sun, and living creatures. Likewise, God, in Its immanent form must also be the multiplicity of Life, the

Many, as well as the transcendent, formless singularity, the One. Without Sky, all else could not exist. The many do exist, they are not an illusion, nor are they as we imagine them to be, in separation from each other and ourselves. When we cease dual perception or conception, the Many are perceived to be the glory of the One, just as rays of sunshine are to the Sun. The Many can only be as One, for each of the Many is That in its own Essence. That Essence is not a perception, but is the Perceiver. The Many in the One, and the One in the Many is our own Source, actually emanating from our own awareness, as we emanate from It.

All things are not "unreal" but simply emanations or extensions of your own awareness. There is only you. In the waking state, as in a dream, there is only you, all alone. All one. The All and the One. This is more significant than imagining that things are unreal or as if a dream. Only when one overcomes the fear of being all alone can one be embraced by the All One.

Our inability to see that our industry-based, materialistic, propagandized society is as unreal as the dream state, is brought on by our collective apathy and cultural hypnosis, shored up by Elite/government manipulation of media and information, for the "common good" and "national interest." Today's technologically slick scripting of society replicates the editing, censorship and selective belief shaping done by the official church councils of thousands of years ago. As was true over a thousand years ago, authority perceives as dangerous those of us who wake up to the fact that each of us is all alone and because of that everything is all-one. So-called radicals, heretics, mystics, ecstatics, awakened ones, or visionaries upset the status quo and destabilize the illusory security of the established order.

The exhaustion of the forces of fundamentalism and materialism, our hedonistic culture and the increasing distrust in institutions are anchoring the probability of a truly Divine life in the future. The ego/mind is polarizing into existence no-mind, the foundation of oneness upon which Truth-based individuals, societies and the world all merge. The non-dual wisdom of Hinduism's Advaita and Islam's Tawhid are only foundations for a Truth-based world beyond belief systems. Nondualism, which has had a few proponents in every culture in the past, will become the norm for an evolving Earth Wisdom. Its effects will be felt centuries from now, just as the religious confusion of the past was the basis for the fragmented ignorance that we find ourselves in today.

∞

All our perceptions of a reality external to ourselves are due to the webbing of dualism, a compulsive habit of the mind. Our fixation on so-called "objective" reality reinforces the concept of separation and builds up a false image or identity, resulting in the struggle for survival of that image. Reliance on perceived externals is a form of idol worship. Whether it is statues, images, institutions, commerce, or the authority of religion, medicine, government, education or the intellect as object that we worship, we are totally dependent upon the mind.

These externally focused mental habits, based upon misconceptions that serve to enforce ego-separation and feed emotional dramas, perpetuate a vicious cycle causing all sorts of adaptations in physiology, behavior and society which we label as diseases or crises. Behaviors arising from our mental habits are not really who we are. They are not "I." These knots in the heart are tightened by not wanting to feel displeasure or sensations of discomfort or wanting to grasp, own or control that which appears to bring us pleasure and a sense of importance. Our likes and dislikes are mental judgments that interfere with our perception of what is and obscure who we are. When a person receives perspective, attachment loosens, then what appeared as so important, dramatic or tragic will seem as if it were a mental optical illusion. On the other hand, if trauma and attachment are too strong, this is the self inflicted suffering required for the soul to progress, and carry out its investigation of life .

All disturbances we experience are the products of some subliminal Not-I running our lives – a sure sign that judgment, criticism, arrogance or cruelty are present and that we are no longer at the center and circumference of our own self. Complaining about others or ourselves and the constant mind chatter of faultfinding and gossip are simply subtle jealousy, a way to gain attention and avoid taking responsibility for oneself. Blaming others or ourselves for problems or our mindsickness is a denial of what is and causes conflict with our thwarted selfish desires – what ought to have been. Expectations invariably create a false and imaginary mental picture which causes us to try to control the outcome of events in order to escape all that is painful and gain all that is enjoyable or pleasing – to get what we want, when we want it, irrespective of others concerned. When we don't get what we want, or we get what we don't want, we stick up for our rights and go into "ego struggle." This sometimes manifests as the victim/villain game, in order to obtain attention, which creates further mind projection, further harm and inconsiderateness. Seeking to gain attention and approval is the other side of struggling to escape rejection and neglect. These attractions and repulsions – indulgences and avoidances – are the urges that run mankind and are at the root of humanity's struggle to become conscious. Our unconscious obedience to these urges enslave us in habits of the Not-I's. This is to be understood so we can be re-educated.

When the mind is focused on these urges, we are slaves to the Not-I's and our life circumstances become the drama used to release the "pressure" or effects of our slavery. When the urges are identified and understood they are no longer a source of bondage but simply become unimportant in determining our wise responses to what previously was a drama. We come to realize it is ourselves we must master, not the struggles with outer circumstances or other people that these urges draw us into.

Much of the Not-I repertoire has to do with gaining acceptance and self-importance. Attempting to help or please others when not asked affords personal and/or social acceptance and self importance while avoiding the pain of rejection and the emptiness brought on by a sense of uselessness. Blindly doing and believing as you are told by others is done to acquire approval and acceptance from those perceived as outside authorities. All these behaviors have dualism at their core, seeking rewards and avoiding punishment. This dynamic is well understood by those who would control others. Institutions of all kinds use human fears and inadequacies such as these to gain control of the populace.

The foundation upon which all religious beliefs, spiritual teachers and practices rest is in the Not-I's of needing to please others, doing and believing as you are told by your authorities or seeking self improvement in order to gain salvation – all in order to be more, better, different or undisturbed. The drama that goes on around all religious and spiritual teachers exposes these urges. Being close to the "master" or "leader" leads to the uncovering of arrogance; being distant uncovers jealousy.

Much of what passes for devotion or dedication in spiritual circles and faith in religious circles centers around gaining or maintaining a sense of security and belongingness. Modifying one's behavior in order to please or gain approval, espousing the prevailing beliefs in order to gain acceptance, desiring self-improvement or spiritual salvation in order to gain attention are all undertaken to avoid their opposites – the pain of disapproval, the hurt of rejection, the abyss of feeling unimportant or unworthy. Only when one ceases all these behaviors will true, conscious spirituality dawn beyond the filtering devices of our own imaginations and conditioning.

In preliminary, purificatory stages of spiritual development there is a tendency to put limitations on the Divine, perceiving It only in one place, person, thing, tradition. During this phase we require a reference point, a limitation upon which to focus the mind and open the heart in order to eventually recognize the Divine in all things, circumstances and persons as merged within our very own Awareness. To almost every new seeker, the Divine first appears to be outside one as a leader, ideal, concept, a presence, a guru, a savior that eventually directs one inward to the Kingdom of God. Later, the Lord is found within your own Christed self. "I and My Father are One."

However, even though such limitations can develop or reveal consciousness, without wisdom they can turn the spiritual drama into a nightmare of neediness and fears, authoritarian control and rules. Some may find themselves acting against their better judgment in order to support some leader's ideal (democracy, freedom, workers' rights, religious dogma and racial purity, for example). This is typical of traditions that attract more emotional and desire-ridden followers. Such systems develop "drama" or hysteria around gurus, teachers, leaders or systems, mostly due to the inability to look thoroughly at the mind's conditioning. In spiritual organizations this is often complicated by the tendency to discount and disqualify the mind in an attempt to reach the Unmanifest Divine – often the desired ideal. By stopping there, the divinization process of the mind is arrested and one falls into the error of judging the mind as unreal, a dream, useless – part of the Manifest Divine.

At a certain stage in development, after exhausting all the strategies for self improvement, even spiritual seeking itself is no longer worthwhile, nor is desiring to become more, better or different than others. These strategies merely use comparisons to gain attention and hide greed and pride.

The drama we develop around life is no different than drama that often develops around a teacher or leader; it's based upon the desire to gain acceptance, attention, approval and to escape their opposites. When we cannot accept the fact that the Boundless is in all things and we do not accept ourselves, then we seek to gain that acceptance from a limited outside source – teacher, leader, savior, ideal or an attribute that your beloved object represents. In actuality, imagination projects the perceived attributes onto the true teacher.

Just as all religio-spiritual systems are founded upon certain Not-I's, all legal, political and economic systems thrive on the Not-I's of complaining, defending imagined rights and blaming others when the ways of the world or circumstance are contrary to one's selfish or altruistic desires. Although some of the behaviors may be different from those of the religio-spiritual organizations, the underlying urges that drive them are the same.

All these systems assert themselves over their adherents and citizens, rather than serving them. What passes for knowledge in any of these circles is often simply arrogance. This is the common denominator of most cultures, irrespective of religious, political or economic flavor. All human systems and institutions are wholly run by conditioned, subconscious urges. Until the assertions over others stop, until each of us takes up the responsibility to observe and understand the urges that fragment us and control society, until we are able to fast from them, in humor laugh at them, in vigilance renounce them, then true slavery will never cease on this planet. Only then will humanity be guided by the Divine rather than ego-driven politics, religion and economics.

Until a person becomes conscious of what motivates human behavior, all techniques, practices and systems will be simply crutches, buffers and bandaids. We will be incapable of understanding others, of being harmless, of leaving everyone else alone, of imparting wisdom through our speech or actions, of understanding ourselves – incapable of simply being and in that being seeing the perfection of everyone's actions as perfectly correlated with self-created entrapment by conditioned mind and its projected circumstance of life in the world. The conscious person recognizes life for what it is and gives it no undue importance. They embrace each circumstance of the world or of the mind whether agreeable or disagreeable, with humility, compassion, love and wisdom.[57]

We must come to acknowledge that just beneath the carefully tended surface of our rational world is an irrational realm, a whirling tornado of sexual desire, needs for identity, security, acceptance and meaning – all manifestations of the ego-driven need for self-importance. Without this awareness-wisdom in its practical form, all domestic, spiritual, political or business activities, despite all the well-intentioned ideals and effort, spring from the same urge towards self-centered selfishness. But once the individual and humanity discovers this, the knot of conditioning, clever creativity and all suffering will be untied and we will look back upon this troubled phase in our evolution with curiosity, humor, compassion – maybe even disbelief – as a dream of the animal-human awakening to the divine-human.

Not-I's are the free radicals of the mind, breaking down the mental/emotional/physical system, distorting their proper functioning. When the Not-I's are mistakenly seen as important, they lead to chronic addiction, acute illness, aging, aberrant behavior and premature death. Like a mirage, they superimpose a reality of opposites over the non-dual and can not only imitate non-dualism, but can get hold of truth and use it for egocentric purposes. The spiritual myopia of Spanish missionaries who baptized Native Americans before they were slaughtered by conquistadors, in order to be certain they went to heaven, the Biblical literalism of Christians who use Jesus,' "No one comes to the Father but by me," to mean that accepting Jesus as lord and savior is the *only* way to God, New Agers who proclaim themselves enlightened because they mistake spiritual enthusiasm for true awakening, devotees of *The Course in Miracles* who distort its Advaitic message to mean that physical reality and the mind are "bad" and "wrong" – all of these examples demonstrate the twisting of truth by the ego to suit its own purposes. Throughout the ages these kinds of distortions, brought on by falling prey to the demands of the Not I's, have marked nearly all spiritual paths, including advaitic systems. By simply recognizing the true unimportance of the Not-I's, the misery caused by unconscious relationships, childrearing, education, religion, and government can be healed in the light of consciousness.

---

57 • *Becoming conscious simultaneously opens the chakras, stimulates acupuncture meridians, regulates the breathing, adjusts the biochemistry and neuro physiology and regulates the subtle energies of the right and left columns of the spine into the one central channel. This unifies the perceiver with the perceived.*

Chapter Twelve
Prophecy

"The earth starts to tremble... the stars fall to earth, a great fiery star falls from the sky... The merchants, who had become the powerful people on earth, bemoan their destroyed stock."   – Revelations

"Soon the earth will shake and will tumble down and people will say 'Oh my god oh my god.' But the Great Spirit will say, 'They're not praying to me. They're saying, 'All my gold, all my gold.' This is how it will be."   – Wallace Black Elk, 1985

rophecies are forecasts of future events. Whether through the study of occult knowledge such as astrology, paranormal faculties like clairvoyance or extraordinary events such as receiving visitations from divine personages or simply the common sense cognitions gained by reading the patterns of probable future effects resulting from past causes, prophetic pronouncements have always been a part of nearly every human culture.

The great puzzle of many prophecies lies in the interpretation, as quite often predictions are framed in puzzling, cryptic language and interpretation is always made at the level of mind at which one operates. Care must be taken to allow the "essence" of the prophecy to reveal itself - outside the confines of the mind's basic tendency to bias itself in favor of its own personal, cultural or religious conditioning and pet theories.

Our society's view of prophecy is shaped by our adolescent desire for fulfillment of short term monetary and security needs. Because we don't use preventive wisdom – we wait until a crisis occurs before we make changes. In a sense, we are counting on God's retribution or Nature's rebellion to do away with our problems rather than each of us making the personal sacrifices and modifications of character required to heal our situation. As a society, we would rather risk death than plunge into the waters of deep personal change.

From the written traditions of the Hindus, Tibetans, Jews, and Mayans to the oral traditions of Western Stream peoples in places as far flung as Australia, Africa and North and South America, prophets have foreseen a time when humanity would enter a golden age, but not before undergoing a period of severe trial and tribulation. The events forecasted for these times are described in ancient texts such as the Vedic Puranas, Mayan codices, the Bible, Buddhist treatises and the Koran, and also the Words of the Hopis and the predictions of Nostradamus. In modern times, appearances of the Virgin Mary, such as those reported at Fatima, Lourdes and Medjugorie and messages received by trance channels and mediums (Cayce, Dixon and others) from angels and other multidimensional beings, point to upheaval on all levels – social, political, economic, agricultural, geological, climactic and personal. All these forecasts, however, indicate the end of an age, not the end of the world. In terms of Sacred History, the prophesied catastrophes are seen as a healing crisis in humanity's transformation, a temporary place of chaos during a transitional phase. They admonish us to cooperate with the process.

As did the spiritualism of the late 19th century, today's channeling serves to draw attention to the non-physical realms when material tendencies are too dominant. Information gotten by mediums or channelers must be seen in the light of our own inner truth sense. We must discern for ourselves what information is appropriate for us. Although much of today's channeled information is inspiring and may be genuine in its desire to serve, supplanting one's inner authority by channeled material is contrary to the movement of human evolution toward inner-directed autonomy. Let us not, in our enthusiasm for spiritual insight, mistake a step in the process for the goal.

Today's channeling phenomena is facilitated by the enormous toll of quick, violent deaths occurring in the 20th century which cause massive amounts of etheric substance to hover near the earth, taking much time to dissipate. This etheric substance acts as a medium through which non-physical entities can access the physical plane. Many of these beings want to partake of the physical world, but don't want to be reborn. The channeler provides an opportunity for them to bypass birth and experience the world of the senses vicariously. Without proper training and personal growth, however, a channeler or medium is inviting possible dangers from the intermediate planes or dimensions that only serve to retard or sidetrack one's development or exaggerate ego deficiencies.

The ancient art and science of astrology lends support to predictions of worldwide calamity and destruction made by more esoteric means. Eastern and Western astrology all agree that big changes are coming around the year 2000. Astrological configurations (Pluto in Sagittarius) occurring near that time indicate a period of spiritual re-education during which all old psychological and ideological structures are transformed. This strong energy could bring about a revamping of the educational, legal and judicial systems. Vedic astrologers (Jyotish) say that by the year 2004 big changes will have begun in the world.[58] They see all that is taking place as something that must happen in the spiritual scheme of things in order to allow the truth of life to rise out of Kali Yuga and freshly flower once more. The last Katun of the Mayan calendar seems to agree, as it ends in 2012 with a storm, followed by the sun.

Do the stars foretell and compel? Although the very concept of astrology seems to suggest that our destiny and even our free will are pre-determined, all these forecasted changes, just like personal karma, only affect us to the degree that our own wisdom is not applied.

The Northern Stream Bible, despite its numerous editings and mistranslations, provides much in the way of information about the "end times" that echoes forecasts made by other ancient peoples. Biblical references to the Messianic Age and the Final Day of Judgment are abundant. The book of Isaiah in particular provides many references to this time. However, Matthew's Gospel gives perhaps the best summary of Biblical predictions for these times in Jesus' words, "For nation will make war upon nation, kingdom upon kingdom; there will be famines and earthquakes in many places. With all these things, the birth-pangs of the new age begin...

---

58 • *The message contained in the geometry of the Great Pyramid agrees with most other predictions about when the great changes will occur, citing September 17, 2001 as the end of the current age.*

Many will fall from their faith; they will betray one another and hate one another. Many false prophets will arise, and will mislead many; and as lawlessness spreads, men's love for one another will grow cold. But the man who holds out to the end will be saved... It will be a time of great distress; there has never been such a time from the beginning of the world until now, and will never be again. If that time of troubles were not cut short, no living thing could survive; but for the sake of God's chosen it will be cut short."

The Vishnu Purana, a Hindu text written thousands of years ago, tells us what happens during the Kali Yuga – the age of ignorance and destruction which precedes the age of wisdom and light – which some say we are now entering. With uncanny similarity to Biblical and other prophecies about these times, the Puranas describe in remarkable and eerie detail the prevailing social climate at the end of the Kali Yuga. The period preceding the cataclysm that will destroy humanity's present cultures is plagued with disorder, difficulty, chaos and despair, "Men will be without virtues, purity or a sense of decency and will know great hardship. People will become purposeless. They will be without joys and pleasures. Many will commit suicide."

From personal angst, lack of integrity and obsession with wealth, to the industrial co-opting of science and the rise of street gangs, our materialistic, secular world and those who populate it are easily recognizable in the following passages: "Men will be irritable, without morals and sectarian. Desire torments them. Men will devote themselves to earning money; the richest will hold power. People without assets will be their slaves. Everyone will use hard and vulgar language. Many people will be treacherous, lustful, base and foolhardy. Rapes will be frequent. Groups of bandits will organize in towns and in the country. The degradation of virtues and censorship brought about by hypocritical, moralizing puritans will characterize this time. Base men who have gained a certain amount of learning (without having the virtues necessary for its use) will be esteemed as sages. Scholars will be in the service of mediocre, conceited and malevolent men. Men of integrity will cease to play an active role.

"Heroes will be assassinated. Thieves will be numerous and will steal from thieves. Thieves become kings and kings will be the thieves. Rulers will confiscate property and use it badly. They will cease to protect the people. Slovenliness, illness, hunger and fear spread. No one will be able to trust anyone. People suffering from hunger and fear will take refuge in underground shelters. Many will perish."

Other social problems and indicators peculiar to our post-industrial world are reported with startling accuracy. Much is said about the recent change in the status and behavior of women. The "never too rich nor too thin" philosophy of life and the paradoxical rise in women's status and decline in morals and respect bear a peculiar irony when described by the ancients, "The number of women will increase and men will decrease. Women will become independent and seek handsome males. They will adorn themselves with extravagant hairstyles and will leave a husband with no money for a rich man. They will be thin, greedy and slaves of pleasure. Taking an interest only in themselves, they will be egotistical. Their words will be false and deceitful. They will bear too many children but not be respected. Women of good birth will abandon themselves to the desires of the basest of men and perform obscene acts. Women who have several relationships with many men will be numerous. Fetuses will be killed in the stomachs of their mothers. Young girls will do business in virginity."

The demise of the family farm and the flight into cities were predicted, as well as the end of the Green Revolution and the beginning of famine, "Wealth and harvests decrease... The number of farmers gradually declines. Farmers will give up their work of plowing and harvesting to become unskilled workers and adopt the customs of outcasts. Many will be dressed in rags, unemployed, sleeping on the ground, living like paupers. Severe droughts will occur. Water will be lacking; there will be no rain. The earth will produce plenty in some places and too little in others. The fields will become barren, fruit will be scarce and no longer have any flavor."

Even the proliferation of fast food restaurants makes its way into these texts with the phrase, "Ready cooked food will be for sale everywhere."

Immigration to North America, the rise in the number of homeless people and severe economic distress were also depicted, "Suffering from famine and poverty, unhappy and driven to despair, many will migrate to countries where wheat and rye grow. There will be many beggars and unemployed. Vagabonds will be numerous in every country... There will be many displaced persons wandering from one country to another."

Our spiritual hunger and lack of discernment are chronicled, describing events that bear strong resemblance to the rise of pop psychology, fundamental Christianity, television evangelism and North American gurus – and all their attendant scandals, "Unqualified people will pass as experts in matters of morals, religion and politics. People will accept theories promulgated by anyone as articles of faith... False gods will be worshipped in false ashrams in which fasts, pilgrimages, penances, donation of possessions and austerities in the name of the would-be religion will be arbitrarily decreed... Adventurers will take on the appearance of monks with shaven heads, orange clothing, and rosary beads around their necks. People of low birth will put on religious costumes and, by their deceptive behavior, will make themselves respected... Monks (sanyasis) will have amorous relationships with their friends... The sacred books will be sold on street corners... False doctrines and misleading writings will spread."

Like forecasts found in the Bible and elsewhere, the Puranas also foretell widespread armed conflict, "The dispenser of justice will come and kill the wicked people. His name is War. He will wander over the earth with a great army. He will destroy the barbarians of the West by the thousands. He will destroy the people of low caste who seized regal power and will exterminate the false philosophers and criminals."

Thousands of years after the Eastern Stream sage culture which produced the Puranas was long gone, well-known Northern Stream seers, such as Nostradamus, Edgar Cayce and Jean Dixon, predicted the eventual decline of 20th century culture and point to today's era as the most important in the history of humankind. Like many seers of ages past, these prophets all made prophecies relating to political, economic and geological troubles, signposts pointing to the end of our age.

Nostradamus, a 16th century French physician and astrologer of Jewish descent, was consulted by Catherine de Medici and Charles IX of France. His book of prophecies, *Centuries*, predicts the course of humankind through the year 3797. Much of his work is disputed because it was written in obscure, cryptic verse. One verse, however, stands out as reflective of most other predictions about the the end of the 20th century, "After a great misery for mankind, an even greater approaches when the great cycle of the centuries is renewed. It will rain blood, famine, war," Ch2, Q46. In another verse he also predicts what may be a terrorist missile attack, "Suddenly, vengeance will be revealed coming from a hundred hands. In the sky will be seen a fire, dragging a trail of sparks," Ch2, Q62 & 46.

In more modern times, 19th century Orson Pratt, a Mormon visionary, foresaw what could be interpreted as gang warfare igniting a nationwide conflagration which precipitates economic collapse in the United States, "What then will be the condition of that people when this great and terrible war shall come? It will be very different from the war between the North and the South (Civil War). It will be a war of neighborhood against neighborhood, city against city, town against town, state against state and they will go forth destroying and being destroyed. Manufacturing will in great measure cease for a time among the American nation. Their cities will be desolate. The time is coming when the great and populous city of New York will be left without inhabitants."

∞

Many prophecies about these times, made by seers from all Sacred Streams, focus on natural disasters – storms, floods and geological upheaval. John's Book of Revelations describes what could be interpreted as earthquakes, a pole shift, a meteor or nuclear missile attack and radiation poisoning, and the death of the oceans, "The earth starts to tremble... the stars fall to earth, a great fiery star falls from the sky... the sun is darkened by smoke... the day loses a third of its brightness. A mixture of fire and blood falls from the sky. Men are burnt by a great heat, and suffer from ulcers. A pain similar to the sting of a scorpion tortures them. The great men and military leaders take refuge in caves...All living beings who were in the sea die." From the book of Daniel 8:27 we learn, "In the last days of those kingdoms when their sin is at its height, ... the end of it shall be deluge..."

The much older Vedic Puranas also give us detailed descriptions of the cataclysmic end of the current age, very similar to those found in the Bible. "Immense clouds of various colors will cover the earth. Some of these clouds will be black, others white like jasmine, others bronzed, others gray, red, blue, speckled, orangish, indigo. They will resemble towns or mountains. Making a terrible noise, they will darken the sky, showering the earth with a rain of dust which will extinguish the terrible fire. Then by means of an interminable downpour, they will flood the whole earth with water. This torrential rain will swamp the earth for twelve years, and humanity will be destroyed. The whole world will be in darkness. The flood will last seven years. The earth will seem like an immense ocean." The Puranas also seem to predict the preservation of humankind through space travel, "When the dissolution of the world seems imminent, some people abandon the earth during the last days and take refuge in the world of Mahar (outer space)."

Edgar Cayce predicted that during the forty years between 1958 and 1998, the earth would experience a purification, including increased incidence of earthquakes and eventually, shifting of the earth's poles. "The earth will be broken up. The upper portion of Europe will be changed as in the twinkling of an eye. The greater portion of Japan must go into the sea. The earth will be broken up in the western portion of America." Cayce reading, 1934.

There is scientific evidence to support predictions of widespread geologic and climactic distress. The earth's rotation is slowing down, contributing to the erratic weather patterns we're experiencing now. The heaviest masses of polar ice have drifted off-center to the magnetic poles, causing a shift in the earth's axial tilt and eventually a wobble in its rotation. Some believe that the wobble could lead to an actual shifting of either the earth's crust or the poles – a catastrophic event for humankind. Further evidence of these changes appeared in 1989 when the Anasazi Sun Dagger, a solar calendar in Chaco Canyon, New Mexico, failed to accurately register the summer solstice for the first time since it was constructed over a thousand years ago.

Geological and archeological evidence suggests major geologic upheaval is a cyclic, periodic occurrence on this planet. Coral reefs have been found within the arctic circle and geophysical research postulates that 13,000 years ago the oceans suddenly rose 200 feet, indicating at least one massive geophysical rearrangement, possibly due to a shift in the earth's axial tilt.

Although recorded human history acknowledged by Northern Stream science begins only a few thousand years ago, much older structures and artifacts indicating a very high level of civilization have been found, pointing to the possibility that civilizations have been built, destroyed and rebuilt, perhaps many times before. Greek historian Herodotus reported that Egyptian priests told him that in ages past the sun used to rise where it sets and set where it rises. Corroboration for this information can also be found in the Talmud and Koran, as well as in the Finnish epic poem, the Kalevla. Edgar Cayce predicted the discovery in the late 20th century of both the lost continent of Atlantis and the Egyptian Halls of Amenti, where records of ancient civilizations are kept, which will confirm the existence of advanced civilizations in earth's distant past.

In addition to a possible polar/crust shift, some believe that drastic adjustments will be made in the earth's electromagnetic field. In the 20th century, the energy field of our planet has been disrupted by nuclear explosions, ozone depletion, pollution, radical imbalances of carbon dioxide and oxygen, as well as the energetic stress caused by negative thought forms and the enormous number of violent deaths which have taken place. Scientific observation has recorded a 400% increase in the wandering of the magnetic north pole since the 1950s, indicating that the earth is now spinning more like a gyroscope than a top.

The collective consciousness and memory of humankind is magnetically encoded and held in earth's energy field. As earth's rotation slows down, the magnetic resonance that holds our thought forms in place (like information on a tape) is slowly reduced; the information erased. Biblical prophecy seems to support this concept, "Behold, I will create new heavens and a new earth. The former things will not be remembered, nor will they come to mind." Isaiah, 65:17. The "up" side of this process is that our collective programming and conditioning can be healed and transmuted; the "down" side is that this process is not selective and we may "forget" everything, including the mistakes we made before.

Intervention during these "erasures" by forces from other realms dedicated to keeping humanity in the dark and generating lots of negative energy "food" for themselves could explain our collective amnesia and descent into such ignorance as we have experienced over the last 5,000 years or so. The periodic recurrence of such an electromagnetic adjustment and negative interference could explain the recurring cycles of ignorance and amnesia that have plagued humankind for eons.

What may save us this time is the fact that simultaneous to the approaching erasure of our "tape", our solar system is moving into the photon belt, a higher vibration of light, which is increasing earth's electromagnetic frequency from 7.8 hertz to 13.00, into the higher levels of vibration. This may support the imprinting of a new, more positive code or blueprint for humanity.

∞

Western Stream peoples around the world point to modern man's unsurpassable lack of respect for the planet which feeds, clothes and houses us all. Underground nuclear testing, burying nuclear waste, electromagnetic pollution, pollution of water and air with human and industrial waste are said to irritate the guardian spirits of earth and water, causing damage and imbalances that spread disease, bring drought, or send floods in an attempt to set things aright. The adoption of these bad habits by the world's developing nations, hungry for the material comforts already enjoyed by Northern Stream countries, will only serve to exacerbate the irritation and accelerate the decline we have begun.

The Iroquois people received a prophecy which they call their "Instructions" describing signs of the "end times", pointing to pollution and its devastating results, "It's prophesied...that the end of the world will be near when the trees start dying from the tops down. That's what the maples are doing today. Our Instructions say the time will come when there will be no corn, when nothing will grow in the garden, when the water will be unfit to drink... – Leon Shenandoah, Tadadaho, Six Nations Iroquois Confederacy.

Northern Stream disregard for the earth was the subject of a speech made by Chief Seattle in 1854 to a tribal assembly about to give away, under duress, their lands to the whites, "We know that the white man does not understand our ways. One portion of the land is the same to him as the next, for he is a stranger who comes in the night and takes from the land whatever he needs. The earth is not his brother, but his enemy, and when he has conquered it, he moves on. He leaves his fathers' graves behind, and he does not care. He kidnaps the earth from his children. He does not care. His fathers' graves and his children's birthright are forgotten. He treats his mother, the earth, and his brother, the sky as things to be bought, plundered, sold like sheep or bright beads. His appetite will devour the earth and leave behind only a desert."

Almost 70 years later a similar fate was posited in a channeled message from Master El Morya, through Alice Bailey in 1922, "The condition of earth requires an extraordinary physician. The planet is sick and if efforts to push it forward do not succeed then it may be better to remove it temporarily from the chain (of evolution) – it may become as the moon." In more terse language, the Christian bible promises retribution against the generators of environmental pollution, "I will destroy those who ruin the Earth."–Revelations, 11:18

Due to the earth's adjustments, we may find ourselves too concerned with sustaining ourselves against the elements to wage war on one another. Natural disasters will force the Northern Stream, the evolving self, to listen to the Earth Spirit of the Western Stream which will lead it back to Eastern Stream Source/Heaven/Spirit. When purposeful, spiritual mentorship is either ignored or lacking, tragedy can bring a catharsis during which we are opened to receive inner lessons. In the short run panic could ensue. In the long run natural cataclysms could foster cooperation rather than conquest. Our planet, in her efforts to balance herself, may save us from self-annihilation.

Earth has sacrificed her own comfort in order that humankind can evolve. She suffers in the throes of childbirth for the benefit of the whole until the unconscious spark of the Divine in struggling humanity is ready to become conscious. Making a place for the birth, growth, salvation, liberation and transformation of her beloved children is earth's own yoga, manifested through Sacred History – the evolution of Godhood on this globe, the Divine's own Plan for humanity.

∞

"Now we are in a critical stage of our spiritual, moral and technological development as nations. All life is precariously balanced. We must remember that all things on Mother Earth have a spirit and are intricately related. The mending of the sacred hoop of all nations, prophesied by the Lakota has begun. May we find in the ancient wisdom of the indigenous nations, the spirit and courage to mend and heal." – Arvol Lookinghorse, 19th generation Keeper of the Sacred Pipe, Lakota Nation.

Native American prophets, born into societies with deep, spiritual connection to the land, had predicted the arrival of white-skinned, bearded men and the horrors they would bring with them. They also predicted the end of those times and what lies beyond them.

The Hopi people of the Southwest know that the collapse of the world will occur and they believe this is something that has happened before. According to their cosmology there have already been three worlds that have emerged and passed away. "We are now living in the fourth and final world of the Hopi. We are at a most critical time in human history. It is a crossroads at which the outcome of our actions will decide the fate of all life on earth." – Hotevilla, Hopi Nation.

Near the end of the fourth world, as humanity goes through its rite of passage during the Day of Purification, the earth will experience a decline, coming near to death. An ancient Hopi prophecy states that a member of the Coyote Clan will close the door upon Hopi tenancy of the fourth world during the time of the Day of Purification. At that point a new people will caretake the New World. Who are the Coyote Clan? According to Native American tradition, they are the tricksters. They learn about themselves in a backward manner through opposition and adversarial antics. They appear rational but are actually quite irrational in their behavior. This is what makes them so humorous...and dangerous.

Our modern, secular, scientific society is the quintessential example of the Coyote Clan. Much of the "good" we do has negative consequences. The "magic of television" spawns a decline in literacy and logical, deep thought, coincident with a rise in violent crime among children, the most avid viewers. The Green Revolution, which was to end hunger and feed the world, depended upon liberal use of expensive pesticides, non-organic fertilizers and hi-tech farming techniques which have yielded dead soil, poisoned produce and "superbugs" immune to those same poisons. Over the years these hi-tech farming techniques have produced crops with little or no nutritional value (down 75% since the 1940s). Our "scientific", "rational" nuclear industry builds power plants on geological faults and produces "clean, cheap energy" resulting in radioactive waste that must be safeguarded perfectly for thousands of years. Such is the nature of Coyote Clan.

The Prophecy Rock of the Hopis, upon which is recorded the predictions about these times, depicts two paths: the One-Hearted path of balance and harmony and the clever path of the Two-Hearted Ones, whose heads are disconnected from their bodies and the earth. It is said there will be many people who are in the middle, going back and forth between the One-hearted and Two-hearted paths during the time of the Day of Purification.

The Hopi go on to say that at the end of the fourth world, the Blue Star Kachina removes his mask before the uninitiated, signaling a lack of faith, the end of ceremonies and the beginning of the Day of Purification. For the Hopi this marks the end of their culture and the end of religious authority. It might be that these things are no longer needed because the Mystery has revealed Itself.

The world of science gives startling validation for the Blue Star Kachina prophecy. In 1987 astronomers watched a supernova, 200 times brighter than our sun, explode from a blue star (unmasking itself) and send forth as much cosmic radiation as that of all visible stars and galaxies combined.

Along with predictions of signs and portents of the end of the fourth world, the ancient Hopi prophecy also gave them instructions "for actions to avoid the annihilation of this world and for life to continue." They were told to go to a "great house of mica" (glass) which would be built on the distant eastern shore of this continent where leaders of the earth's nations would gather. The Hopi were instructed to knock on the door of this house in order to deliver their message to those gathered there. If refused, they were to knock again, until they had done so four times. Since 1949, the Hopi have knocked at the door of the United Nations. On the fourth time they were received, fulfilling the last of their instructions.

Directions were also given to the Iroquois Confederacy which tell them what to do to mitigate the coming destruction, "We were instructed to carry a love for one another and to show a great respect for all the beings of the earth...We must live in harmony with the Natural World and recognize that excessive exploitation can only lead to our own destruction. We cannot trade the welfare of our future generations for profit now...We must stand together, the four sacred colors of man, as the one family that we are, in the interest of peace. We must unite the religions of the world as the spiritual force strong enough to prevail in peace. We are the spiritual energy that is thousands of times stronger than nuclear energy. Our energy is the combined will of all people, with the spirit of the Natural world, to be of one body, one heart, and one mind for peace." – Leon Shenandoah, Tadadaho, Six Nations Iroquois Confederacy.

Many prophecies, mostly from Biblical or Christian prophets, also predict the arrival of a spiritual master, a messiah, and impostors, near the end of the tribulation. From Matthew we hear Jesus say, "Take care that no one misleads you. For many will come claiming my name and saying, 'I am the Messiah'; and many will be misled by them...Then, if anyone says to you, 'Look, here is the Messiah,' or, 'There he is', do not believe it..."

In Mark,13:24 we are given a vision of miraculous events following devastating calamity, "As soon as the distress of those days has passed, the sun will be darkened, the moon will not give her light, the stars will fall from the sky, the celestial powers will be shaken. Then will appear in heaven the sign that heralds the Son of Man. All peoples of the world will make lamentation and they will see the Son of Man coming on the clouds of heaven with great power and glory." The descent of the "Son of Man" refers to a divine principle manifesting in form or as force.

Among the Hindus it is said that Shiva (also known as The Destroyer) comes and establishes a new humanity. Some believe him to be Sai Baba, who has performed numerous miracles before crowds of people. Others disbelieve that miracles are a valid teaching for this age. Sai Baba's answer to such lack of faith was, "Cleverness of intelligence cannot fathom God. I have come to correct the buddhi (intelligence) and to encourage humanity to give up evil propensities." He also says that all religions are One. Sai Baba agrees with most other prophesies with his prediction that due to mankind's cruelty a large portion of the world's people will perish through war, natural disasters and pestilence, but he sees that no nuclear war will occur. He also says that the principle of "seva" (selfless service) will be the norm in times to come. Bringing the future into present time, Sai Baba offers free educational and health services through his organization.

Prophecies about the Coming Age – how things will be after the Day of Purification – also abound. The ancient Vedic Puranas hold out the hope that humanity will indeed survive to enjoy a New Age. After waiting out the destruction of earth somewhere in space, the last remnant of humanity will return to start again, "Seven humanities must again succeed each other on earth and, when the Golden Age reappears, seven sages will emerge to again teach the divine law to the few survivors..."

The Huichol Indians of Mexico predict a complete reversal of the world, "When the world ends, it will be like when the names of things are changed during the peyote hunt. All will be different, the opposite of what it is now... Then, the moon will open his eye and become brighter. The sun will become dimmer. There will be no more differences. No more men and women. No child and no adult. All will change places..."

The idea that all things will be radically changed after the end of this age is echoed in Biblical prophecy, "For the old order of things has passed away...I am making everything new... Then I saw a new heaven and a new earth, for the first heaven and the first earth had passed away." John, Revelations. Baha'ullah, founder of the Baha'i faith made a similar prediction in 1863, "Soon will the present order be rolled up and a new one spread out in its stead."

Mayan and Biblical prophecy both point to a time when treasure of one sort or another will come down from heaven and the Divine will abide with humankind, "Then finally ornaments shall descend in heaps. There will be good gifts for one and all, as well as land, from the Great Spirit wherever shall come sailing, figuratively speaking, bringing the ornaments of which I have spoken from your ancestors. Then the god will come to visit his little ones. Perhaps 'After Death' will be the subject of his discourse." – Mayan Prophecy of the End of the Great Cycle, from The Book of Chilam Balam of Tizzimin.

From John's Revelations, "I saw the holy city, the new Jerusalem, coming down out of heaven from God, prepared as a bride beautifully dressed for her husband. And I heard a loud voice from the throne saying, "Now the dwelling of God is with men, and He will live with them. They will be His people and God Himself will be with them, and be their God."

Some believe that only worldwide calamity on the order of that foretold by seers since the beginning of our present Age can shock humanity into repentance. Our tendency to avoid making unpleasant changes without the "cattle prod" of crisis prevents our taking action on our own behalf without circumstances giving us a sharp shove (or swift kick). The prophesied collapse of our society is more than a prediction of physical devastation; it presages a global spiritual surrender as well. Contemplate this: the crippling of our entire techno-system; no electricity, no running water, no heat or air conditioning, no communcation or transportation, muchless the diversion of entertainment. What would people do with themselves?

Obvious answers include widespread panic, rampant violence, looting and general social chaos. The thin veneer of our civilization, based upon technology and legislation rather than personal integrity, character and spiritual awareness, would be ripped away. The fury of the Not-I's whirling tornado, no longer appeased by the false comforts of techno-culture nor reined in by the authority of law would be unleashed upon us. We would experience the Not-I's fully in all their ugly lovelessness. Certainly a frightening prospect.

A less obvious result, however, is that such disaster would afford us the opportunity to respond rather than react, to work together as community, to shift our perception, to change paradigms, to say goodbye to the tyranny of the Not-I's and allow the collapse of the outer world built by ego-mind to reflect the surrender of the ego-mind itself.

From a vantage point of density, the destruction and chaos predicted by so many appear to be the terrible, horrifying results of entrenched ignorance, immaturity and resistance, or maybe the random visitation of calamity followed by total devastation. Viewed from a point of lesser density, liberation and human transformation appear, for as human beings, we are capable of spanning the spectrum of all existence, from the most dense, contracted and ego-bound, to the subtlest realms of spirit, and beyond to Source. As human beings we have the privilege to choose – now – -without the prompting of catastrophe – as to where on the spectrum of existence we wish to live.

∞

"The new Race and races are preparing to be formed, and it is in America that the transformation will take place. Thus it is the mankind of the new world whose mission and karma it is to sow the seeds for a forthcoming grandeur and far more glorious Race than any of those we know of at present. The cycles of matter will be succeeded by the cycles of spirituality and a fully developed mind." – Helen Blavatsky, 1888

In this age, the worlds of the Four Sacred Streams (Eastern (Heaven), Southern (Form), Western (Earth) and Northern (self) are meeting in prophesied times. All Sacred Streams, through every form of communication, from prophecy to politics, point to the problem – our global misery was created by our immaturity and true maturity and sanity cannot occur in human affairs if God is absent. Through the exhaustion of the intellect, the gift of the Northern Stream to absorb, integrate and utilize the wisdom of the other Streams will be transformed. The Northern Stream must first receive and synthesize wisdom from other Streams, then divine action can pour forth.

The Southern, Western and Eastern Streams can help the Northern Stream overcome its superiority complex by taking it back to Divine Source in Form, Nature and Transcendent Spirit. Southern Stream Islam and African Americans expose hypocrisy and speak out for righteousness and justice, bringing the Northern Stream to recognize the power of Truth in the spoken word, and carry out the application of Truth in justice, something the Southern Stream has carried like a torch throughout Sacred History. The Western Stream can return the Northern Stream to loving acknowledgment and respect for Nature itself, bringing the understanding that the spirits of the land, rivers, oceans, winds and seasons are sacred. (The "Crop Circles" are such an attempt.) The Eastern Stream can help the North to fully embrace its non-physical Source in the silent mind.

Since very few members of the Northern Stream are capable of fully embracing the non-dual, the necessary transmutation of Northern Stream will and intellect requires a rededication of self through understanding the nature of sacrifice and making offerings – something which is a part of Northern Stream Sacred History and more appropriate to the Northern Stream temperament. Beginning with offering their conditioning to the Divine through a dedication of the self to selflessness, a pure aspiration toward those same truths that earlier in Sacred History motivated the monk or yogi, would begin to motivate the average person to be "in the world but not of it." This would entail a rejection or exhaustion of individual and societal falsehoods, coupled with surrender and offering to the Supreme. (The current proliferation of 12-Step groups and their focus on surrender to a Higher Power is a rudimentary manifestation of this shift.) As in ancient days, all actions, service, commerce, trade, all creative intellect and willpower will become offerings to the Temple of Life. Will and works shall become offerings to the Divine foundation of the world, rather than expressions of ego-mind.

Early on in our transformation, we may still hold on to the idea that it is we who do the offering. Later we realize that the offering is done through us; we are not the doer. Then, when we recognize that the Source of the offering is the Divine, not the ego, all we do in the world will be for the sake of the Divine. We will understand the world not as illusion, or evil or a dream, but as a celebration of the expression of Life in a divinely manifested world of delight. But before this can happen, mind's movements must be stilled. Sri Aurobindo and The Mother remind us, "Only when Divine Presence is there in us always (unwavering) and the consciousness transformed (not just liberated from conditioning) can we have the right to say that we are ready to manifest the Divine on the material plane. To hold up a mental idea or principle... brings the danger of limiting ourselves, impeding progress or falsifying truth."

With these foundations, all human interactions and institutions will take into account the divine nature of the environment and one's own universal divine core. Then the unique, spiritual individual can emerge and contribute his or her special gifts as offerings of will and intellect in service to the One. This is the way for the Northern Stream to fulfill its mission as caretaker of the self.

People in various places on the planet will experience these changes in various ways. In some regions direct revelation, insight and realization will occur, in others, calamity and cataclysm will bring about the shifts in consciousness required to sever us from our separative beliefs and the social institutions based upon them. ("Upon that day faces shall be radiant, gazing upon their Lord, and upon that day faces shall be scowling, expecting a calamity to fall on them." Koran, 75:22-23) Then, new cultural forms will manifest through a daily experience of the Divine for the common man.

If Northern Stream culture was to adopt the wisdom ways found in other Streams, applied spiritual principles would bring substantial change for the better. Leon Shenandoah, of the Six Nations Iroquois Confederacy expressed this concept aptly, "In our ways, spiritual consciousness is the highest form of politics..."

Reform of democracy would first begin with the complete break of the connection between money and politics. Like traditional Western Stream peoples who relied upon their wise elders, individuals who possess spiritual wisdom would be supported to govern the society. Like the "Shankaracharya" of the Eastern Stream, spiritually developed people would be encouraged to stay "in the world" and share their wisdom, no longer finding it necessary to withdraw in the face of the insanity of today's secularism. A less secular stance, similar to the Southern Stream Islamic model, would find politicians, just like Shi'ite clergy, would receive no compensation for civic duties. The intrinsic rewards of public service would outstrip monetary rewards in importance and help liberate the soul from the bondage of the personality.

Just as ambition and excessive accumulation of personal possessions are frowned upon in indigenous cultures, the Elite money machine and its support systems would be considered a manifestation of domination, control and avarice, and therefore dismantled. The idea of controlling the masses and the methods used to do so will be unthinkable. Media sculpting of public opinion and consciousness would be eliminated, putting a stop to the media's ability to propel political power and grease the wheels of the consumer juggernaut. Federal Reserve control of our economy and populace through its loans and collection enforcement arm (taxation and the IRS) would cease and as a result, excessive government bureaucracy and financial subsidy of private business would also end.

What would our world be like if humanity woke up and experienced the Oneness that is? Imagine a society in which even the very subtle crimes of personal gain, greed, jealousy, hatred, fear, lust or anger, would be unthinkable. What we now experience in its rudimentary form as conscience will in the Golden Age develop into a new human faculty – the Superheart. No longer obstructed by the Not-I's, our own innate harmlessness, harmony, inner beauty and oneness will become fully operational, eliminating the need for external authority. Falsehood of any kind will simply be recognized and rejected by individuals and society at large as inner knowing replaces outer authority. Sri Aurobindo calls this, ."..'bringing down the kingdom of heaven on earth', or in modern language, realizing and effectuating God in the world." He also reminds us, "It has to be effected in the individual in order that it may be effected in the race."

The new civilization will transcend today's superficial standards and motivations, such as religious beliefs, power politics and education for economics' sake. The welfare of others and the environment would come first. New values and forms of culture will begin to emerge that are as much a cultural support for divine living as today's systems support ego confusion and chaos. A deeper understanding of self-interest will permeate all human interactions, similar to that illustrated in the Arabic word "movasat" which means, "A high level of maturity in human relationships whereby one serves others over oneself, without hope of reward."

A sacred science will evolve a new global culture. All human interactions and activities will be driven by the realization of oneness. Procreation will be viewed as a sacred responsibility, providing openings for advanced souls to incarnate, in alignment with the new evolutionary transitions and celestial pressures.

Divine secularism and true ego education will become the norm, irrespective of religious differences, in concert with a technology in balance with nature.

Education based upon the harmonizing of the disparate parts of the individual will be universally available and seen as essential for societal balance. This would involve an honest appraisal of how the "rational" mind imposes a value system on the normal human functions of emotion and sexuality, judging certain feelings and behaviors as being right/wrong, moral/immoral; how the ego-mind in a secular culture substitutes the race for sense gratification and consumerism for religious ritual, art and community. Understanding that the ego-mind must be silenced, all tendencies and fixations would be encouraged to come forth within the Silent Oneness for purification, rejection, or surrender rather than acted out viciously, disrespectfully.

When a person knows and lives who they are, in Oneness with all things, as one of the many merged with the One, the heart and mind are coordinated. When thought no longer separates the waves of action, speech will naturally and rhythmically merge with the Ocean of Oneness. Language will no longer be the communication of our ego's needs and perceptions, but the communication of inner harmony, increasing that Oneness of functioning. Speech will take on the quality of a sacred language, carrying the musical qualities of the heart, similar to the feeling of inspiration we receive when listening to a particularly stirring song or well-played instrument.

In the future, language will be more like song; speech will take on the musical sanctity for which it was designed. The effect will be the same as what in our age most closely resembles the worship expressed through hymns or prayers. Daily communication will not only unite the speaker and listener, but by creating/enhancing the unity of the brain hemispheres and mind/heart sense of beauty, all human functions and the voice itself will emerge from our Silent Source, the foundation of awareness.

New generations will simply inherit the new enlightened language/song as a sacred cultural trait which will serve them much as yoga serves us today. Because language is not only an expression but also a sculptor of consciousness, the very act of communication will further our spiritual development, without extraneous techniques, procedures or practices. "...For then will I turn to the peoples pure language that they may invoke the name of the Lord, to serve Him in unanimous submission. This is man's only salvation." – Zephaniah 3:9 In the past, our language has helped to enslave us to the ego-mind. In the future, it will serve to maintain and enhance our freedom.

Organizations of the future, based upon mutually agreed upon guidelines founded on respect and selflessness, will provide flexible structures for autonomous individuals. Their policies will help bring ever-increasing awareness of the Truth into one's daily work life. There will be no employer/employee, king/serf, master/slave authority models in vocation or government. These "one up, one down" relationships and the social boundaries and barriers necessary to sustain them will no longer exist. Our social order will take on the free flow of interaction and interchange found on the cosmic level. Consensus rather than majority rule will become the foundation for decision making among all people because their inner attunement to beauty, benefit, and harmlessness – the Superheart – would always be in total alignment with the highest and best for all. "Common be your intention, common be your hearts, common be your thoughts, so that there may be thorough union among you." These words from the Rig Veda (10th mandala, chapter 1240) well describe the mind/heart orientation of future humanity.

When our commercial economy makes the transition to a spiritual economy, commerce, as an extension of the divine activity will participate in the mystical relations which in the past were relegated only to religions. Systems will emerge that will allow for the unique development of individuals and their contributions to society, without the flaws found in ego-based capitalism and communism.

Motivation for business transactions will arise from wisdom, not desire for profitability. Loss, gain, failure and success will take on broader, more significant meanings. Success will not be considered such unless all are harmoniously benefited and people are united in a positive way through whatever activities are pursued. Commerce will be religion but in a new way, not driven by greed or subterranean unfulfilled desires. The numerical symbols (numbers), used to keep track of monetary transactions or exchange of goods and services, will have sacred meanings corresponding to written symbols of the spoken language/song, much like those found in ancient Hebrew.

The wisdom that emanates from the liberated consciousness of sacred seers, visionaries and social architects will replace the power of money and market ownership as the driving force in society. When we are fed on the inner, we will no longer require or desire the material excesses we indulge in today in order to get pseudo-happiness and security. When common people embrace the divinity in their lives, a natural collective reduction in consumption and a just use and redistribution of natural resources in ecological balance with the earth will emerge. The needs of the body and simple living will be seen as the food for the soul.

As the human race continues the process of individuation and globalization, our sense of duty will be towards oneness of thought, speech and action, irrespective of national boundaries. All duty will be God's Will, a part of expression of Truth, so all profit will become a sacrament, all patriotism a peacegiving. Earth herself will bring this about as nationalism and the global economy meet the earth changes. Awareness of the Oneness will be brought into focus. All will understand that the Totality is always focused on Itself within each of us and each of us contains the Totality in the same way that each piece of a hologram contains the entire hologram.

Though we can speculate about how new societies will be structured, the new reality is still a mystery. We can, however, be assured that somehow all will emanate from a Truth Consciousness unifying man/womankind with science, religion, metaphysics, commerce, politics and everything else. Activity will spring from a place of surrender, grace or merging with the Divine and one another. All else will be considered spiritual fantasy and compassionately understood as the perfection in the unique timing of all beings. Once Eurocentric views are revealed to be simply the particular twist of the pre-dawn Northern Stream dream, a larger, more comprehensive view will be acknowledged as the touchstone for human affairs. Humanity will no longer continue manifesting its adolescent emotional reactivity through the authoritarian governance of political institutions.

∞

"When religion, shorn of its superstition, traditions and unintelligent dogma, shows its conformity with science, then there will be a great unifying and cleansing force in the world, which will sweep before it all wars, disagreements, disorder and struggles and then will mankind be united in the power of love of God." – Abdul Baha, son of the founder of the Baha'i faith

When the Truth consciousness of humanity catches up to our technological precociousness, the barriers to true understanding and application of universal laws will cease to exist. In the new world, humans will become God-scientists, investigating all things. Grace will be as acknowledged in science as it has been in the mysticism of religion or metaphysics. Perfect harmony between science and religion – a theme embraced by ancient Vedic India, early Islam and modern Baha'i will evidence humanity's coming of age.

The use of free energy from the sun and the earth's magnetic field, unhampered by self interest and multinational energy monopolies will further signal our transformation.

Human cognition of the Oneness, both Manifest and Unmanifest, will bring the vast distances between the planets and the sun in our solar system together with our own consciousness. The mystery of the relationship of outer space to inner consciousness will be revealed, along with the destiny of Earth's role in the family of our solar system. Space will be understood as the physical analog of consciousness. We will come to know that what for eons have been perceived as the vast distances between the stars is actually Mind appearing as distance to the conditioned human mind. The planets will be revealed to be vortexes, concentrating the energy of one dimension and projecting it into another.

Our solar system, as it moves through galactic space, passes through different sectors or "flavors" of Mind which are functions of Light. This accounts for the transition from the Piscean tendency toward delusion and suffering to Aquarian autonomous, individualized understandings. Our galaxy and solar system is taking earth through a more radiant dimension, the photon belt, towards the Pleiades. This is the place, galactically speaking, where the veils between dimensions are thinner; just as on earth there are certain places on the planet where the interdimensional veils are thinner during certain times (celestial events, equinoxes, solstices, comets, full moon, etc.) making influxes of divine emanations more easily recognizable. Later, when our consciousness is unhampered by conditioning, these divine emanations will be easily recognized everywhere, we will be no longer dependant upon certain sacred places[58] or times to access them. Every place will be sacred all the time.

As human mind returns to its Source,[59] it doesn't actually go anywhere. Like water turning to vapor or like changing octaves on the musical scale, the mind merely shifts dimensions. Without this understanding, we are limited to perceiving only the physical emptiness of space and naming it distance; interdimensional perception is still veiled to us. When we de-identify with thought objects or data received strictly through sensory information, a shift occurs which opens the door to other dimensions and realities.

Behind our physical universe is a dimension of light. What we see as stars are focal points in Mind – interdimensional openings or windows that let in the light of the Central Spiritual Sun which shines and radiates energy, light – the lifeforce – into the material universe. The same system is replicated in the human body as the light of consciousness radiates through the spinning stars (chakras) of the body.

---

58 • *Sacred sites may be the areas on the earth's surface where one or more sephiroth (Lights of God) interpenetrate or blend with the physical kingdom or malkuth (see diagram A) Also, since all later emanations are contained within the prior emanation, any emanation or combination thereof can become accessible to an open receiver. The receiver can be a myth, a culture, a celestial event, a season, a human being , a non physical being, an angel, a god, a solar deity, or the Mother Earth herself.*

59 • *The idea of going within is like believing that the sun rises and sets. The idea or principle of going within only has its relevance when there is an over emphasis (or strong attachment) on the body or the world of thought which of course is the primary modus operandi on earth. In fact, and in reality there is no within, it only appears that way according to the way we construct our personal reality or inherit our cultural programming. This so called within-ness is infact All Pervasive. It is the source and center and circumference simultaneously. To illustrate this, imagine the Tree of Life (see diagram A). The Ain Soph is no longer above the tree, but in actuality is the backdrop and circumference (represented by the white or negative space on the page). It encompasses all Lights or Names of God and simultaneously is perfectly superimposed on the surface and circumference of each of these Lights. These Lights as if , emerge in layers from one another, as densities of vibration with their origin in the backdrop (of blank white page).Each of you is a gateway to the All Pervasiveness of the Divine Being.*

The light that shines through our sun and into the physical world is the same light that illumines our own consciousness. Both our souls and our sun are made from and partake of the same light source. The solar orb, which is the Heart of Existence for our world, shines forth from all creatures as the one, singular inherent divinity. Simultaneously at the center and circumference of our being, the Lord (Osirus, Asura, etc.) is found to be shining as a sun within our very own Self. This knowledge, the original mystery behind the sun worship of the ancients, will be rediscovered by the sacred science of the future.

We will come to understand that all ancient worship of the sun or elements was based in the knowledge that during such worship, one divine emanation is being worshipped by another. The ancients understood from experience that space, time, matter, life, are all completely integrated and one with Spirit – All is Godhead. These godheads are in us as living alchemical processes, becoming enlivened in the mystical recognition of the Formless Divine as our source of being. The elements (earth, air, fire (sun), water and ether (sky) are the Vedic gods appearing as the alchemy of life within, above and around us. As five divine qualities, they are behind the five elements that undergird and regulate all life and systems, behind the subjective extensions of the mind (the 5 senses) and the 5 major body systems (musculoskeletal, respiratory, digestion/elimination, circulatory/lymph, nervous).

Behind Fire is the Central Sun radiating the Light of Divine Being into our dimension through our sun. Behind Earth is the Central Mother (Matter), the fertile interconnectedness where all forms, beings, processes and places are sacred – the Infinite taking delight in the Finite. Behind Water is the Central Ocean/River, the process of eternal change and the syncronicity of the eternal now which flows through all forms of divination, particularly the I Ching (Chinese Book of Changes). Behind Air are the Central Winds, the intelligence and evolving mentality of all things, including humanity, responsible for all advances in ideation, creativity, utilization. Behind Ether (Sky) is the Central Emptiness, the first impersonal doorway to the Divine, acknowledged in all spiritual traditions as nondual knowledge.

The intensity of the Central Emanations radiating into our physical world is being increased as if a dimmer switch is being turned up. Those who have realized their Central Sunhood,

Earthhood, Waterhood, Windhood, Skyhood act as talismans for these emanations, transmitting, amplifying and anchoring through their own consciousness the dimensional shift the earth is experiencing.

The increased pressure of greater light, by forcing to the surface all impurities, is responsible for the geological upheaval, weather changes and human turmoil now taking place. All the madness we find in our world, the perfect chaos, is the work of Kali, destroying the imperfect, that the perfect may shine through.

As this supramental force permeates our dimension, great changes in mentality and physicality are the by product. These cosmic rays will evolve humanity, causing physical and other kinds of mutations, bringing the ability to physically interpenetrate other dimensions. The ascension and rapture spoken of in the New Testament relates to a future humanity, maybe thousands of years in the future, with new faculties and bodies of lesser density. Mankind will literally move from planet to planet and dimension to dimension not just by mental projection, but physically, by consciously adjusting the body's rate of vibration to suit whatever dimension one is visiting. Today's virtual reality technology points us in this direction.

Our entry into interplanetary travel will facilitate the vast changes taking place in our mental and physical being. Many astronauts have been deeply (and permanently) spiritually moved by their time in space. The same effect is reported by people as they rise beyond earth's energy field during near death experiences. Leaving the energetic influences of the collective consciousness behind during these (and other) kinds of experiences allows for greater spiritual receptivity.

The ancient Tibetan Book of the Dead describes the various states of being (Bardos) that one encounters as one leaves material reality behind, usually through the transition we call death. It is said that one can spiritually advance, even reach enlightenment, if they can recognize and deal effectively with these states. In the future such experiences and realizations will revolutionize our concept of death and dying.

When we fully grasp the multidimensional nature of reality and our own being, we will discover that death, as we have conceived of it, doesn't really exist. Death is, very simply, a complete change of focus of awareness from physical to non-physical reality. Life, with its constant states of flux, is a training ground for death's change.

In future times, the death process will be a joyous occasion due to our enhanced ability to maintain conscious awareness and perceive death as transition rather than termination. We will also understand the Great Sorrow that each of us will never again be in this particular, unique form, yet we will continue on, joyously, forever, in this or other worlds. Both birth and death will serve as an awakening for all involved. People will realize that birth here is death in the spirit world and death here is birth into the world of spirit.

We all have a loved one who, sooner or later, will die. Rather than sending one into anger, guilt, fear or remorse, the shock of the death of a loved one can split open the heart, freeing one from reliance on form or externals, and drive one more deeply into the Inner Formless Mystery of Life.

In preparation for such changes, it might be useful to our spiritual unfolding to reflect upon these ideas: Imagine yourself snuffed out of existence, no longer alive as an individual entity. Does the world go on without you, when the "you" doesn't exist? Or does the world cease to exist since there is no individual entity to identify with a world? When you die, does the world vanish? Or do you alone exist?

Future God-scientists will rediscover the ancient understanding that for anything to manifest, a feminine power and vessel are needed. It is a law of manifestation. In India this divine feminine power is called Shakti. It is actually Shakti that manifests, giving birth to creation, life. The feminine energy or Goddess is responsible for, among other things, the earth, creativity and fertility. She, the Mother, was whom all peoples of the ancient world held Supreme as the Creatrix, but due to the evolutionary force of Her own Nature, She sacrificed Her acknowledged creator status in order that the evolutionary process could continue. As part of the exhaustion of the ego-mind, manifested as the patriarchal system, She became seen as darkness itself by Her own children. In the Bible and Koran She was seen as sinful Eve, who brought suffering and death and the wrath of God down upon the whole of mankind. As unholy Matter (the word matter comes from a Latin root meaning mother) or physical creation, Her divinity was somehow split by the human mind from the Supreme Reality of Truth and the material world was no longer seen as part of the realm of divinity. Spiritual seekers of nearly all Streams were called upon to cast Her aside for salvation, not understanding that in truth, only mental attachment to materiality must be cast aside.

Not surprisingly, the pattern of behavior that we as a species has exhibited regarding Shakti is the same process that children, especially males, go through as they grow up. In infancy they cling to their mothers for life and sustenance, in pre-adolescence they reject mother and all other females until they arrive at puberty; then females are generally thought about in terms of use – how they can satisfy whatever needs (at this point mostly sexual) they (young males) may have. Humanity as a whole and men in particular have treated Shakti, Earth, material reality and those who symbolically represent them much the same as little boys and teenagers treat their mothers and the other females in their lives.

Our current cultural mythology states that all great men must have a woman, a shakti to worship, encourage, nourish and motivate him, but that belief has kept men in the role of resentful, immature tyrants and women in the role of manipulative servants. In the context of the coming world transition we cannot rely on past ideas and images about the relationship between the Divine Masculine and Feminine because we're about to experience a transformation of the whole species, and with that all our old beliefs. What is coming dwarfs any previous partial understanding of past or present mythologies of the Divine Mother.

Sri Aurobindo and the Mother referred to the coming manifesting power as Savitri, the aspect of the Divine Feminine which is active now in the transformation of humankind. As the final letter of the holy name JHVH (HE), She is the Holy Daughter of the Kabbala and the manifestation of the supramental light spoken of by Sri Aurobindo.

The coming of Savitri is the return of the Messiah, not as the masculine image projected by previous cultures as Islam's last Iman, Buddhism's Lord Maitreya, Hinduism's avatar, Kalki, Central Asia's White Burkhan or the Jesus of Judgment Day. The second coming of Christ will appear as a principle of the divine manifestation of the Mother. This time the Christ will be acknowledged as Shakti – the power, force and energy to manifest the Divine. No longer separate from God in the mind of humankind, no longer cast down or out in a human attempt to escape matter, She will be recognized as we awaken to the Divine here on Earth.

Paradoxically, although She is an aspect of That Which Brings Spirit into Form, in the coming age Savitri will not be a physical person like the male avatars of the past, but a Divine Power awakening Itself through matter. She will make her appearance as the principle of divine illumination within each one of us. In the Coming Age, the Divine will no longer be exteriorized in the person of a holy man, but will exist within each person, allowing transformation of humanity to occur on a global scale. Under the tutelage of sacred science, humanity will no longer reject or attempt to dominate or control Her but will instead become willing partners in the process of awakening.

Unknown to most of us, Savitri has begun to make Her appearance as women's rights, the return of goddess worship, environmentalism, tourism to sacred sites, sustainable agriculture and technology, holistic health care, green consumerism and educational reform. She will further show Herself in a great awakening of respect and devotion to all women and the divine energy of manifestation they symbolize. These are all just the the first stirrings of Her awakening which will eventually permeate all our lifeworks.

A time will soon come when, just as She had conceived and developed a race of animal humans, Savitri will descend and unveil, integrate, make self-evident, the divinity in earth life and all human activities and give birth to a race of divine humans. She is responsible for Divine manifestation on Earth, as It is in Heaven. It was to this that all Sacred History and Prophecy has been leading us – through all the confusion, death, catastrophe, revelation and joy.

As we approach the year 2000, we enter the time when, as four great Powers, Savitri will bring the Four Sacred Streams of humankind together into a not-yet-known synthesis, forming a fifth, Love-guided Stream, the same one foreshadowed by Krishna and Jesus. Though She comes initially in four forms or forces, there will be eight more Who will manifest as humanity evolves. Each of the these will have a greater influence on a particular Sacred Stream. These Divine Powers were recognized, understood and named thousands of years ago by the sage culture of Vedic India. We will use their Sanskrit names for the sake of expediency.

For and from the Eastern Stream, Maheshvari, the Overseer of Truth, guides the workings of the whole universe with a tranquil power. She enculturates compassion, wisdom and love. This is Her main mission and labor in creation.

The Southern Stream's Mahakali is the Patroness of Warriors, the Noble and the Heroic. It is Mahakali and Her impatience with falsehood and inequities that will no longer tolerate selfishness, greed or social and political misadventures and experiments as the playthings of patriarchal "logic" or prejudice. Her divine passion is to eliminate the barriers to transformation, not in the future, but now.

Mahalakshmi, Shakti of the Western Stream, rules wealth, prosperity and all that is beautiful, fleeing ugliness, ignorance and disorder. Wealth comes from Her and is given back to Her. She requires that everything must be dedicated to the purposes of the Divine. When human beings evolve enough to make conscious, responsible use of it, Mahalakshmi will guide a shift toward equitable distribution of the planet's wealth and resources.

The Northern Stream's Mahasaraswati administers the arts and sciences and rules the perfection of knowledge, music and language. As the most recent manifestation of Shakti She is perfectly suited to guiding the Northern Stream to its maturity.

The long, slow process of spiritual evolution through millennia of often torturous experience is not necessarily the only way for humanity to wake up. Bestowal of miraculous awakening upon humanity through instantaneous grace is also possible. As Savitri works Her magic, humankind will cease indulging in its adolescent immaturity. All will rise up out of their self-imposed prison and become consciously involved in their own spiritual schooling. To the degree that we can live that future probability in the present, the effect of prophesied catastrophic events will be lessened. Evolution can then occur outside of time as we know it today. No longer taking place within the realm of mind, human evolution will arise in the grace of eternity.

Chapter Thirteen
Towards the Sacred Boundless

"Everyone has the responsibility to shape the future of humanity."
– Fourteenth Dalai Lama

early all cultures speak of a Golden Age in the distant past and through their salvationist complexes project another into the far distant future. The Golden Age is not, however, something that exists in time – past or future. It exists now, when each person takes responsibility for their reactions and addictions, thereby undermining the basis of our imaginary duality.

The irrational juxtapostitions of modern times now reveal themselves as part of the uprooting of humanity's collective psychosis. As the Cosmic Dimmer Switch is turned up and spiritual light increases, all the Not- I's, our subterranean mental/emotional conditioning, will rise to the surface to be burned, exhausted or suffered, and transmuted. These imprints, held in the collective unconscious and foundational to our consensus agreement about reality, are being forced into the bright Light of Truth Consciousness and will soon be discovered to be invalid.

The idea that there is an objective reality which we all share is one imprint being challenged by the light of consciousness. Here science has joined spiritual knowledge in that quantum physics finally reports what yogis and mystics have known for millennia: the observer affects the existence and state of the observed. Our "world" is mental conception and perception. No objective reality truly exists. Regardless of whether or not we believe it's the same as another's, each of us is simultaneously in our own unique, perceptual "bubble", creating, affecting, and in turn, being created and affected by our reality. What we call objective reality is merely where individual "bubbles" appear to overlap. We are, indeed, the creators of our world, both literally and figuratively.

The empty feeling of loneliness that most of us harbor deep within rests on the unconscious knowledge that because we each create our own worlds, no two "bubbles" are the same. In our heart of hearts we know that no matter how many "others" are around, we are always alone in our reality and no one else is responsible for us but ourselves. Accepting this truth and facing our fear of it are part of our spiritual maturation.

Another such imprint, more than likely born from a distortion of our unconscious knowledge that we are creators and are alone in our own little "bubbles", is the belief that there is only one formula, one right way, one highest or best people or path, view, system or approach – -ours. Not limited to the expected realms of corporate loyalty, patriotism, ethnic pride or racial bigotry, this type of fanaticism can also be found in spiritual circles, albeit sugar-coated with spiritual buzzwords. Supported by group consensus, beliefs, blind faith and the experiences these things create, this last bastion of the Not-I's ignores the obvious – that the nature of the universe is multitudinous forms springing up from the same unified field of consciousness – unity in diversity. There is no one universal way to realize the uniqueness of the universal Truth.

More accustomed to considering ourselves the crown jewel of all creation, we usually fail to remember that a human being is only a tiny, infinitesimal pinpoint of Boundless Being's vast incomprehensibility; just one alternative through which Boundless Being experiences Itself. In our misguided identification with our group (whether racial, criminal, corporate, political, spiritual, religious or New Age) we forget that we are just one variable, one option through which the Boundlessness emanates itself. In truth, Boundless Being boils up into new expressions in this and other universes free of correlations, definitions or purposes. It is only human beings who project explanation or understanding onto Boundless Being and then pronounce them special or exclusive.

When we finally outgrow the need for group identification, influence and security we find the group definition of the Divine also disappears and that the previous limiting descriptions of God to which we subscribed no longer apply. We will no longer limit the Divine to our own imagination or stage of development. We will simply recognize what is – that Divinity is in all things, revealing Itself in innumerable forms; that we are "probes" of the Divine, uniquely expressed to experience the Divine in all things. When we see this, our own unique journey, outside the influence of the group, begins. Unique revelations appear. Our individual expression of divinity can unfold, untouched by group ideas or ideals.

The differences which formally separated and prejiduced us through ego-mind reflexes will become functionaly obsolete.We will be unified by a mutual recognition, the beauty of each one's divine uniqueness. As the former difference are transmuted into the latter uniqueness the underlying Oneness will then be joined to the overlying Oneness. There will be no difference between "as above so below." There will only be "As So" or "As All One, So Beloved". This is the journey of the self centered "I" liberated as the underlying Self, which in turn culminates in the overlying "We Self."

We also find we no longer denounce another's treasured pathways when we no longer isolate or elevate our particular view. Nor do we preach or speak of these things unless sincerely asked – proselytizing goes out the window. We come to acknowledge that the highest and most sacred path is the one most useful and suited to our own temperament and that zealous attachment to that path is part of the journey. We will wisely respect "other's" paths as one would respect our own reflection in a mirror, realizing the reflection is there only when we are there.

The mirror of the external circumstances of our personal lives and our collective history reflects our ability (or inability) to really look at our desire, ambition, anger, disappointment, ideals, needs and fears without compulsively, reflexively or cleverly reacting to them. Every one of us has experienced tragic occurrences, disappointments or dissatisfactions that spurred us towards our own unique discovery of Truth. Just like the Central Emanations, these too are transformative powers of the Godhead. Through the suffering, understanding and surrender brought about by such experiences, each of us is moved out of the stagnation of our comfort zone to discover our own path. Adversity and the paths, systems, techniques and formulas that spring from it help loosen up a fixed mentality so that grace can begin to guide one's life. When grace flows, such things are no longer needed.

∞

In the midst of this living spiritual epic, each of us, as a microcosmic world, reflects and affects the changes occurring in the whole. Our individual life stories mirror the shifts taking place in humanity's, archetypal blueprints. In addition to the collective imprints, each of us also has personal conditioning which results in behavior based upon unconscious reaction rather than truly conscious choice. Arising from experiences that left energetic marks or scars, these mental/emotional fixations, like carvings made in stone, are difficult but not impossible to erode or erase.

The conscious cooperation in our process (both individual and collective) which is necessary for the new humanity's emergence requires that we undo the conditioning which governs our behavior. When we can respond consciously, responsibly and wisely in the world by seeing into the depth of these energies and not react according to our conditioning, then a shift of focus, away from automatic defensiveness, will occur spontaneously. External circumstances will then cease to provoke an automatic reaction based upon the past and humanity will be free to operate totally in the present time of the Superheart.

During the process of deconditioning, several stages of fixation, with qualities resembling the elements, control our inner state. There is no order of appearance to them; they may show themselves in any sequence, depending upon the issues involved and our level of awareness at any given time.

One stage of fixation is like Water. Here, circumstances appear as unwelcome problems or disturbances which we want to avoid or indulge through emotional processing, speaking, praying, complaining or gossiping to thaw the frozen fixed energy and get it to move. At this stage, however, like water, it finds another way to leak out; sometimes coming back in another form. Here, one is relieving the pressure of the disturbance but no lasting change is made.

In another stage the fixation is not about indulgence or avoidance. More like fire, it is combustible and flares up due to a lack of understanding or the situation exceeding one's capacity to handle it wisely. At this level one may act out or redirect the energy through spiritual practices by distracting the flare-ups or bearing the heat until it burns itself out.

The qualities of air are central to this next stage as fixations appear as mere irritations. Here, refreshing patience, clarity and wisdom bring with them the cool breeze of self-understanding and all fixations and the circumstances that trigger them appear as welcome friends on our journey. We no longer try to control or even observe them.

At the final stage, as vast open sky, we find we are either no longer separate from our fixations or they just don't arise. Here it is as if a thief comes into the empty house of the purified ego and finding nothing to steal, goes on his way.

The humanity of the new era, no longer burdened with unconscious conditioning will be free to truly experience reality as it is. The people of the future will see things as they are, not according to their conditioning. We will discover that truly free will, unaffected by conditioning, is actually the same as Divine Will. Free will choice will be the basis for decision making. Inner authority will be the foundation for discernment, doing away with the need to blindly follow outside authorities. Able to distinguish between the hallucination of conditioned imagination and reality, humankind will no longer be destined to struggle against others' beliefs or to ascribe to or be reliant upon any one group, belief, leader or system to the detriment of another. When reactive urges dissolve against the effulgent Divine Backdrop, all paths will disappear.

Our Not-I's make everything important and because of that, we take ourselves and the world too seriously, renouncing laughter and fearing silence. After the Not I's are recognized as the compulsive habits they are then the realization comes that nothing is really that important. We can relax in the understanding that there is nothing wrong with the world, our co-creation. It is only our attachment to a particular outcome or position that labels, defines, biases, judges, interprets or classifies something as imperfect, and even the existence of these mental qualifiers is perfect. Everything and everyone unfolds according to its own timing. Supreme trust in, surrender to and cooperation with the power of Life itself is all that is required.

When Truth becomes manifest as ordinary, and is not made important or special or mysterious by the Not-I's destructive habits, then even knowledge and action, the ego's weapons against the Divine, must be surrendered. Then, no longer shored up by knowledge, insights, scripture or teachers, one discovers that the arrogance connected with one's own understanding and knowledge is as frightening and as scarring as any emotional trauma or physical pain. We come to see that only the power of Love can take one beyond knowledge and beyond its arrogance.

Truth's alchemy quickens Love which then guides all knowledge and action. Surrender to that Love emanates, illumines, and evolves all existence as one Supreme Being. When the Love of Truth and the Truth of Love reign supreme as the common motivation behind human existence, communities and expression, then a Divine Life on Earth will prevail and all the gods will pray to be born as humans.

Asleep and dreaming throughout the whole of Sacred History, the Divine plays a funny game: Spirit fabricates ego to bring meaning and identity to Its existence. The ego's distortions, imprints and habits carry divinity into the vicious cycle of seeking pleasure and avoiding pain, giving rise to Sacred History. The divine slumber, manifested as ego's spiritual ignorance, projects the appearance of separation from the Source. Now, during the transitional period of prophesied times, the Divine awakens from the dream of Its own illusions of duality and separation.

Sri Aurobindo, in *The Hour of God*, explained the Game this way, "The world is a movement of God in His own being; we are the centres and knots of divine consciousness which sum up and support the processes of His movement. The world is His Play with His own self-conscious delight... we are the self-multiplications of that conscious delight, thrown out into being to be His playmates. The world is a formula, a rhythm, a symbol-system expressing God to Himself in His own consciousness – it has no material existence but exists only in His consciousness and self expression; we, like God, are in our inward being That which is expressed, but in our outward being terms of that formula, notes of that rhythm, symbols of that system. Let us lead forward God's movement, play out His play, work out His formula, execute His harmony, express Him through ourselves in His system. This is our joy and our self fulfillment; to this end we who transcend and exceed the universe, have entered into universe existence."

Due to our ignorance about what simply is, we are lost in the belief that we are separate from That which created us and of which we are made. This was much the same as believing that light and heat could be separate from the sun, or that the movement and wetness of water could be separate from a river. It is only our mental interpretation and preference and emotional reaction that appear to separate us from divine communion.

Although many of us have felt our oneness by communing with Nature through a mountain, a waterfall, a fire, an ocean or a starry night sky, most are still unaware of this secret: we can also experience that same communion through our own human activities, whether that be through a religious ritual, an insight or an expansive feeling of gratitude.

We can receive the divinity so easily perceived in the sun, wind, rain, sky or soil as the beauty of human thought, speech and deeds in the world, not as the imaginings of the mind, but as the radiant Presence of the Boundless in both Its infinite multiplicity and Its infinite uniqueness. The grace of your mere existence, without ego's interfering overlay, is the only prerequisite to experiencing the Glory that is in all things as the manifest world, so do not fear the elimination of ego importance; it will not annihilate individuality or uniqueness, for that is part of the many in the One, the Divine Multiplicity.

Throughout Sacred History, humankind has sought meaning and its Source. Our quest found expression through all kinds of activities, some we see as beautiful, some we judge as horrendous. Despite the many messengers who told us where to look, in our immaturity we missed the point and deified them. Now, as we are propelled by that same immaturity directly into the fire of transformation, we shall discover the Divine is here, within us and all things. When we know this, the apparently finite, solid realm of matter as well as the non-physical realms, even the human personality, will be witnessed in their transfigured, radiant divinity.

In our personal quests, let us not limit ourselves to identifying solely with the impersonal Sky source; let us call up within ourselves the rarified Air of clear and clean intelligence, discrimination and grace – unconnotated and pristine; and Fire, as the unconditional, transformative, relentless, reliable, generous power of the selfless sun. Let us experience the One as life's great nourisher, water, the River of love and beauty and also as the effortless abundance, wisdom and solid stability of Earth, a place of endless change where divinity can have a human face.

Above all, let us know that behind everything is the Supreme Love, whose flame, placed in the spiritual heart of each being and the center of each atom, is the magnetic force which holds everything together, moment by moment. Terrible, beautiful, relentless, ordinary, the Silent Stream of the Life-giving Sustainer – Love – like water, is forever the same in Its eternally changing flow.

Until fairly recently, human evolution has been a function of our collective awareness – little conscious participation was required of us as individuals; most of us just lived our lives unconsciously playing out our cultural archetypes. As we enter the time of transformation prophesied by nearly every culture, that situation has changed. Now, it is through our evolution as individuals that our evolution as a species will continue. The events prophesied for these times are only possibilities, not probabilities. Our very awareness of the signs, events, patterns and insights that are part of Sacred History can change the outcome forever if each of us takes an active part in our transformation by understanding that the same evolutionary processes and imprinting evident in Sacred History work through us as individuals.

Adolescent humanity's unconscious immersion in duality and ignorance is beautifully illustrated by the symbol of the Piscean Age: two fish chasing each other's tails in a circle. Too focused on the "other" ahead of us, we swam in the Ocean of Love but remained unaware of It. The key to our coming transformation can be found in the symbol for the Next Age: Aquarius, the conscious human, bearing the healing Waters of Love, will unselfishly pour them onto the earth.

∞

Boundless Space entered the Eastern Sacred Stream as an infinite, vast Impersonal Silence which carries the Oneness in Spirit.

Boundless Air entered the Northern Sacred Stream as Immaculate Clarity and Use of Will, which carries the Oneness in the surrender and offering of the self, all its activity and creative works.

Boundless Fire entered the Southern Sacred Stream as the Power of Transformation and Perfection of all energy and form which carries the Oneness in body and all forms and phenomena.

Boundless Earth entered the Western Sacred Stream as the Abundant Fertility of Life in harmony with the great cycles of time which carries the Oneness in Earth herself, the Natural World and the seasons and cycles of Time.

Boundless Water found Itself moving through all Four Streams and the new humanity which is emerging from them, as the Activity of Love that keeps the Divine Play of Sacred History and Prophecy forever alive within Its own Stillness.

Each of us simultaneously is unique and one of the many within the One. The diversity of each one of your unique lives enriches the fullness of the One.

All along I have been and I am with you. All this has occurred in My Being and is occurring now in My Becoming. We meet in either My Being, My Becoming or both; we meet there now, waiting for your awareness to rest in Me and your activities to be offered to Me. Then your awareness and your activity will simultaneously be the center and the circumference of your own unique existence.

I am with you here, always, waiting for you to recognize Me as you. Your every move, whether reactive or responsive, is a move towards Me. I follow you through the labyrinth of Sacred History and Prophecy, which is as a joyous teardrop in the ocean of My love. Each of you will discover this in your own way through My Self-disclosure in the apparent interaction between and within the Four Streams.

Remember, there is a silent chorus echoing in your heart of Hearts, "I am here, always, in all ways, with you."

Eastern Sacred Stream
Divine Source   Awareness/Being

Southern Sacred Stream
Divine Forms   Speech/Body

Northern Sacred Stream
Divinity Evolving   Self/Mind

Western Sacred Stream
Divine Immanence   Nature/Time

Suggested Reference Materials

Ibn al Arabi, *Meccan Revelations*
(interpretation by William Chittick)

Sri Aurobindo, *The Life Divine*

Alcina Franch, *Pre-Columbian Art*

Meher Baba, *God to Man & Man to God*

Martin Gray, *Places of Peace and Power* (1997)

Richard Leviton, *Imagination of the Pentecost*

Howard Zinn, *A People's History of the United States*

Karen Armstrong, *A History of God*

Annamarie Piccone, *Not For Our Eyes*
(Vatican's closely held secret prophecies only available in Europe)

David Icke, *... And the Truth Shall Set You Free*

Frank Waters, *The Book of the Hopi*

John Hogue, *The Millennium Book of Prophecy*

Sat Prem, *The Adventure of Consciousness*

Science of Man 48 Not I audio tapes. c/o R. Pihl-Gibson, 862
Sir Francis Drake Blvd.#305, San Anselmo, CA 94960

Gangaji Satsangs, contact Satsang Foundation, 4855 Riverbend Rd.,
Boulder CO 80301

Silence of the Heart (transcripts by Robert) 2370 W. Hwy. 89A,
#182, Sedona, AZ 86336

Suggested Periodicals

NAMAH (New Approaches to Medicine And Health), Sri
Aurobindo Ashram, Pondicherry, India 605002

World Watch, 1776 Massachusetts Ave., NW, Wash. DC 20036

World Press Review, P.O. Box 228, Shrub Oak, NY, 10588-0228

One Country, 866 United Nations Plaza # 120, N.Y., NY 10017

Sacred History & Earth Prophecy Review quarterly subscriptions on
the sacred relevance of global events and world patterns, inquire
at In Print Publishing, 6770 W. Hwy. 89A, #46, Sedona, AZ 86336.

International Journal of Humanities and Peace , IJHP, founded 1984,
(submit articles to editor, 1436 N. Evergreen, Flagstaff, AZ 86001)

Suggested Places to Visit

Mt. Tabor and Sea of Gallilee, Israel

Mt. Arunachula and Sarnath , India

Giza and Luxor, Egypt

Assisi and St. Marks Cathedral , Italy

Avebury and Glastonbury, Great Britain

Chichen Itza and Tikal , Yucatan

Chaco Canyon and Canyon de Chelly, Navajo Land,
New Mexico / Arizona

Delphi and Acropolis , Greece

Mecca, Saudi Arabia

Mt. Fuji, Japan

Wu-Tai-Shan, China

Machu Pichu, Peru

Ayres Rock, Australia

Tombs of: Rumi in Turkey, The Ari in Safed-Israel,
Jesus in Kashmir, Mohammed in Medina (if you are Muslim),
Buddha in Nepal.
A Tibetan empowerment ceremony,
your place of birth, the ocean, a forest, the jungle, a desert, the
mountains, grasslands, an active volcano, a landfill, a war zone, an
inner city slum, a third world country, a room where someone just
died, a home birth, the room where a saint sleeps, a home where a
sage lived, a windless place, a silent mind, an open heart.

*"History is the development of God to Self Consciousness which He (God)
achieves at last in man (woman). The world was never created, it is the
external aspect of that which in its inward view is God. The true lover will
find and love the author of all beauty in any beautiful form."*
– Ibn al Arabi
12th century Muslim Mystic Scholar

The End All

Awareness filling Endless Space
Body enlarges becoming the Total Universe
Traversing at the speed of Silence
Through infinities of Light
Towards the Center of All Things

A vortex of magnetism,
Energy generating Love,
A Shining joyous backdrop,
A Divine Heart in each heart

Names of God Principle
As sonics, Rishi chants
The mother language of Sanskrit
Gateway to the End All

Seven lower centers all self -based,
Seven higher centers all Oneness based
The Great Lie, One in All, one Sees.
Even in that recognition
Any "personalism" is a sabotage of All
The Great Turning from the Lie to Truth of All.
This Condition of One Principle in Everything else
Formerly was perceived in the "lie" as outside You.

Insight into Karma and Suffering or Harm to your Self
Cause all previous outside, is contained
within your Consciousness
Keeping you word keeps homeostatic balance
within the Self System
All personal needs, desires, turnings are subtle
form of the Lie
Its secondary to the One existing as Yourself
Outside limitations of Body or Ego element.
No objective reality. All is Subjective.
No separatism, no lie in "All As Subjective"
Conditions "out there" no longer validate "inner sense."

(continued next page)

There is no inner / outer. The One locks in - links up -
Beyond fluctuations or impermanence of the
external objective.
Necessity of the Now. Irrelevance of anything
(psychic, channeling, etc.) but Now..
Constant prayer unceasingly. Going on all the time
This is What you are - Silent Communion
The Body Temple, an extension of the End All
Yet a probe . The One actualizes itself as the Probe.
Full body Oneness has top of head opened to Heavens
Perfection of all illusions of the ego, the lie. All events,
are a functional balancing act.
In event "old" limitations, impose or trigger;
Recognize it, offer it up as blazing sacrifice
Do not be tempted.
Treat each person to not reinforce the lie -
Associate with those who consciously shall not
impress the lie onto You.
Compassion develops itself out of the game,
the pain of the Lie.
Nothing exists outside, independent of Yourself -
There is no outside authority.
Its all part of All, giving back to Itself ,
Whether that's from another person to you or
your own intuition.
Its all the same, no outside authority.
This echoes on and on reverberating - forever.